My Dearest Patcy

THE EARLY YEARS of MARTHA WASHINGTON

A Novel

BARBARA J. VEST

My Dearest Patcy

THE EARLY YEARS *of* MARTHA WASHINGTON

A Novel

BARBARA J. VEST

Cover design by Beth Farrell
Interior design by Karen Schober

This is a work of fiction. Names, characters, places and
incidents, though based on fact, are purely the product of the author's imagination or are used
fictiously and are not to be read or
interpreted as historical fact.

Published by Elton-Wolf Publishing
Seattle, Washington

ISBN: 1-58619-100-4
Library of Congress Catalogue Number: 2003113565

08 07 06 05 04 1 2 3 4 5

First Edition January 2004

Printed in Canada

ELTON-WOLF PUBLISHING

2505 Second Avenue Suite 515 Seattle, Washington 98121
Tel 206.748.0345 Fax 206.748.0343
www.elton-wolf.com info@elton-wolf.com

To my loyal husband Jim
My loving daughter Michelle
My beautiful granddaughter Whitney

Love sought is good, but given unsought is better.

—*Twelfth Night*, William Shakespeare

ACKNOWLEDGEMENTS

When I retired in 1999, one of my first replacement activities was to become a volunteer at the Washington State History Museum. The museum was busy setting up a traveling exhibit called "George Washington, the Man and his Myth," which was also the name of the beautifully written guide to help docents explain the pictures and artifacts. James Flexner's biography, "Washington, the Indispensable Man," was offered as an informational tool to brush up on George's life. I became deeply interested in renewing my acquaintance with George Washington and promptly marched to my local library and checked out several other biographies. (I had not read about cherry trees and not telling lies since elementary school.)Having always had an interest in our first ladies, Martha Washington became a prominent piece of my readings. My innate curiosity led me into questioning why so little information was available about Martha's early life. A book was not on the agenda at that point! Two biographies, one written by Elswyth Thane, the other by Dorothy Clarke Wilson, did an admirable job telling the story of Martha's life after she married George. "There must be a story somewhere, telling about her first marriage and the four children she gave birth to," I told myself. So I went to work.

My matriculation into the world of research began at my local Lakewood library which became my port of call. Once Martha's family tree was located, I was ready to begin. Rose Jeter and her helpful resource staff flawlessly warmed up their computers helping me search for obscure names or dates. Our statewide lending library was amazing. Sometimes, I borrowed resources three or four different times to make sure I had my facts stated correctly. My hunt also took me to the East Coast where I visited Mount Vernon, The Fairfax Museum, Jamestown, Colonial Williamsburg, Carter's Grove and Richmond, Va.

There are many people who helped keep me on track; offering encouragement and enthusiasm to this project. My family gave me impetus to keep going, especially, my daughter Michelle. She gave long hours and expertise in helping format the manuscript. Jim, my husband, never lost faith for finding a publisher. First time authors are not high on priority lists. A very special thank you to Val Dumond, my editor and loyal mentor; Mary Thompson, Research Specialist from Mount Vernon's Ladies Association; Stephanie Jacobi, Visual Resource Manager, The Virginia Historical Society; and Holly Bailey, Washington and Lee University, Richmond, Virginia. Thanks for making this addition possible. The city of Colonial Williamsburg, Virginia, whose docents patiently demonstrated the daily lives of the colonials; and the people at Microlynx who gave unstinting time to the complexities of technology and patiently rescued me numerous times.

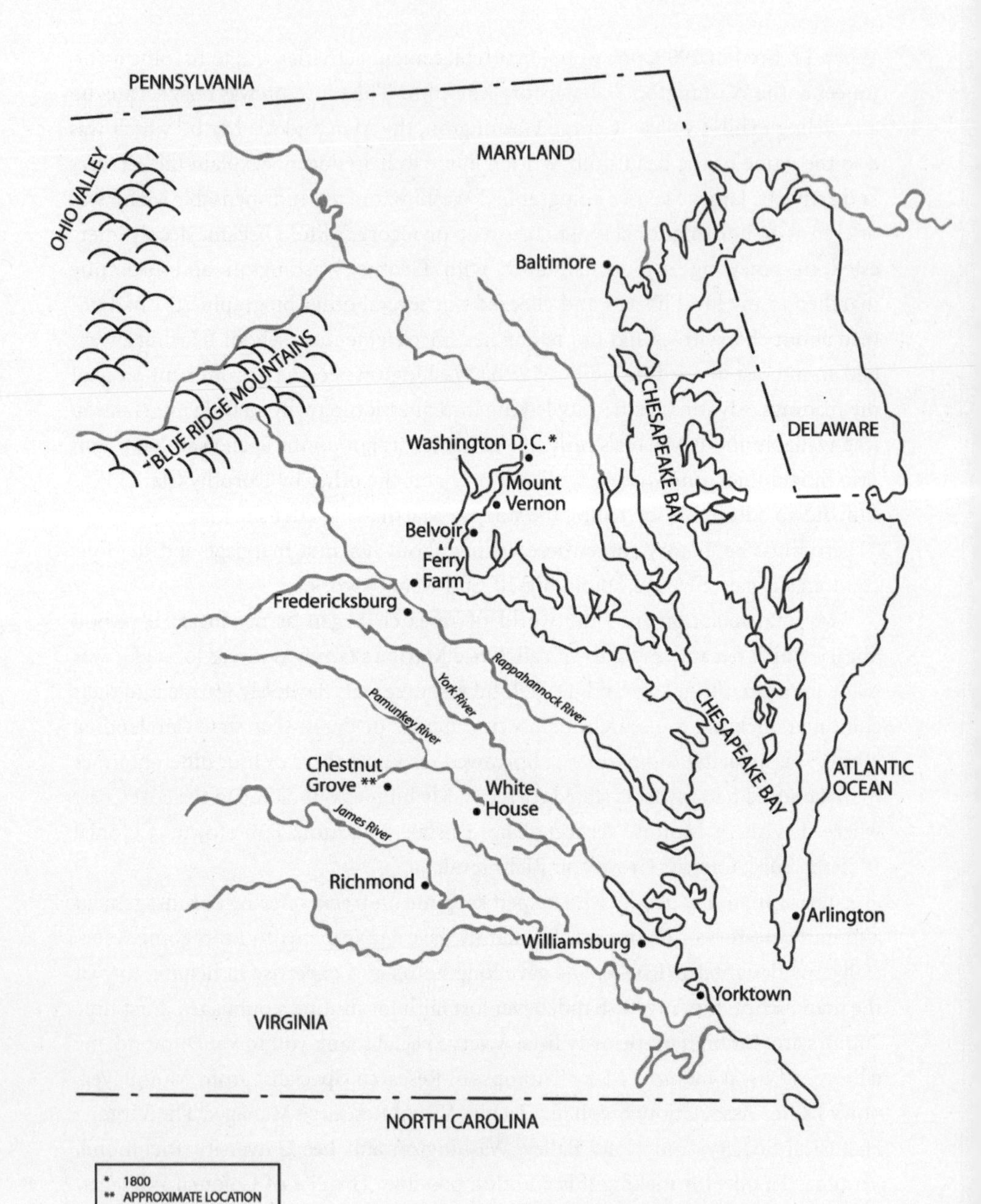
PENNSYLVANIA
MARYLAND
OHIO VALLEY
BLUE RIDGE MOUNTAINS
Baltimore
CHESAPEAKE BAY
DELAWARE
Washington D.C. *
Mount Vernon
Belvoir
Ferry Farm
Fredericksburg
Rappahannock River
York River
Pamunkey River
CHESAPEAKE BAY
ATLANTIC OCEAN
Chestnut Grove **
White House
James River
Richmond
Arlington
Williamsburg
Yorktown
VIRGINIA
NORTH CAROLINA
* 1800
** APPROXIMATE LOCATION

CONTENTS

PROLOGUE

Who was the woman who came into the world as a daughter born to a farmer who had respectable holdings but not wealth, and his wife, the daughter of a preacher? Her place in history sings as a couplet—"George and Martha". . ."Martha and George"—not unlike bread and butter—peaches and cream—wine and cheese.

Much has been written about George Washington, the dynamic and powerful man whose place in history is recorded forever in books, periodicals, and journals as the "Father of Our Country." This is not his story; nor is it the story of the woman who lived for forty years with America's first icon; rather this narrative is the story of the girl, the oldest of eight children whose parents gave them the gifts of infinite love and security, unyielding religious conviction, and the high ethical and moral principles of colonial times. This empyreal upbringing set the stage for the main event, whose benchmark is January 6, 1759, the day Martha married George. This tale begins on June 2, 1731, her birthdate.

We know Martha preceeded George in birth by eight months and succeeded him in death by two and a half years; however, there are few records of her first twenty-seven years, before she married George. Most historians dedicate several sentences to describing her, as a "wealthy widow who had four children, two of which died in infancy, before she met and married him." In fact, she may have been the wealthiest woman in Virginia and her two oldest children were over four years old when they died, hardly infants by present day standards. How did Martha's humble beginnings elevate her into the Virginia aristocracy, leaving her a widow at an early age?

The few known facts about Martha Jones Dandridge Custis Washington are here assembled into a story that brings alive her parents, siblings, slaves, first husband, and children, in the setting of colonial life during the eighteenth century. Few recorded journals, few letters, and little documentation of stories about Martha's early life have been passed down through the Dandridge-Custis generations. A prodigious study of the life and times of colonial days preceded this interpretation, though one can only imagine the dialogue that passed between the players in this narrative.

On the landing in Jamestown in 1607 of colonists who were only men and boys looking for gold and other treasures, the newcomers discovered only "faire meddowes and goodly tall trees." The value of this early discovery went unrecognized for several years as the colony struggled for survival because of impure water and swampy land that caused sickness and death. Although they showed little initial enterprise, the men were taught agrarian skills and how to live from the land by the numerous Indians who inhabited Virginia, headed by Chief Powhatan. With little at first but lumber to ship back to England, the colonists then learned from the Indians the possible worth of tobacco as a commodity the English would clamor to import.

By the late 1600s, new settlers came in large numbers. There were nearly two hundred fifty thousand people living in the colonies by 1700, with the greatest numbers in the southern colonies. Many came because they were offered either free land or land at a low cost. Under English law, all colonial land belonged to the king, who issued charters to settlers. An ordinary charter gave a settler one hundred acres to farm. Each farmer could keep fifty acres of his chartered land for himself. The other half reverted to the king, but farmers could buy back from the crown as many acres as their purse would allow, priced at five shillings per acre.

The majority of immigrating planters owned fifty to one hundred acres and worked hard to plant, harvest, and market their products. Owning a plantation with over a thousand acres moved owners into the next tier of a developing middle social strata. The landed gentry of England were granted large charters from the crown. Lord Thomas Fairfax, for example, was a member of an influential English family who was given five million, two hundred thousand acres of land in Virginia and West Virginia. Many ancestral dynasties transferred to the colonies, bringing an unbroken aristocracy to the Americas. Large plantations required overseers, field hands, and service hands for planting and harvesting. Slavery gripped the large plantation ownership by 1670. This institution had a profound effect on the social structure, which added to their power and recognition.

Land acquisition was the objective of second and third generation American colonists, in the New World of the early eighteenth century. Expanding their fathers' and grandfathers' plantations, their determination was to procure the means to be landed gentry in the English manner. This drive succeeded in establishing a hard-working, remarkable aristocracy that contributed to the social consciousness of the Virginia tideland planters. They attended to a classical education for their sons, aspired to reverent religious beliefs and exerted themselves to establish and maintain an orderly society. The wealthier the planters, the more politically and socially powerful they were.

Quality of life improved with an expanding population, expansion into the western frontier, and procurement of more land. Lavish homes were built, horse-drawn carriages and luxurious furniture were imported from England, as were the latest English fashions. Schoolmasters were hired to teach the planters' children. Libraries in the homes were filled with the classics and books of law, history, and science. Williamsburg became the capitol of Virginia, and with it came a legislative assembly that met twice a year. This drew the representatives and their wives into town, where social gatherings brought entertainment, gaiety, and matchmaking.

When the General Assembly gathered, Williamsburg became a metropolitan city. Most town folks complained about the "Publick Times" because of the overflowing inns, boarding houses, private homes, and taverns, called ordinaries. Streets were filled with carriages that journeyed back and forth from the Governor's Palace to the Capitol. The Duke of Gloucester Street, the mile-long main street, was over-crowded with men rushing to the House of Burgesses or the General Council meetings, while gaily dressed women, the wives of elected officials, filled the dressmaking, apothecary, and wig-making shops.

The profile of the colonial woman in the second half of the 1700s depended on her station in life. Wives of southern planters, with large households to oversee, had slaves to handle the menial tasks of housekeeping. The lady of the house had the job of administering the duties of the staff; scheduling and organizing the cleaning, changing of linens, soap-making and candle-making, weaving of cloth and clothes-making, preparing and storing of foodstuffs, baking, cooking and planning of menus, as well as caring for the children. She was expected to teach her daughters the aristocratic expectations of directing homes of their own. She also taught the girls the basics of reading and writing, primarily so they could read the Scriptures. Her sons either had a live-in tutor to teach reading, mathematics, the natural sciences, Latin, and French, or they were sent away to boarding school before sailing to England to receive a higher education.

Plantation wives, in total, had the responsibilities of all household duties, child rearing, conjugal obligations, and offering of southern hospitality as hostesses to numerous house guests, many uninvited.

Legally, colonial women were allotted inferior status. They were the chattel of their husbands. All decisions were made by the men. Most women deferred to their husbands to choose the designs of and to purchase their fashions. Women did not make contracts or wills, exercise rights over their children, could not sue nor bring suit in court, execute a deed nor administer an estate. The right of women to vote was a century and a half away.

YOUNG MARTHA

1731–1747

June, 1731 "Push! push! Mis Dandridge. That babin is sure to come soon." Mim wiped Frances's forehead with a wet cloth that was almost as steamy as the humidity of the day. Frances Dandridge had started her labor the previous afternoon—slowly at first, with a feeling of apprehension mixed with the familiar twinge of her soon-to-return women's monthlies. She knew the baby was nearly there because she remembered her own mother bearing the pain of child-birth many times. Twice Frances had assisted with one child born alive and one born dead. She had always felt that was her fault because of her clumsy treatment of the baby boy, who had trouble getting out his first newborn cry. The stifling heat was creating fear in Frances as she relived the day when that tragedy had happened, watching her mother struggle for relief from the heat and the pain from the child who refused to release himself from her womb.

The faraway clouds on the horizon kept bumping into each other, creating a deafening sound which kept getting closer and closer. Frances remembered how her mother always explained the summer thunder as music from the Lord giving substance and blessings to thirsty crops. John remained out in the fields, preparing for the advent of a summer storm. He was fretful and unsettled, knowing that Frances was suffering during her first labor of childbirth. Mim had assured him at dinnertime that the time was near.

John took in a deep breath as his shoulders straightened in pride, knowing that his firstborn was due anytime. He tried to sort out the reason for the churning in his stomach. He wanted to believe it was a feeling of excitement, instead of worry for the health of Frances, who had promised him a houseful of boys.

The sky was a mixture of green and blue, blending into an ominous, indigo color. John knew the thunder drawing closer meant more rain, a raging wind, and more of those persistent mosquitoes. He reached into his pocket for a handkerchief to wipe his moist brow. He grimaced as he realized he had given it to Old Joe, to wrap around his nose when it started to bleed profusely. John pondered Joe's persistent bleeding. Always it happened on days when the wind blew and the rain poured.

Joe had been with the Dandridge family for thirteen years. John had paid twenty-five pounds for him at an auction which included his woman, Mim, who was nearly fourteen at that time. John Dandridge figured she would bring strong boys into this world to help with the field work. John's bargain had gained him only Mim herself, for Mim had never given birth to a child of her own.

Frances lay quietly on the saturated sheets, which were moist from the oppressive humidity, but mostly from the sweat melting from her body. Her head twisted as she tried to look down into the closed eyes of her little gift from Heaven. Slipping in and out of sleep, Frances raised her head and called, "Mim, Mim, please go outside and send someone to find Mr. Dandridge. Just say he's supposed to come upstairs to see me and don't tell him anything else!"

Frances laid her head down, giving out an almost silent whimper. She knew that John would be a protective, kind, and loving father. Her feelings vacillated from euphoric happiness to a gnawing sense of disappointment. With a faint smile she repeated to herself, "June 2, 1731 born to John Dandridge and Frances Orlando Jones Dandridge, their first child." Much needed sleep overtook her as she drifted slowly into a deep slumber, her baby girl lying beside her, also sleeping soundly.[1]

1739 Martha danced around her unmade bed. Rarely did her usual quiet manner permit such merriment, but it was her eighth birthday and Papa had promised her a trip into Williamsburg. Mim worked fastidiously to wind Martha's silky, sable-colored hair into a braid that would be curled into a circle and pinned at the nape of her neck.

"Mis Martha, if you don't fasten yourself to that chair now your pa is gonna go to town without you!" It was unusual for Mim to speak to Martha with a sharp tongue. Martha's ways were civil, obedient, and trustworthy. Her behavior was such a contrast to her three high-spirited younger brothers—John, William and Bartholomew—who, nonetheless, never seemed to be in any trouble with the adults, especially Papa. The boys were not invited to make the journey into Williamsburg, which meant Martha would have her father all to herself for nearly a week.

The journey was anticipated by the Dandridge boys even though they were staying home. Trips always meant that toys and candies from England would be brought back to them. Mother always needed powder for mixing ink and new quill pens for her letter writing. She asked Martha to bring home a catalogue full of the latest English fashions.

This trip was unusual because Old Joe was to accompany Martha and her father, so that a doctor could look over the bothersome problem of the incessant nosebleeds he had been afflicted with since childhood. This was not the sort of treatment slaves usually received from their owners but John Dandridge was adamant that Joe be given the best medical advice available.

"Patcy, hurry along now—we'll miss the boat," Papa called to his beloved daughter from the bottom of the stairway. John Dandridge had given her the pet-name of Patcy several hours after her birth. Frances seldom used the name "Patcy" when addressing Martha but her younger brothers, imitating their father, always called her that.

Chestnut Grove, the tranquil settlement where the Dandridge family lived, was scarcely a quarter mile from the tidal Pamunkey River. A barge travelled back and forth between Chestnut Grove and Williamsburg twice a month, a journey which was nearly twenty-five miles by land. Since river travel saved several hours, the Dandridge family diligently planned their trips around the schedule of the barge.[2]

"Papa, Papa, wait! I need for Mim to finish my hair and wrap my satchel. We have plenty of time," returned Martha quickly.

"The horses and wagon are here and the boys are anxious to go with us to the river. I promised John he could drive the team back home," shouted Papa. Frances Dandridge, who had been in the nursery feeding her three-month-old daughter, Anna Maria, sprinted down the stairs, quickly manipulating the buttons on the bodice of her dress. As she approached the landing, she regained her composure, cleared her throat, and calmly said, "Mr. Dandridge, you promised me that John would never drive the wagon unless you or one of our field hands was there to oversee the ride."

"Frances, darlin', I've told you before that he is a natural handling the horses. Well, I'd trust him to drive all the way to Williamsburg by himself."

"Please, John, he is only seven years old, and with you away for several days, I don't know what I would do if something happened." She pleaded with her sable eyes as she waited for her husband to promise that someone else would safely bring the boys back.

"Darlin', I could never turn away from those big, dark eyes of yours. Of course, I'll make sure John has plenty of attention and help." He leaned over and caressed Frances. "You get plenty of rest whilst I'm gone. That baby girl needs a mother who can provide healthy sustenance." The tender moment of parting was interrupted as Martha and Mim flew down the stairs, with the satchel all tightly wrapped with a leather strap and Martha's hair firmly in place. They giggled as they stopped short at the discovery of Mother and Papa embracing at the bottom of the stairs.

"Hurry along now, Papa, we'll miss the boat," Martha chortled, as she mimicked her father. Then she slipped around their joined forms and scurried out the door to the waiting wagon.

Martha Jones Dandridge knew this was to be the best day of her life. The subtle wind blowing above the river brushed against her face. She gazed into the swirling water. Undulating ripples suggested forms, just as the white puffy clouds overhead did. She saw people moving quickly, coaches pulled by trotting horses, large houses with enormous trees blowing in the wind, all the things she remembered from her first visit to Williamsburg the year before.

Startled, Martha saw her father jump to his feet and give directions to the head boatman. "Pull the pole forward and quickly! Joe, move yourself over to show Mr. Westerly how to guide this boat." Joe moved with caution because he had barged with Mr. Westerly before and knew he didn't like unsolicited help.

The boat was newly built, with a six-foot beam instead of the usual four feet and a length of fifteen feet, adding more space for transporting goods to Williamsburg. A boat crew usually required two men, but with the added width and length this one needed an extra man.

"Set yourself down, blacky. My men only take orders from me," bellowed Mr. Westerly as he thrust Joe toward the side.

"Now, now, Westerly, Joe here can navigate these waters with one hand tied behind his back. The wind's calm so's we shouldn't have any trouble settin' on course," Mr. Dandridge said. "One more pair of hands will assure a safe trip." Mr. Westerly jerked his head to one side, motioning for Joe to grasp the pole and start poling.

No longer fearing a confrontation, Martha settled back down on her hard seat knowing that Papa had diplomatically avoided an unpleasant situation with Westerly. She had overheard Pa tell Mother that he sure hoped that Bo Bolling would be the head boatman today. Papa didn't care for Mr. Westerly, because he treated his subordinates so poorly.

"What can I get for my best girl?" asked Papa. "Mim prepared a basket for us and your favorite crispy chicken is just awaitin' to be eaten."

"I couldn't eat now, Papa," Martha answered. "My tummy is clenchin' with excitement. Maybe later. How much longer will it be before we get there?" she asked impatiently.

"You watch the sun, and when it disappears behind Ball Mountain, we'll be close to the fork. Keep your eye on Old Joe, because he'll be workin' harder as we approach the currents." Martha knew how worried Pa was about the nosebleeds. She knew how her father depended on Joe for advice on farming their difficult soil and his way of handling all the farmhands.

The currents could become troublesome if the winds were westerly where the Pamunkey River forked into the York River. Old Joe assisted the regular deckhands to keep from turning around and heading back into the Pamunkey. The slight winds left the currents unagitated as the transition was safely made from one river to another. They would soon be at Queen's Creek Landing, and that meant Williamsburg was only a mile away.[3]

"Patcy darlin', are you sure you don't want a bite of bread and a chicken leg?" asked Papa, stepping around two barrels to reach his daughter.

"Papa, I couldn't eat anything right now. I'm busy watching to make sure our barge doesn't get caught in the whirlpool."

Papa carefully studied Martha's face and realized she was suffering some worry about the safety of the river trip.

"Now darlin', no need to worry. This may be the calmest and quietest trip we've ever made down the river. You have so many surprises ahead today, my little birthday girl! We'll be in Williamsburg in 'most an hour." Papa pressed his lips against Martha's shiny forehead while she surveyed the water below just one more time to make sure the currents remained steady.

The barge slowly paralleled the unsteady wooden dock. The winds were northerly which caused the stern to float itself away from the dock. The bow was comfortable as it laid into the wharf, but the dockhands scurried aft, using their poles to push the stern back toward the dock. Martha took in a deep breath. The air which enveloped her smelled like the Williamsburg she remembered. Martha had only visited the capital once before, to attend the funeral of her Aunt Unity who was married to Papa's brother Uncle William.[4] Martha had always felt a self-punishing guilt about the visit because she felt little sense of mourning for someone she hardly knew.

As far back as Martha could remember, Papa had told her stories about Williamsburg during "Publick Times," which always generated a city full of high spirits, comradeship, numerous business dealings, and the renewal of old friendships with family and friends. Plantation life can be solitary for a girl who has only robust brothers. However, she loved helping with baby Anna Maria, now called Nancy, and anticipated her sister's companionship as she grew older. After Aunt Unity's funeral service, her cousin Nathaniel had come home with the Dandridge family and spent nearly all the summer before returning to Williamsburg.[5] Nate was like an older brother to Martha. He could do so many things—read, write, spell, recite, and decipher. And could he ride! He promised Martha he would teach her to ride on his next visit to their farm in Chestnut Grove.

A dazzling black carriage waited by the dock. Sitting proudly holding the reins was Nate, waving his arm high above his head, shouting, "Patcy, Uncle John! Over here." He jumped carefully from the beautiful horse-drawn vehicle and dashed toward the wharf.

Martha returned Nate's greeting by shouting, "Nate, Nate, come help us. Papa is going straight to give his papers to Mr. Carter, and I'm going straight to your house."

Nate reached for Martha's hand as she nearly jumped into his arms. He reached under her shoulders and gently lifted and swirled around to place her safely on the dock.

"Oh Nate, how I have longed to see you and talk to you. I have so much to tell you."

Nate quickly kissed her cheek and said, "I have so much to tell you! Come quickly and see our new carriage. It just arrived from London and it is the pride of our family. Pa let me come to get you and it is the first time he let me drive it all by myself. Everyone in Williamsburg wants a drive, but I promised Pa I'd bring you and Uncle John right home."

Martha paused for a minute while she waited for the dizziness in her head to diminish. Seven hours on the barge made her lightheaded as she stepped lightly on firm ground.

Nate said, "You're just gettin' your land legs. You'll be all right in a little bit."

Old Joe was unloading the baggage and the food basket while Papa opened his valise and arranged the papers inside. He jumped from the rocking barge and met Nate with a hardy handshake. "Hello, Nate my boy, you have grown at least a foot since I last saw you."

"Yes, Sir. Pa says he's sure I'll be a tall one," he said, grinning and returning the handshake. "Come and see the new carriage. It is very easy to drive. It's light in weight and Pa says it's flexible. He told me I couldn't call it a buggy or a wagon 'cause it's a carriage!"

John Dandridge looked forward to his semiannual trip into Williamsburg. "*This will be a hasty visit because of all the responsibilities back in Chestnut Grove*," he reminded himself as he took in a deep breath of tidewater air. John loved the cool breeze blowing off the Chesapeake Bay. Going to Williamsburg in the summertime always meant a drop in temperature, which also meant good sleeping weather. Inland weather was nearly unbearable in June, especially with the nuisance of the enormous mosquitoes. The tidelands escaped many of the insects that were so bothersome to the plateau folks, but it was a mixed blessing because the Chesapeake lands had their own breed of bugs.

Old Joe, his arms loaded with luggage, rambled toward the carriage. Once in place, it became obvious that the fine new carriage could not hold two satchels, one valise, a large and overweight food basket filled with fresh goods from the Dandridge farm, and four people.

"Joe, you remember where brother William's house is, don't you?" asked John Dandridge.

Knowing what was coming, Joe replied, "Yes, Sir." He stumbled backwards and lowered his head. Mr. Dandridge and Martha, with Nate driving, were already seated in the carriage.

Joe had poled most of the trip down the Pamunkey and the York River. Even though it had been an easier day because of the calm waters, he felt like a field hand who had just finished a twelve-hour day in a blistering sun. His powerful appetite reminded him that he had not had food since leaving home early that morning.

"You follow us at your own speed, Joe. There'll be cool sleepin' in the hay. The breeze is comin' up," said Mr. Dandridge. The carriage lunged forward while three heads jerked back and then forward in unison.

The dust billowed into Joe's sweaty face as he patiently waited to regain sight of the speeding carriage. "That boy will kill all of 'um before they get home," Old Joe said, shaking his head in disbelief. As the dust dissipated, Joe could see that the carriage continued to travel at an unsafe speed. He watched until it disappeared into the dusk, then turned and walked back to the barge, which was being unloaded by the deck-hands. "Are ya willin' to let me help for some water and maybe a hunk of bread?" Joe asked Westerly, the boss.

Mr. Westerly was an overfed, round man with unusually short arms and legs. His head was as round as his middle and rimmed with a ring of unkempt, bright red hair. His body odor reminded Joe of dried tobbaco soaked in a brine of body sweat. "We don' need no help. We don' have no bread nor water either. Now git, black man!"

Joe began walking the one-mile trip into Williamsburg on the dusty road that led to the Francis Street house of William Dandridge. He knew what lay ahead, little or no food and a bed of hay to share with the horses, cows, and chickens. He knew it would be a long time until morning.

The activity outside Martha's bedroom window was a mixture of conversation between her father and her uncle, street noise from the wagons, and clopping horses heading for the morning meetings at the Virginia Capitol. Martha recognized the voices of her father and her uncle, but there was a stranger whose voice was nearly inaudible. Both Mr. Dandridges returned sonorously that they would not pay that outrageous money for an acreage that already had five years of growing tobacco leaving only two years for growing healthy plants.

"Now, you look here, man. We know what kind of business you're running!" Papa blurted.

"You're trading with man alike, be it Indians, sea pirates or your own kind." Uncle Will pleaded with Papa to lower his tone a bit.

Papa ignored his brother and continued, "Why, I'd never let anyone cheat me into thinkin' that your deal was worthy of contemplation. It isn't even respectable, you unscrupulous shyster!" Papa turned and went into the stable wiping his forehead with the back of his hand.

Martha was on her feet, peering out of the open window. She held the transparent curtain lumped into her fist in an attempt to hide her curious face. She loved her Pa so deeply that she had to swallow the tears that lodged in her eyes and fell into the back of her throat, making it ache. She had never heard her father speak so loudly, nor had she ever witnessed such anger.

The two Dandridge brothers had now been joined by Nate who had also heard the acrimonious conversation.

"Pa, can I help?" asked Nate.

"No, Nate. Please get the carriage ready. Uncle John and I need to be on our way to the meeting which starts soon. I'm going to say good-by to Mr. Carter here and we'll be off."

When Nate reached the stable, he could see his uncle speaking in low tones to Old Joe who was grooming the horse. He could read Joe's furrowed brow but he couldn't understand what Uncle John was saying. Joe nodded his head toward Nate, silently rolling his eyes to let John know that someone had entered the stable.

"Good mornin', Nate. Come in. We're gettin' ready to hitch up," John Dandridge said.

"I'll be glad to help, but can you tell me what happened with Mr. Carter, Uncle John?" John shook his head and lowered his eyes.

By midmorning Nate and Martha had their heads together, laughing and talking over mugs of hot water with warm milk, and fresh biscuits and honey. Nate gave Martha a confidence that seemed to escape her at home and other social gatherings. His gift to her was his ability to listen to her every word and then give needed advice, encouragement, and assurance. There had not been a word spoken about the confrontation between her father, uncle, and the stranger that morning. Martha would like to forget what happened, but her memory wouldn't let her tuck it away.

Nate, always perceptive, opened the subject. "Did you hear the conversation between Pa, your father, and Mr. Carter early this morning?" asked Nate. "I was worried they might have awakened you and I know how tired you were last night."

Martha reluctantly admitted, "Yes, I did, and I am so scared! I have never heard my Papa so angry. Why did it happen?"

Nate studied Martha's face, amazed by her intellect, which he thought was far beyond her eight years.

"Your father said it had to do with a piece of land that my father and yours want to buy, but it is nearly useless acreage and Mr. Carter wants way too much for it," answered Nate carefully. He did know more about the land deal but didn't think Martha could be interested in what the circumstances were about. He also knew that if the land deal went through, it meant that Nate and his father would be moving to the plateau, closer to Martha and her family. He had been hopeful that he could save that information and present it to her as a special birthday gift. "We'll have to walk to Gloucester Street, cause the carriage is already there, and Joe can't bring it back because Doc Walters is goin' to look over him today," Nate said with a large grin. "Come on, we'd better get our day started. You'll need to have a rest this afternoon so's you can be ready for the assembly tonight."

"I'll be ready before you are, Nathaniel Dandridge," laughed Martha, as she jumped up and sprinted up the stairs. Her hair was fluttering behind her small head as she took two steps at a time. She didn't have Mim to pin it back for her, but she didn't care. She loved having her hair fall down her back, even though she knew her mother wouldn't approve.

Martha quickly dressed and brushed her long, shiny hair, her thoughts flashing back to the early morning confrontation. She knew her father had planned an important meeting with a Mr. Carter. This had been arranged several months ago so that it could be held during Publick Times in Williamsburg. Martha told herself that it would take a long time to forget this morning's incident. "I'll ask Papa what happened on the way back to Chestnut Grove."

Martha and Nate sat on a bench in front of the apothecary, watching the men who were turned out in their knee breeches and stockings with garish buckles on the shoes. Each wore a coat and vest. Their coats had sweeping skirts and deep cuffs with large buttons. All wore fashionable powdered wigs. The women relished the shops. They swept in and out, looking over the latest English fashions. "I can't remember ever seeing such beautiful dresses," sighed Martha. "Mother has the drawings in her catalogue but they're so colorful when you actually see them."

"Wait until tonight when everyone meets at the Governor's Palace. The richest planters and their wives will be there," said Nate. "The Spotwoods and the Custis family will be there. Everyone says that John Custis is a crabby old man who gives orders to everyone in sight, but mostly to his children. There isn't a Mrs. Custis. Mr. Byrd, who loves to pester and pinch women, will be there."

"Mr. Bird? Is that his real name? You mean he has a name like dog or cat?" Martha's laughter rolled from her lips. "I bet he looks like a bird?—probably with long skinny legs covered with his silk stockings, a grandee who preens like a peacock!"

"His name is really Mr. Byrd, B-y-r-d," said Nate, breaking up at Martha's question. "Pa says it used to be spelled B-i-r-d, but his ancestors in England changed the spelling so's it would look and sound like a family in a higher class; and yes, he is a grandee, with property and influence.[6] His wife just ignores him while he plays cards or dances with every young girl. He will even ask the chambermaids to dance, but they must always refuse. Mrs. Chiswell probably won't come tonight. At the last assembly, Mr. Byrd threw her onto an upstairs bed and tried to kiss her until she couldn't breathe. Everyone said Mrs. Byrd cried all the way home," Nate laughed.[7]

"You just made that story up, Nate Dandridge. You've been reading those books," said the unbelieving Martha. "Do you think Mr. Carter will be there?"

"Maybe. He travels some. He wasn't here for the last party," answered Nate. "Let's walk to the Capitol. Maybe we can sneak in and watch the powdered wigs at work."

"I want to go the the apothecary first. I promised the boys I'd bring them something."

Gloucester Street was lined with towering oak trees. The day was sultry but the on-shore breeze turned the trees into overhead fans, keeping those underneath cool. The townfolk's houses lined the main street. All were uniform, two-story dwellings with decorative front doors and clear glass windows and they all seemed to be freshly painted.

"Come on, I'll race you to Market Square," shouted Nate. " You'll love looking over the huge Berkshire hogs. Their bacon's the best! They just came in on *The Morning Star* a couple of days ago. There are passenger pigeons, too. Come on. The last one there's a rotten egg."

Martha had a diminutive body. She was small boned with delicate hands and tiny feet. Her legs were no match for Nate's, whose elongated legs were quick and steady. "Wait, wait, you're too fast, come back."

Turning around, Nate ran back and picked Martha up and threw her over his shoulder. "There, now there won't be any race. It will be a tie."

"Put me down, Nathaniel Dandridge!" Martha kicked her feet and started to cry. "I can do my own running and I'm not a rotten egg."

"Martha Dandridge, you are the prettiest egg in the whole of Virginia. Let's go on so's you can buy yourself a birthday present. Come on, pretty girl, we need to do some shopping for the boys, and you promised your mother to bring her some catalogues and the latest Virginia Gazette."

Dr. Walter's house was located on the east side of Williamsburg. His home was distinguished by the brilliant red color painted on the wooden siding. Most people called it the Cardinal House because the color matched the numerous cardinals that lived in the oak trees that lined Gloucester Street. Old Joe felt uncomfortable approaching the house. Mr. Dandridge was to meet Joe on the stoop at one o'clock. He was unsure of the time but his stomach clarified that food would be an appropriate prospect. Mr. William's house servant had allowed that a bowl of white beans with a hard biscuit was adequate for a field hand's breakfast. Joe often felt light-headed and suffered from frequent piercing pains in his lower abdomen. The nosebleeds seemed to be coming more often and lasting longer. "I'm grateful Mr. John is concerned about 'um, but I know the Lord will do with me just as He pleases," Joe said to himself. "No doctor will take care of an old black man, anyway."

At that moment, the front door opened and standing in the doorway was a large gray-haired black woman with her apron wrapped around her arms, which were crossed and lying across her large bosom. "You git offen the porch, blacky, now!" screeched the woman. "This isn' no place for a lowclass black man. We ain' gonna feed no one no how. Now git!" She waved her strong black arms in Joe's face.

Joe thought her arms looked like the legs of an oversized ox as they flapped and fluttered in his face. "I'm waitin' for Mr. Dandridge. He is taking me for to see Doc Walters," said Joe, as he used his long arms to protect his face and upper body.

"My footin! Doc Walters never fixed no black man," retorted the woman. Her heavy lips were round and wide as saliva sprayed Joe's face. "Besides, no white man would fix a man who has a nose as big as a mule."

Joe looked down at his feet in embarrassment. He couldn't find the words to explain to the woman why he was waiting on the porch for Mr. Dandridge. "If'n you don' mind, I'll be waitin' in back 'til Mr. Dandridge gits here," he said softly. Joe turned and stumbled across the dried grass, and found a large full oak tree behind the house. He sat down between two exposed tree roots but found that comfort was difficult for a man of Joe's size. "Please, Lord, given me the strength to git back to Ches'nut Grove and my woman," prayed Joe to himself. "Will'amsbur' is no place for a black field hand." Joe lay back, putting his weary head against the coarse, uneven tree trunk and fell into an unsettled sleep.

John Dandridge felt the disappointment and frustration of his only full day in Williamsburg. The morning began with the vain attempt to bargain with Franklin Carter, who owned five hundred acres of tobacco land promised to the Dandridge brothers. Neither John nor Will had ridden out to look over the property, but Carter had promised high quality soil with seven prosperous years of tobacco growing. Included in the land price was an introduction to Mr. Carter's English factor who would then assure the sale of the Dandridge tobacco for a small percentage. John and Will looked forward to the prospect of shipping more tobacco to London and Bristol. The English believed tobacco to be a magic drug that cured most ailments. Since the late 1690s sales had been growing with enormous profits for the colonist planters.

It was by accident that John Dandridge learned of the land sale. Several months ago he was preparing his journals to report land sales in Kent County to the Land Assessor in Williamsburg. As County Clerk, John dutifully fulfilled this obligation twice a year. John owned only five hundred acres of land, which hardly qualified him as an aristocratic planter, but the Clerk's job availed him of inside information of land bought and sold and made him privy to land put on the market. This piece came to his attention for two reasons. First, the land had been measured and surveyed by a very reliable A. Washington, whose signature was on the survey. Secondly, the proximity to Chestnut Grove made the acquisition even more attractive. There was a single pile home with four rooms and two fireplaces, a barn, and a freshwater well on the property. William and John wanted to expand their holdings, and had used forbearance in waiting for the piece that met their criteria of price and location. Certainly, the owner was a reputable man. Mr. Carter had achieved wealth and reputation as a land owner and grower. He also had bartered artifacts from the Indians and then shipped the items to England for sale to the curious English who wanted to know more about New World savages.

Franklin Carter and John Dandridge had corresponded several times and negotiated a temporary sales agreement that suited both parties. The spring meeting in Williamsburg was to draw the sale to a close with concurrence on several items. Before John's arrival in the capital, Will made an appointment with the Land Assessor to search records for verification of land measurements. The western movements into the Shenandoah Valley for land acquisition had created a "land rush" that equalled the Old World colonization of the New World. Record-keeping efficiency was unreliable to the point that rumors and innuendo were included in most conversations of the Williamsburg elite.

William Dandridge was a frequent dinner guest in many upper-class homes. He was a lively conversationalist with keen observation skills, using both his eyes and ears. He delighted both sexes with his ability to reconnoiter and then mimic his information sources. Since becoming a widower a year before, he was on numerous guest lists to even the numbers at dining tables, especially if there was an available woman invited. Match-making was a very old game and it hadn't escaped life in the colonies. It was at a recent party that Will learned that rascals pretending to be land surveyors had invaded Virginia. They used high-quality circumferentors "or brass, magnetic, compasses" mounted on tripods. They had chain men working the chain lines for authenticity. These scalawags had no idea how to use the equipment but were quick to collect a fee and leave a worthless survey behind.

Three days before John and Martha's arrival in Williamsburg, Will had learned that the land survey might be bogus. What he didn't know was how much Franklin Carter knew or didn't know about the survey. The Carter reputation seemed honorable enough, but recently Franklin was preoccupied, and oftentimes unavailable for discussion on any matter. Other men showed concern for the dramatic change and had no compunction about debating Franklin's transformation.

The previous night, John and William had a grave conversation about the discrepancies in the survey. Will poured John a second glass of brandy as they examined the plat of the property which was located approximately five miles north of the Dandridge farm at Chestnut Grove. The survey appeared immaculate, with many details which, unfortunately, caught the attention of both men. The elaborate compass card had been carefully drawn and perfectly measured, but the neglectful surveyor had used the wrong directions on each of the points. The drawing showed the direction to be southwest. There was also a drawn profile of a nearby mountain but the only rises north of Chestnut Grove were rolling hills. Will shared with John the concerns about recent unreliable surveys. Will had become suspicious when he discovered the directional errors, and visited the Assessor the following day. The land they were buying was, indeed, the parcel on the survey. But it was not north of Chestnut Grove, it was south, and it had already been growing tobacco for five years!

Before retiring, the two brothers decided they must confront Mr. Carter with this information the first thing in the morning. They had their documentation and they planned to announce that there would be no further negotiation, and that the only discussion would be with an attorney in good repute and the Virginia State Land Assessor.

Mr. Carter's reaction to the discovery was, as expected, a complete denial. He insisted that he was also duped by the survey if, indeed, it was counterfeit. He asked to take the plat to the Assessor himself to clarify the records. The brothers agreed that the three men would go together, but Mr. Carter declared that he would be unavailable because he was expected at the Council meeting at nine o'clock. Will suggested to John that they begin researching the survey and gather all the available information and meet Mr. Carter at his convenience in the afternoon for further discussion.[8]

Joe tried to raise himself from the cramped position between the two tree roots. His right foot and lower leg tingled as he put full weight on both legs. The blazing afternoon sun ignited his body into a parched, water-deprived condition while he watched his sweat drip like rainfall on a treetop. He bent his head back to survey the location of the sun and knew the time was late afternoon. "*Where is'n Mr. Dandridge?*" Joe thought to himself.

Joe knew that John Dandridge's preoccupation resulted from his concern with the Carter land deal. Mr. John was a man of great integrity and honesty, and pity to the man who tried to deceive him on any matter. Joe was a long-time confidant to John Dandridge and knew about the land purchase. John had asked Old Joe to journey to the acreage and inspect it for its veracity. Joe had packed food, water, and a light blanket into the Dandridge wagon where he would sleep during the two nights he would be gone. He started out on a burning hot April day that ended with a thunder and lightning storm. Joe turned the wagon around because the nose bleeds reappeared with disabling fury. He knew the nose bleeds always depleted his strength and resulted in fatigue that usually lasted for several days. Mr. John, with his usual calm, sent Joe to his cabin for rest and recovery, but several days later John suggested he accompany them to Williamsburg to see Doc Walters.

"*I guess I'll be heading back to Mr. Will's house and wait for Mr. John,*" Joe thought. He knew he needed water and food. Unexpectedly, Joe remembered he was to drive the Dandridges back home. Mr. John had dropped Joe by the doctor's house and said he would be back by one o'clock. John Dandridge's ethics made punctuality a priority, so Joe realized there must be an emergency. He started the trek back to Mr. William's home on foot. Fatigue consumed his body as he lumbered through the dusty streets and onto a path that spewed powdery dust into his mouth and eyes. The William Dandridge house seemed miles away.

Martha and Nate gaily kicked rocks partially hidden by the swirling dust on the footpath as they walked back to the Dandridge home. "You're going to miss your nap this afternoon. You'll need a tubbing instead," laughed Nate.

Martha's arms were full of packages and she felt so proud of the gifts she had purchased for her three brothers and mother. Papa told Martha that it was time the boys learned their letters so they could start reading the Bible, and learn to cipher to help with the receipts. Martha bought materials for each boy to make a journal for practicing their letters. She knew they would be disappointed if she didn't bring a toy, so she also purchased a brand new game called Diabolo. The shop lady told Martha the game was played in all of Europe, especially by the children in the court of King George. Martha knew her brothers loved tops, and this new top could be whipped in the air to see how high it would go. Another challenge for John, Will, and Bart would be to see if the top could be caught in different bodily positions. "*Mother will want the boys outside to play this game,*" Martha thought as she smiled to herself. Her biggest thrill, however, was the birthday present she had bought for herself.

Martha and Nate had entered the apothecary, which also sold all kinds of books, books about balms and fever powders, Greek and Latin grammars, Plutarch, Rousseau, and the latest novels from London. Nate suggested a book about Pocahontas, but Martha didn't want him to know about her reading deficiencies. Under the guise of a proficient reader, she found a dance manual with diagrammed instructions. Martha squealed with delight and shouted for Nate to give approval to her choice. Martha, almost giddy, said, "Mother promised a dance tutor would come to our house and teach me fine dancing, but now I can teach myself with this manual! Papa will be so proud. Oh, I can't wait to get home. Nate, will you help me when we get back to your house?"

The afternoon wasn't nearly long enough for Martha to shop, observe the people and admire the extraordinary Capitol building, the Governor's Palace, Bruton Parish Church, and the rows of beautifully painted two-story houses. The elegant carriages brilliantly paraded up and down Gloucester Street, adorned with black drivers in their finest ruffled white shirts, with necks stiff and eyes looking straight ahead. She soon learned to tell the difference between the visitors and the towns-people by their clothing. "Nate, I have had the best time today. I would like to live in Williamsburg someday. Only thing is that I want to wear beautiful dresses like the rich women wear," Martha said.

The tall oak trees furnished shade like an open umbrella over Martha and Nate.

The usual afternoon Chesapeake breezes were at rest for the moment, depleting the air of movement and comfort. "Why aren't there more trees in Williamsburg? I can barely get my breath out in this hot sun," Martha whined. "Mother would be very angry if she could see me without my bonnet."

Nate grasped Martha's elbows and guided her across Gloucester Street as two wagons, drivers, and horses came face to face with one another. Both drivers pulled their reins and slowed as the two children carefully crossed in between. "Fire is always a big worry so there's not too many trees growing in Williamsburg.[9] Hurry on now, we'll be home soon where there's a big oak tree for us to sit under," Nate said. "Here, let me carry some of your presents so you can rest your arms."

"It's not my arms that are tired. It's my feet!" answered Martha. "Come on. Let's hurry so's I can take off my shoes and give my toes some air."

Franklin Carter was a second-generation American. He owned fifteen thousand acres of prime farm land which was worked by indentured laborers and nearly a hundred slaves. Mr. Carter personally supervised all plantings of crops, mostly tobacco, working from morning to night. He owned a grist mill and a sawmill, traded with the Indians, and trafficked in slaves. He realized that his businesses and stable reputation were in jeopardy after his dealings with the Dandridge brothers. He felt himself to be a man of great ambition and energy, but this latest problem from what he thought was a misunderstanding, clearly substantiated his worst nightmare. His lack of trust in his attorney Jonathan Milton, who was his brother-in-law, had defiled the sale. Franklin was heavily invested and frequently in need of ready cash. He relied on his attorney to find ways to improve the cash flow.

After leaving John Dandridge's home, Mr. Carter made haste to Jonathan Milton's law office. Mr. Carter's wife, Ann, had insisted that her brother should shoulder the responsibility of managing all of their business accounts. With reluctance, Carter agreed, knowing full well that Jonathan was capable of fabricating schemes of real estate promotion to increase revenues.

Carter quickly opened the law office door and found Jonathan with his feet on his desk, reading the latest Virginia Gazette. "Get yourself up and out of that chair!" Carter blurted, grabbing his shirt. "What have you done to the plat on the land the Dandridges were going to buy? I know you have falsified the land survey."

"Set yourself down," answered Jonathan. "I have no idea what you are talking about. We have worked together and you know I have never done any transactions without your knowledge. Calm down and tell me what it is you want."

"You know I've borrowed money from the Bank of Baltimore and I'm on the line to pay up in three months for the acres out west in the Shenandoah. I put up the deeds for both the clean northwest piece out by Chestnut Creek and the southeast piece that is farmed by the Hampton family. The Dandridge brothers want the northwest site but somehow they think they're getting a piece with a house and an unspoiled land. Now, my *dear* brother-in-law, you tell me how and why, when I had a shoo-in sale, we end with this skullduggery? So help me, I'll fix you so's you never practice law anywhere in Virginia again."

Jonathan Milton was a tall and much-too-lean man. His begrimed, coal-black hair was pulled back into a cue tied with a once-white ribbon. His ruffled, white shirt had a grimy ring surrounding his unusually long neck. His irritating habit of cleaning his craggy fingernails with a pocketknife, never in his own privacy, provoked everyone in his company. Jonathan had worked hard to pay Carter's bank indebtedness before the deadline. Shortly after taking over the Carter accounts, Jonathan realized he had access to the net worth of his sister and brother-in-law. It seemed reasonable to share in their wealth even though most of it was on paper. His schemes were mostly legitimate, but at times he couldn't resist risking terms that netted him more than the usual commission paid by Franklin. The Chestnut Creek sale was a temptation Jonathan couldn't ignore. He handled all correspondence during the negotiations between John Dandridge and Franklin Carter. The northern piece was mortgaged for twenty-five pounds, as was the southern piece. Carter then purchased the Shenandoah piece free and clear, using the money from the mortgaged property. When Carter decided to sell the Chestnut Creek land to John Dandridge, he set a price of fifty pounds, which would pay the mortgages.

In the meantime, the Crown made inordinate demands of taxation on the colonists, causing an inflationary spiral. Jonathan, using Carter's name as he negotiated the sale to the Dandridge brothers, precipitously and without Carter's knowledge, raised the price to one hundred pounds. His plan was to pay the Bank of Baltimore their fifty pounds leaving Carter two pieces of land, the Shenandoah and the southern farms with a farm house free and clear. This arrangement seemed foolproof, and irresistible because it netted Jonathan a percentage of the sale as well as fifty pounds that no one would know about.

Jonathan hadn't known that the wrong survey had been sent to John Dandridge. John and Will had been very excited to think there was a home on the plat, which would mean Will and Nate could move from Williamsburg to the farm to grow tobacco.

Jonathan tried to put his devious mind to work to solve this mix-up. "Franklin, I need some time to look into the situation. Can you give me that favor?" Jonathan's confusion caused his head to whirl. He reached his shaky hand into the bucket used for drinking water and sponged his flushed face.

"I'll give you five minutes to settle this trickery! My reputation as an honest man is out on the line and your chances to continue lawyering, if I have my way, may be at an end," said a scowling Carter. He moved toward the door on unsteady feet. He turned toward Jonathan and pointed his trembling hand. "You'd better pray for an honest answer on this matter, or pray you'll be goin' to Heaven instead of that other place," he said, slamming the door behind him.

Jonathan quickly realized that in his haste to covertly extract fifty pounds for himself he had somehow switched surveys. The negotiations had been made through a messenger, explicitly regarding the one hundred pound price. When the Dandridges asked to see the plat, he had sent the southern survey by mistake. Apparently John Dandridge was so excited about the house and outbuildings, he had not carefully studied the location. Jonathan pondered the plausibility of this possible explanation. He was aggrieved at his own untidy business methods, thinking "*Carter will take his future business away in any case.*" Jonathan wanted to own the land himself and lease it to the Dandridges. He envisaged giving Franklin the bill of sale and fifty pounds. Jonathan would then convert the title into his name, lease the land to the Dandridge brothers, retire the loan to the Bank of Baltimore, have fifty pounds profit and own five hundred acres free and clear.

SPRING 1745 The dogwood branches were laden with white blossoms, open and reaching for the brilliant spring sunshine. The daylight hours stretched longer into the early evening providing opportunity to the Dandridge family for catching up on the days' events, which were numerous. Mother always looked forward to her children's enjoyment of outside activities, especially the boys. John, at the age of thirteen, had become a necessary member of the planting and harvesting team of the plantation. Papa was very proud of his ability to read and decipher the receipts. William was still struggling with letters and numbers, at age eleven, while Bartholomew, at age eight, had mastered all the letters giving him fluency and ability to do his lessons as well as to help Will with his. Papa, who loved to give his girls nicknames, called seven-year-old Anna Maria "Nancy." The burgeoning Dandridge family now included Mother's namesake, Frances, aged one. Mother always knew that each time a new baby was about to arrive Papa would drop to his knees each night to ask the Lord for another boy.

Martha's petite body barely reached five feet, but proportionally, her small waist corresponded with her bosom and hips, likening her shape to the work of a prodigious sculptor. Her dark hair kept the glimmering sheen as though sunlight was always shining through it. The ebony eyes blended with her fair and unblemished complexion. Martha, at fourteen, was growing into a young woman with gracious manners, a benevolent sense of kindness, a strong Christian conviction, and an intuitive judgment of the character of others.

Frances Jones Dandridge wanted her children to become learned in the basics of reading the Bible. "Reading is the key to salvation," Mother repeatedly told her children. Martha knew that her mother had little schooling herself and that her father was a far better tutor than her mother. However, Papa also insisted that each child be able to read the Scriptures. Frances took the responsibility, making sure each of her children achieved Bible reading. Martha's mother had a quick mind to memorize, which was how she read the Bible. Her grandfather and her father were ministers, and with the repetitiveness of the daily Scripture readings each morning and evening as she was growing up, Frances was able to remember the chapters and verses that were her grandfather's favorites. This was an unfathomed secret that Frances held within herself forever.

It was Papa who tutored the children in learning their letters and numbers, when time permitted. Old Joe had begged Mr. Dandridge to teach him to read, which was a request that only a slave held in the highest reverence by his owner would dare ask. Papa agreed, then stopped the lessons when he learned from his brother William that some of the other plantation owners had heard the rumor that John Dandridge was "tryin' to teach his slave to read." The children loved Joe and begged Papa to let him, "learn with 'um." But Papa, thereafter, always made sure that Joe had other plantation duties.

Heaven itself could not possibly be as cloudless, warm, and full of color and scents as Virginia in the springtime, Martha's favorite time of year. The wild azaleas, rhododendrons, blue lobelia, morning glory, and violets were in full bloom, filling the air with wonderful aromas.

Springtime was also planting time. Papa and Uncle Will carefully planned the right time to drop the seeds into the warm April soil. The Dandridge brothers were not considered wealthy plantation farmers with hired overseers to supervise the slaves, so they meticulously supervised all aspects of planting. The brothers had had several successful years growing healthy plants, and were relieved when the return enabled them to receive a land grant to further expand their farm, by fifty acres. Both brothers increased the number of slaves to help with the tobacco, but were still considered outside the circle of the rich planters.

Martha dashed down the staircase, braiding her hair into one pigtail as she ran into the parlor. Mother was feeding Franny while she directed Nancy in the threading of a needle so she could finish her embroidery. Nancy always struggled with the needles. Papa teased her, saying, "God gave her ears that could hear all the way to Williamsburg, but eyes that couldn't see across the room."

"Mother, I'm riding over to see Nate today. I can't wait to see all the blooming flowers along the way, and besides, Nate is going to give me a riding lesson. I'll be home early afternoon." With that she leaned over and kissed her mother gently on the cheek. Baby Frances smiled broadly, asking with her eyes for a kiss, too.

"Which horse are you taking? Not Princess! She is with foal and cranky," Mother asked, hardly taking a breath. "Does your father know you are going all the way over to Chestnut Creek for a riding lesson?" Frances Dandridge's dark eyes flashed, while her brow wrinkled across her forehead.

"Yes, Papa knows, and no, I'm not taking Princess, I'm taking Fatima and I'll be back early afternoon," Martha answered with respect and patience, troubled by her mother's behavior. She quickly shrugged her shoulders, knowing her mother was showing her concern and love for her with her look of displeasure. "I'll be careful, Mother, I promise."

Martha thought Nate would always be the love of her life, and she was just as sure that she was his. He had been her mentor in proper manners, especially Williamsburg manners, and he influenced her choices when picking cotton and silk for new clothes. He always told her that the color white was not as regal as the color purple like the English Royalty wore, but it was the color the angels wore, and she was an angel and should always wear it! And besides, it was his favorite color.

Nate also taught Martha how to ride. He knew that Martha would never be considered a competent rider. Her ninety-five pounds was hardly a match for the small pony of seven hundred pounds she first learned to ride. Both Princess and Fatima were Tennessee Walking Horses, which had a comfortable running walk and a smooth canter, but both horses sensed Martha's reluctance to take charge. John Dandridge had asked Nate to teach his children to ride, and Nate felt pleased and confident with the assignment. Young John, especially, could handle horses easily and adroitly. The other two boys would season with experience.

Martha's nightly prayers always included thanks to the Lord for working His ways to allow Nate to live closer to her. It now seemed that he had lived near the Pamunkey River at Chestnut Creek forever, but she remembered it was the spring of 1740 when the house was finally finished and the family were settled in, in time for planting. Martha's thoughts drifted back to that dreadful morning when her father and Uncle Will had the argument with a Mr. Carter in Williamsburg. She wasn't sure what had caused Papa to burst out with such anger, the like of which she had never seen before and hoped she would never see again. Someday she wanted to ask Nate about the incident again, but every time she remembered that day, she was usually giving prayers and ready for bed. Mother had told Martha that it had to do with the land Uncle William owned in Chestnut Creek, and to just be happy that they now lived close by.

Martha's thoughts continued to focus on the Virginia spring. The flowers bloomed profusely along the way to Nate's house. Fatima seemed to respond to the reins as Martha gently asked the horse to please behave and just canter. Fatima seemed to allow Martha control, but she often felt that Fatima was as mistrusting of her as she was of the horse. The ride to Uncle Will's took nearly an hour, which passed quickly because of Martha's reverie. She saw the old oak tree with a double, gnarled trunk she always used as a landmark. The debate about cutting it down and using it in the construction of the house had ended when her brother John said, "The Lord would never forgive the Dandridge family if the wood was going to be used to walk on. It is too pretty and it needs to be kept alive so's the Lord can enjoy it, too."

Martha shifted her weight back into the saddle as she pressured the reins slightly to slow Fatima down. She waved at Nate as Fatima eased to a complete stop. Martha gripped the reins and the horse's mane with her left hand, but forgot to grab the pommel before she swung her right leg over the rump of the horse. She moved so quickly that Nate could not warn her to put her right leg next to her left leg, move her hand to the cantle, and then jump down. Hanging precariously and still clinging to Fatima's mane, Martha's petite legs dangled as she lost her grip. She fell on her backside, raising dry dirt into her eyes, nose, and ears, as well as Nate's. She lay for a minute, half laughing and half crying. Nate helped her get herself upright and discovered her face was flushed and her hands sweaty. It was Nate who had suggested Martha ride full saddle instead of sidesaddle. He was sure her tiny body would have more control over the horse.

"Hello, cousin. Welcome to a day of learning how to gallop and dismount a horse," Nate chortled.

"Nate Dandridge, you tell anyone what just happened, why, I'll never, never talk to you ever again! Besides, I'll tell Uncle Will it was you who took Carter Lee's cap right off his head at Church last Sunday."

Nate, with his hands on his hips, threw his head backward and bellowed a deep laugh that emanated from his backbone. "If you tell my Pa that I took the cap, I'll tell Uncle John it was you, and you hid it under little Frances's quilt which was wet from where she threw up! Then we'll both have to 'fess up that we took it, the two of us."

Martha dusted herself off. She combined her laugh with Nate's infectious laughter as the two proceeded up the hill to the William Dandridge home.

A slight wind from the north developed, causing the dry dust to swirl and float through the air. The two cousins giggled while Nate grabbed his tricorn from his head, and began slapping it against Martha's backside to remove the fine, powdery dirt from her long petticoat.

"Not so hard, Nathaniel. After all Martha is our guest and how will she explain the hole you are about to pound into her skirt?"

Martha dabbed her eyes with her hanky. "Aunt Euphany! Hello." The familiar voice belonged to Euphany Wallace Dandridge, Uncle William's new wife. She was a large-boned woman, slightly plump, with large hands. Her face was never without a smile and Martha was extremely fond of her Aunt Euphany, especially when she played her harpsichord when the family gathered at Chestnut Creek. Her hands danced across the keys, stretching across nearly two octaves. Martha always unconsciously tucked her small hands behind her back when she watched Euphany play.

"Martha, darlin', are you sure you're okay?"

"Yes, I'm fine, the horse is fine, but Nate is being so uncivil to me that I may return home and never come back," Martha replied, her sunny disposition exposed as she began laughing.

"Come up to the house and drink a cool glass of tea before dinner. Nate can take you home in the wagon so's you don't have to ride back by yourself," Aunt Euphany said sympathetically. "You can hitch Fatima onto the back of the wagon, Nate. You won't mind doing that, will you?"

Sunday mornings at the John Dandridge farm bustled with activity. Mother always insisted that the Sabbath be a day of reverence, tranquillity, and quiescence, although Papa and young John still had to feed the livestock, William and Bartholomew took turns milking, and Martha helped with food preparation while Mother took charge of Nancy and Franny. Church meant that fresh, clean clothes were exchanged for the week's dirty ones, with a Saturday bath in between. Mim did not help on Sundays because she and Joe always took the farm wagon full of field-hands to Church over near the Benton farm. Mother's precept was—no loud voices, no disagreements, know your Sunday duties and carry them out, give thanks to the Lord for the week past, and pray for a bountiful week ahead.

The morning sky was cloudless, with an intense sun that already provided insufferable heat. Nate, rising early, was out in the stable getting his wagon and horse ready to take Martha and John to Church with him.

After driving Martha home from Chestnut Creek the day before, Nate spent the night with Uncle John and Aunt Frances. Nate offered to explain why Martha was late arriving home after she had promised to be home early in the afternoon. It was nearly twilight before the two returned. William and Bartholomew were outside watching for Martha and had been instructed by Mother to come and tell her as soon as she came up the road. Bart was the first to see a wagon, but the dust was so thick that he could not determine the driver or the number of people in the wagon. "Mother, Mother," Bart shouted, "someone's coming up the road in a wagon, but I can't see who it is."

Mim was the first person outside, wiping her wet hands on her apron as she came through the door. Her quick eye recognized the visitors. She said "Well, bless, I do think that is Mis'er Nate and Mis Martha." She turned, picked up her skirt and raced like the wind inside the house shouting, "Mis Dandridge, it be Mis Martha."

"I'm glad you have seen me home," Martha said to Nate. "Mother will be worried, Pa too. And look, there are Will and Bart pretending to play when I know they were sent outside to watch for me."

"Your mother knows that time flies by when we are together, and she probably expects you to be late. She'll have a double surprise when she realizes there will be an extra plate at the table. Let me do all the explaining," Nate said. Always masterful, Nate rendered the reason for the delay. His father had needed Nate to help with a heifer delivering her spring calf, and this gave Martha and Nate a late start with the riding lesson.

"Please don't tell Papa about my fall from Fatima. He'll be disappointed 'cause he expects me to be an able rider, and I know I'm not."

Old Joe was hitching the Dandridge wagon to ready it for the rest of the family to ride to Church. St. Peter's Church was the place the plantation families met once a week for conversation, gossip, and perhaps a business transaction or two. The service often lasted over two hours, causing mothers to threaten their restless children or try to be inconspicuous as they nudged their husbands to stop the incessant snoring. The Dandridge brothers and their families always had seats in the middle of the church pews. The conventional standard of seating gave the front of the church to the wealthier planters and the back to the artisans, craftsmen and laborers.[10]

Martha and Nate had great influence in their individual families to always be among the first to arrive at Church. Their game was to watch the right of entry into the front benches of the farmer aristocrats. Many of the planters had homes in Williamsburg as well as their plantation homes. Nate could recite hearsay about many of the St. Peter's members that attended during planting and harvesting time. Martha and Nate both had particular families they waited to see arrive.

Martha's favorite was John Custis, a Councillor in Williamsburg, and his son Daniel. Recently, they were accompanied by a woman too young to be Mr. Custis' wife and too old to be Daniel's. They were always late. They attracted the attention of all the congregation because the unknown woman could never decide where she was going to sit. After several weeks of observation, it became clear that Daniel did not want her near him or his cranky father. During the second hymn, (they were never there for the first hymn) Daniel would politely excuse himself and move into the back row. That Sunday the woman followed Daniel, and during the second verse Mr. Custis followed the woman, and brought her back to the front bench during the third verse.

Martha bent her head to the right to try and attract Nate's attention. She held baby Frances, who was sound asleep. She had Nancy sitting on her right side and Bart on her left. Papa had John and Will on his right, and Mother sat between Nancy and Papa. Mother sat with the fixed look the children always called her Church Face.

Papa gave strict orders that Church was to be Mother's resting place, literally, not metaphorically, because she worked endlessly all week taking care of the baby, minding the older children, leading Bible study, teaching the girls homemaking duties, and managing all the household duties, including directing Mim and the other women who helped with farm duties. Every Sunday Papa's hand lay over Mother's. Martha delighted in the loving way Papa looked at Mother, a look that was always fondly returned.

Nate followed Martha's gesture, with her head moving backward to direct his eyes on the Custis situation. Nate shrugged his shoulders and raised his eyebrows, silently saying he had no idea of what the exchange of seating between the Custis men and the strange woman meant.

Reverend Godfrey began his sermon, *Idleness is the Devil's Work*. Martha tried to stay centered on the homily, but when it stretched well into an hour, her arm, tightly wrapped around baby Frances, became paralyzed. Martha began to shift and squirm on the stone-like bench. Frances whimpered, but Martha bounced her gently and patted her back to keep her quiet. Mother gave Martha a look of gratitude and a warm smile.

The boys became unsettled as the sermon came to an end. This always meant that Reverend Godfrey would give the closing prayer, which sometimes lasted thirty or forty minutes, walk slowly down the aisle, open the door, and then turn to greet all the church members as they passed by.

Bartholomew stood tall as the prayer began, as did all the other parishioners. He began to repeat aloud from memory the first five or six sentences of the prayer, in concert with the Reverend. Papa motioned him to be quiet but Bart seemed not to see or hear Papa as he continued the litany in an almost trancelike state. Will could not contain his burgeoning laughter as young John elbowed him in the ribcage. Will, giving out a fulminating yell, poked John on the shoulder. All the while little Bart raised his voice to sing out, "Praise the Lord our God," in unison with Reverend Godfrey. Mother was horrified that her youngest son would mimic the Reverend. "John, please tell Bartholomew to be quiet! Everyone can hear him and he is making a spectacle of himself."

"You give us life and you take us away. We never question your timing," Bart continued.

In the pew behind the Dandridges was the Thomas family. Robert, laughing audibly, tapped Bart on the shoulder, encouraging him to continue. Mr. Thomas slapped at Robert's hand telling him, "This is a house of worship. Be quiet!"

The Brown twins, sisters who had never married, sat in the pew in front of the Dandridges. Mary sat erect, ignoring the commotion, while Elizabeth, satisfying her curiosity by turning with her usual stern stare, was mesmerized by Bart's ability to repeat the prayer perfectly. Reverend Godfrey stopped the prayer in mid-sentence, and asked, "Has the Lord intervened in the prayer?"

Elizabeth Brown clamored to her feet and shouted, "Yes! Yes. Praise be, the Lord has reached down today and sent us His disciple." There was a buzz of whispers throughout the congregation which progressed into snickers and teehees.

"What? What is this?" Reverend Godfrey's face turned a brilliant crimson. "Who, pray tell brings us the the Word of God, who is this messenger of Christ? Tell me, Miss Brown, who it is!"

Robert Thomas stood up and pointed to Bart, "It's him, Bartholomew Dandridge!"

"Shut up!" said Mr. Thomas, pulling his son into his seat.

The front pews were mostly filled and everyone turned to see who was causing the interruption of the prayer.

"Here—Here, Reverend Godfrey," Elizabeth Brown said, turning and pointing to Bartholomew. "He's come to save us all from the teachings of the Devil." Overcome with her mistaken belief about the reason for Bart's recital, Elizabeth grabbed her dress, pulled it up over her knees and moved into the aisle. She fell upon the floor, waving her arms repeating, "He's come to save us sinners. He's come to save us sinners." Sing-songing, she said, "He'll lead us into the joy of Heaven, oh Lord," shifting herself into a kneeling position. "Praise the Lord. Praise the Lord, our Savior has come," she continued rocking back and forth on her knees.

By now, all the people were out of their seats, trying to bear witness to the religious epiphany. "Hallelujah!" came a shout from the back of the church.

Bartholomew quickly stopped his waggery, knowing his mischievous mimicry was heading him into trouble as he studied first his mother's face, then the actions of Miss Elizabeth Brown.

Mary Brown looked down at her sister with disgust and said, "Get up, you old fool. You sound like one of those Methodists. This church don' do that kinda carryin' on. The next time you say you're headin' for the revival tent, I'll lock ya in the barn!"[11]

"Bring this boy to the altar of the Lord," requested Reverend Godfrey.

Bart looked at Papa with his large Dandridge eyes while his face began to change to the color of a sun-ripened tomato. "Pa, I'm sorry." His tears began to tumble.

The Dandridge family, sitting stonefaced, were fully aware of Bart's ability to remember and recite Reverend Godfrey's closing prayer. The Reverend used, line-for-line verbatim, the same words each Sunday. Mother leaned over her young son to comfort him, because by now he was awash in tears. Papa took Bart by the arm and excused himself and the boy as they passed in front of several people in the same row. "Please, Reverend Godfrey, if you'll excuse us. I'd like to speak to you after the service," Papa said with a quiet congregation listening.

He leaned down and reached for Elizabeth Brown's elbow to help her to her feet. Miss Brown struggled to make sure her dress covered her knees and hung in place around her tightly laced black shoes. She looked around to discover all eyes of the congregation were centered on her. Elizabeth gave a broad smile and waved her arm as though she was pleased with herself. She turned and patted Bart on his head. "Fine boy.

Should spread the Gospel when he's a man."

Bart turned to look at his parents, waiting to read their faces as he thought to himself Mother's Sunday words about silence being golden. The stillness in St. Peter's Church was hard for him to understand; was it approval or condemnation? As if on cue, Franny awakened and gave her dinnertime cry. Martha gently handed her to Mother so she could manage the feeding. Papa, Bart, and Mother, with baby Frances in her arms, set about going down the aisle to the outer door when the Reverend asked the congregation to please be seated.

"Brother Dandridge, please bring the boy to the front. I would like to have him walk out with me and greet all the church members at the door." Papa told Bart to wipe the tears, hold his head up, and walk with Reverend Godfrey. Martha, Nancy, John, and William all followed the Dandridge procession. Upon reaching his the door, the body of members broke with tradition, stood, and gave Bartholomew a standing ovation.

The sweltering Sunday afternoon prompted men to remove their Sunday coats and the women to don bonnets to protect their faces. The children began the ritual of running in the churchyard, playing tag and teasing one another. Bart was the center of attention, and, as any seven-year-old, he especially loved being the focal point of the grown-ups. Uncle William and Aunt Euphany each took one of his hands and reached out, picked him up, and swung him like a swing. The John Dandridge children all lined up to take a turn but Mother said, "No, it was only Bartholomew's turn this time."

The church was a unifying influence on the plantation owners. Usually there was a church picnic or social where the planters could exchange small talk, circulate rumors, snoop, eavesdrop, and hear the latest news from England. The isolation of running a plantation could only be broken if an unexpected guest arrived. The Virginia planters were a hospitable lot who always looked forward to visits, but they occurred so seldom the Sunday services were anticipated for the day of rest, words from the Lord, and fellowship.

The wagon trip back to the Dandridge plantation was quiet, the family observing Mother's old proverb "Speech is silver, silence is golden." Papa wrapped his arm around his wife's shoulders and said, "You know, darlin'? I bet the Reverend will have a new prayer next Sunday."

SPRING 1747 Martha busily packed her bags, readying herself for a trip into Williamsburg. This was her third trip in as many months and she hummed to herself as she viewed her reflection in the mirror. She liked what she saw, especially her new hairdo. Mim had convinced Martha to cut her hair and let it hang loosely around her neck. The cut gave variety to Martha's looks. She could tie a ribbon around her head, letting the hair fall around her face. She could pull her hair back away from her face and tie it in a ribbon, or she could still, with Mim's help, pile it into an upsweep and weave flowers in and out. This was her dress-up hairdo and this was the style she would wear for Nathaniel's wedding to Dorthea Spotswood.

The wedding was to be held in Bruton Parish Church in Williamsburg, the grandest church in Virginia. The only other wedding that Martha had attended was when Uncle William married Euphany Wallace two years earlier. It was held in the parlor of Aunt Euphany's home and though it was beautiful in its simplicity, it could not compare with the plans for Nate and Dorthea. Most weddings took place in the home of either the bride or the groom, but Nate and Dorthea withdrew from colonial tradition and chose Bruton Parish because her late father had organized the building of the church.

Dorthea's father Alexander Spotswood had arrived in Virginia in 1710 as Lieutenant Governor. He soon became a capable administrator and worked hard to advance the development of Virginia. He turned Williamsburg into a showpiece for an enlightened and rational imperial government. His greatest contribution may have been the encouragement of settlement along the colony's western frontier. He led a party of men across the Blue Ridge Mountains and down into the Shenandoah Valley, claiming land for the English Crown all the way to the Mississippi River. Opportunities for personal gain seemed to be strewn at his feet, and, sometimes by devious means, Governor Spotswood accumulated vast land holdings totalling eighty-five thousand acres. While in England, lobbying for confirmation of his estate, he met and married Anne Butler Brayne, goddaughter of the Duke of Ormonde. Several years later, Dorthea was born into an aristocratic Virginia family with titled English ancestors.[12]

Nate's father Colonel William Dandridge served as a captain in the British Navy. His rank easily enabled him to enter Williamsburg society. William and Nathaniel were frequent guests of the Williamsburg elite, and it was at one such assembly that Nate met Dorthea. Nate was attracted by her intelligence and graciousness. She was tall, willowy, and very lean, with a small waist. Her intellect and grace carried over to the ballroom floor where Nate and Dorthea fell in love. Most dancers stopped to observe the two as they glided smoothly in perfect unison to a minuet. It was understood by both families that theirs would be a marriage of love and adoration rather than just a merger of two families to strengthen their economic power by an arrangement of marriage.

The John Dandridge family planned to stay in Uncle Will's Williamsburg home on Francis Street. Mim and Old Joe accompanied the large family to help Mother and Papa manage the children. The Dandridge family planned to stay in Williamsburg for two weeks, spending the first week attending prenuptial parties and the second week attending the postnuptial parties. Nate had moved into town nearly two months earlier to help with preparations and be in attendance for the numerous festivities.

Jun 1, 1747. I promisd mother I wud start a journel as soon as we went to willumsburg for Nates weding. Tomorow is the dae I hav ben dreding becaus Nate well be gon forever. she seys I ned prctice on riting an penmenship. Nate an Dortheea will not liv in Chesnut Crek. I wil mis him so much but I no he is vere happy. He seys I can visit ofen. I lov willumsburg so much but i no things wil never be the same between us. Todey mother and papa gav me a birtdey presen for the weding. It was in a hevey wud box an it wus a dres to ware to the weding tomorow. there is white lase looped all around the white peticoat. The over dres is silk in a pastel blue coler. A neckline that is so lo it wil show mi bosum an a tite fitting bodice an ruffles on the sleves. It is so beutiful I cant wait to ware it. The bigest surprise is silk stokings and silk shoes to match the dres. Uncle Will seys it is mi weding dress. The shoes r big so I will hav to be carful. Let me behav an hav a gud time. all the Dandridge famly wil be there. I am vere xcited. I am glad Mim is here to take care of mi hare Good nite and may tomorow tern out to be the best dey of mi lif. Yours humbly

The wedding day began very early for the Dandridge family. The ceremony was to take place at noontime, which meant Mother had to rise and begin preparations to ready the five oldest children. Franny, at three years, was to stay home with Mim. She was not the usual Dandridge female. Instead of having a mellow disposition like Martha and Anna Maria, Franny was a disorderly and unruly gamine. Papa said she should have been a boy, and even though she was a girl she'd be strong enough to plant and harvest someday. She began the day whimpering with that soon progressed into a boisterous wail. "Why can't I go to Nate's wedding? Patcy and Nancy get to go."

Mother, always restrained and composed, said, "You'll stay with Mim and Joe today. Mim promised to let you help her plan supper, and Joe will take you for a ride on one of Uncle Will's horses."

"I don't want no ride. I want to go with you." Franny's cry had turned into a sob. Mother picked her up and gently rubbed her face and forehead, only to discover she was burning with fever.

"Patcy, please go and get Mim and tell her to bring a cool basin of water and a clean cloth. Then find your father and tell him to please come upstairs." Mother rocked Franny back and forth, trying to soothe her whimper by humming a soft melody.

Go to sleep my pretty baby,

Papa's gone, be back on Mayday.

Mother touched Frances, gently stroking her hair, which was wet with perspiration.

He'll bring you a fork with a shiny spoon,

You'll laugh when you see a man in the moon.

Mim pushed her turban away from her forehead as she quickly entered the bedroom, splashing water from both sides of the pan she was carrying. She reached down to examine the child, and sang out, "Lordy, Mis Dan'ridge, this babin on fire. We uns better get her undressed and wrapped in wet sheets so's her fever break."

"Yes, yes, Mim. I know. I can take care of her. Now go and find Mr. Dandridge and ask him to come here. And do it very quickly." Mother was trying to hide her concern by using her usual calm and melodic voice. Mim rushed through the door, and ran head-on into Mr. Dandridge, with Martha right behind him. "Frances, darlin', what is wrong with our Franny?"

For Mother, the question was too difficult for words as she raised her shoulders into a shrug and lifted her dark brows into an "I don't know," look to her husband, while tears rolled down her cheeks. "Oh, John, I am so worried. This fever came on so quickly. Baby Frances was fine at breakfast and she played after, like she always does. She became very upset when I told her she was to stay with Mim and Joe while we attend Nate and Dorthea's wedding. She is sleeping now, but I know she has a high fever. Do you think we should ask Doctor Walters to come and look at her?"

"She'll be fine when she wakes up. She's always been one to turn upside down if she doesn't get her way. Mim and Joe will take good care of her while we're gone. Now get yourself dressed so's we can be on our way."

Frances Dandridge wouldn't agree to accompany her family to the wedding. Her nightly prayers always asked the Lord to keep her children well, and she never wavered about thanking him each night if the day didn't bring illness or accident to them. She knew that Franny would need her when she woke up. "No, John, I will stay and keep a watchful eye on her. I want to be here when she wakes up. Mim will help, and I'll send Joe for the doctor if I feel it is necessary."

Martha, with tears beginning to fill her eyes, stood by the bedside and listened as her mother and father debated Franny's illness. She knew how long her mother had anticipated Nate's wedding, and said, "Mother, please let me stay with the baby. Your place is with Papa today. Besides, so many of your friends and family will be there, and you haven't visited with the Williamsburg folks in ever so long."

Mother pulled a handkerchief from her apron pocket and wiped her daughter's eyes and nose. "Oh, my dear, precious Patcy. You have looked forward to this day for so long, too. I could never accept your generous offer. Besides, you need the fellowship of people your own age. Nate has always been your best friend, and I do worry when he is gone from the plantation and living in Williamsburg. You go and finish dressing. I'll stay with Franny."

As Martha recognized her mother's soft, yet assertive voice, she left the room so her mother would not see her out-of-control tears as they fell upon her breast. "*Today was supposed to be the day for the Dandridges to rejoice in gaining a new family member and sharing our joy with family and friends*," Martha told herself, "*Please God, watch over Mother in her disappointment and concern for Franny. Help this fever to be only temporary, Amen.*"

Martha crossed the hall and entered the bedroom she shared with Anna Maria, to begin dressing for the wedding. Her tears had washed away but her deep feelings for her mother kept gnawing inside her stomach. Martha thought to herself, "*Why of all days did Franny have to get sick today. I must pay attention to every event today so I can tell Mother when I get back. I want to make sure she will feel like she was there.*"

Mim had laid her beautiful new dress across the bed. The warm late spring day was filled with music coming through the window. The cardinals, robins and whippoorwills sang their songs to each other while a carriage passed by on the street below with a team of horses whose hooves danced in perfect rhythm.

Martha quickly dressed, hoping the skirt and bodice would fit her petite body. "Where is Mim when I need her help? She always can fix things and make them right," Martha said aloud as she gazed at herself in the full length mirror. She slipped into the matching shoes and was not surprised when they did not fit. Mim entered the bedroom at that moment, as the mirror reflected an elfin, fair-skinned, graceful, almost-sixteen year old ready to attend her first social event as a grown-up lady. "Mim, the shoes are too big. They are so beautiful and match the dress, but my feet won't let them stay in place."

Mim took the shoes and stuffed rags into each toe. Handing them back to Martha, she said, "Here, make do with thes'ins. We need to start workin' on yur hair, so sit still while I fix the flowers."

Martha swirled around, waiting for the mirror to give approval. She knew she had never looked or felt so elegant. She dashed across the hall to where Mother was hovering over the baby.

"Shhh, shhh, Franny is still sleeping and the sleep will help her get better," said Mother, with uncertainty. She turned and looked at her oldest daughter, overwhelmed with emotion, "Patcy, now you know why you must be the one to attend the wedding. You have never looked so splendid. Your father will be proud to accompany you today. Come here so I can see you in the light." Mim was standing near the window and reached up quietly to open the heavy drapes. "My darling, I love you so," Mother said, clinging to Martha. Her tears ran down her cheeks and spilled onto the silk bodice of Martha's dress.

"We'll miss you, Mother. I promise to remember everything that happens and tell you as soon as we return."

Bruton Parish Church was on the corner of Duke of Gloucester Street and the Palace Green, a garden leading into the Governor's Palace. The Dandridge family needed two carriages to carry Papa, Martha, Nancy, and the three boys. The carriages left Francis Street in tandem, the two girls and Papa driving in front while Old Joe managed the boys in the second carriage. The entourage turned the corner onto Gloucester Street and came to a complete stop. There was a protracted line of carriages waiting to drop off the guests for the noon wedding. Papa took out his pocket watch and clicked it open. It read eleven thirty-five. "That weddin' music will likely start before we get inside," said Papa. Martha tried to sit calmly, afraid she would wrinkle her dress.

Nancy stood up and asked Martha to take her hand so she could crawl up onto the seat and survey the traffic. "Looks like we are the ninth carriage in line," she reported. Papa told Nancy to sit down and act like a lady or else she'd have to go back to Uncle Will's with Old Joe.

Williamsburg in early June was effusive with flowering white dogwoods, bright red azaleas and pink rhododendrons. Duke of Gloucester Street looked like God knew that this special day had to be blessed with glorious splendor to insure the splendor between the bride and groom. The breeze from the bay seemed to know that today it was to be gentle and almost motionless. The Dandridge family arrived at the church exactly at noon. Nancy carefully gave her gloved hand to a liveryman who was at the curb helping the ladies debark from the carriage. As she stepped onto the grass, she looked back and counted the carriages still lined up. "There are thirteen carriages behind ours, not counting Old Joe's. Do you think the wedding will start without the boys?" Nancy asked. Martha gave her hand to the liveryman. As she stepped down onto the dried grass, her silk slipper fell off. Quickly she thrust her foot into the shoe, as she looked around to see if anyone had witnessed this humiliation.

"Papa, do you think they'll wait to start until all the people are seated in the church?" Martha asked, regaining her composure. Papa was tending to the horse and carriage when one of the liveryman took the reins and said, "Mis Spotswood says we suppos' to put each rig aside for all the guests."

"Thank you, boy. This horse is a mite spunky so's you might want to watch out for his bad disposition," Papa said as he handed over the reins. He turned to answer Martha's question as Joe drove up with the boys. Bartholomew was preparing to jump out of the carriage, when the horse became startled by all the commotion and reared back onto his hind feet.

Ever steady, Old Joe said, "Careful, now, o' friend." He eased the reins and then pulled them back hard. "John, you and Will stay put until I get things settlin' down."

Papa walked in front of the horse to grab the reins and help Joe ground the horse. "Ease up, Joe, ease up!" shouted Papa grabbing the front rein to pull the horse down. As the horse tried to right himself, his right hoof nearly grazed Papa's left shoulder. John hurled himself backward falling on the drive. The girls all surrounded their father to keep him from getting up. "I'm fine, fine. Just help me get up. Where is John? He'll have to take the family into the church while I settle the horse. Patcy, you and Nancy get Will and Bart and go on in."

Martha took motherly control of her younger siblings as they filed into the sanctuary together, without Papa and John. Martha's watchful eyes observed the men escorting the guests to their seats. The line was extensive and several men had their pocket watches open checking the time. There were no young children present. Martha knew that her mother's decision to keep Frances home, even if she had been well, was a sound one. Most of the women wore gowns shipped from London. The silks and cottons were colorfully elegant and fashionable, the latest style. Most wore hoops of steel or whalebone to support their skirts. Martha knew that some of the women were wearing tightly laced corsets to cinch in their waists and push out their bosoms. Nancy nudged Martha to notice an overweight woman and whispered, "I'm afraid they're going to fall out."

"What's going to fall out? asked Bart loudly.

"Sshh!" answered Martha as she put her forefinger to her lips. Nancy fell into uncontrolled laughter.

"What's so funny?" asked Will. "And what is Bart talking about?"

"Nothing that concerns you, so be quiet. We're about to be seated." Martha took another look at the haughty woman and then another look at Nancy, who still was hiding her laughter in her glove. Martha swallowed hard and put her gloved hand over her mouth to stifle her own laughter while both boys still wanted answers to their questions.

Martha and Nancy turned to have one last look, just as Papa and John entered the church. Both girls erased their laughter, straightened their backs and pulled the boys into the line. The Dandridge family entered the church, led by a tall blond-haired man who walked with a limp. Once seated, Nancy whispered, "Who is the man who seated us?"

Martha shrugged and turned toward Papa to ask the same question. Papa shrugged an "I don't know."

The English protocol influenced the seating. The groomsman placed the Dandridge family in the middle pews, which were nearly full, as were the rear pews. The front pews were nearly empty, raising Martha's curiosity. Once again she asked, "Where are all the people?"

"Looks like most are still tryin' to get into the church. Suppose the organ will tell us when things will start," Papa answered in a whisper. With that the pipe organ gave a thunderous sound, causing the Dandridge children to jump in their seats. Papa sat back, entranced with Bach's latest *Toccata and Fugue in D-minor.* He strained to see who was playing the gigantic organ with such style and rhythm, and realized he was an unfamiliar man.

Slowly, the church began to fill. Martha continually reached over Nancy and pulled on Papa's sleeve to ask the names of the aristocrats. Papa suggested she change places with Nancy so she could be less conspicuous with her questions.

The William Byrd family was seated in the second row. When a man, carrying a young child, and a woman entered, Martha asked Papa, "Who are they?"

"They are the Hugh Jones family; he is a professor at William and Mary," answered Pa.[13]

John Custis came in, with a lady on his arm and Daniel walking behind. Martha leaned over and giggled in Nancy's ear, "I wonder if the lady will stay in her seat or move around today?" Rolling her eyes, Nancy shrugged.

Many guests nodded to Papa, which he acknowledged with a return nod. The reverberant organ continued to play Bach with fervor, when Martha realized the organist was repeating the Fugue. "Papa, what time is it? she asked impatiently.

Papa pulled out the watch and said, "Twelve-thirty."

The boys seemed to be sitting peacefully, when Will's stomach began to growl vociferously, throwing the boys into gales of laughter. People continued to enter the church, but found the seats all occupied except for several located next to the Byrds in the second row. There were still many people standing against the walls waiting to be seated. The groomsman carried long benches in to accommodate them, but there were more guests than there were places to sit.

A stylishly dressed man walked down the center aisle, with an attractive woman on his arm and three children following close behind. He turned and inclined his head to recognize Papa with a smile. Papa returned the motion with a reluctant nod. The groomsman placed the family in the second row next to the Byrd family. Martha and Nancy strained to see the family but neither could identify them. In a hushed voice, Martha again asked Papa who they were, and he quietly replied, "The Carter family."

The Dandridge family walked to the Governor's Palace for the post-wedding celebration. It was a day that would be engraved into Martha's memories forever. The Palace, like the Parish Church, was brick, to conform to the prevailing Georgian architecture in Williamsburg. The three-story building had a wide circular drive that would accommodate three carriages side by side. The verdant grounds looked bluish-green with the violets and lobelia in full bloom. The Palace roof supported a small cupola, reflecting a European influence of the Renaissance style. The low brick wall protecting the front of the building supported ten-foot pillars on either side of the entranceway. Each pillar was topped with the coat-of-arms of the English Monarchy all made of stone.

Most of the wedding guests chose to walk to the Palace instead of wasting time trying to manage a carriage. The boys were anxious to see the long tables of sumptuous food prepared for the bride and groom's guests. The girls were anticipating the festivities of music, dancing, and people-watching. Papa was hoping he would hear about new land acquisitions and possibly new export tariffs that were rumored to be coming from the English Parliament. He also planned on politicking for votes to put him in the House of Burgesses.

As the John Dandridge family approached the vestibule, the sound of several horses drew Martha's attention. She turned and watched the arrival of Nathaniel and Dorthea. The carriage was black leather trimmed in gold piping, with a driver sitting in a high seat above the bride and groom and a footman riding on the back, watching over the couple from behind. Both servants were dressed in white shirts with rows of ruffles sewn on the bodice. Their black waist-length jackets were cut to show the frills of the shirts. They wore black pants and white silk stockings. Martha and Nancy waited for Nate and Dorthea to enter the Palace, but were pushed aside by guests equally as anxious to catch a glimpse of the regal couple. "There must be thousands of people here!" the crushed Nancy said to Papa and Martha.

"No, darlin', there are about one hundred and fifty, by my count," answered Papa. "Most all of Williamsburg and many plantation owners are here."

"We haven't been able to talk to Nate this whole past week 'cause he's always so busy with all the parties, and Dorthea giving him so many callings," Nancy whined.

Martha knew that Nate would not walk past the John Dandridges without acknowledging them, but still she felt a deep foreboding that the two cousins' relationship was being changed forever. Martha loved Dorthea, and until the day of their wedding, they had shared Nate harmoniously. She told herself that today wasn't the time to think about the future, but just to remember the carefree days of their childhood. Martha had realized that morning, when she saw herself in the mirror as she prepared for the wedding, that she was no longer a child. Her life was on the threshold of change; her sixteenth birthday was only weeks away and many of her friends were already planning their weddings. "*I wish I could forecast my future. I know I would love to have a wedding like Nate's, especially if I can find someone to love me like Dorthea loves Nate.*"

John, Will, and Bart were feasting on baked ham, barbecue, meat pies, fried sweet potatoes rolled in sugar and cinnamon, sweet cherry and strawberry tarts, and sweet punch. Many plantation friends of the boys moved outside to begin a game of hide and seek. Their stomachs properly filled, the Dandridge boys joined them.

Inside, the crowd consumed the buffet quickly, the men then leaving the women alone to discuss babies, the latest local gossip and the news from London. The men went to an upper-story room to smoke and sip wine and brandy.

Mim hovered over little Frances, sponging her forehead, neck and shoulders with a damp cloth. The song of a robin perched on the windowsill reminded Mim to keep humming into Franny's ear. "Mim, please keep singing or talking. She needs rest, but I don't want her to go sound asleep," instructed Frances Dandridge.

"Sleepin' seems like it be best for her, Mis Dandridge."

"We'll see that she gets sleep in due time." Frances Dandridge struggled to keep her composure as she observed her baby lying motionless. She fell to her knees, keeping her hand on the baby's arm, patting gently between her tiny clenched hand and outstretched arm. "Dear God, please help us from letting her fall into a deep sleep," she prayed. "I know she needs rest, but I'm so afraid of a coma that she won't be able to wake up from," pleaded Frances.

"Mis Dandridge, maybe Doc Walters should have a look," Mim said. "Mr. Dandridge was worrin' maybe he be at the weddin'. I thought Joe be back by now so's he'd go and git him if we think we need him. What does you think?" Mim asked.

Frances' preoccupation with her prayers delayed a response as she looked up and corrected Mim, "What do you think? Let's wait until Mr. Dandridge returns. She isn't as restless now, so maybe her fever is going down a little."

"Yes 'um, Mis Dandridge, I supposin' you're right." Mim's thoughts tried to sort out the confusing English language, "Do and does. . .was and were . . .them and those. Lordy, lordy, how am I ever goin' to keep them things straight?"

The clock on the downstairs mantel chimed four o'clock. Frances was still on her knees beside the bed and Mim was sitting in a rocker next to them. Both had fallen asleep, but neither one had heard the clock in the quiet house. Somehow the clock disturbed the baby. She gave a mournful cry but didn't awaken. Both women were on their feet hovering over the fretful child, feeling her hot face and forehead. "Mim, go and get more cold water while I undress Franny. We're going to wrap her body in cold cloths to try and get the fever down."

While Mim prepared the bath, Frances swiftly pulled the clothes from the baby. She began to softly cry and pray between the tears. "This is the second time I've cried today! The first were tears of joy; Patcy looking so grown-up and beautiful this morning and now dear God, I'm asking you for help to make my little girl better," she sobbed. "Oh God, I've never had a child this sick... Please forgive me for all my sins... I promise to be a better Christian, mother and wife... Please don't let it be yellow fever or typhoid," she moaned. "Dear Lord, please give me strength. *Our Father which are in Heaven... Hallowed be thy name...* " Frances lay across her daughter and realized she was near hysteria. Her sobs and incoherent prayers were broken with catches in her breath.

"Mis Dandridge, I bring the cold water and more rags. Here let me help you up to the chair while I fix baby Frances. You need to rest some more." Mim gave a small shiver because she had never seen Frances Dandridge so troubled. The shivers and shaking overtook Mim as she tried to help Frances to the chair.

"No, no! I'm fine, Mim. Let me bathe the child," sobbed Frances. "*Thy Kingdom come... Thy will be done... on earth as it is in Heaven.* Please God, help me do what I have to do."

"Mis Dandridge, we can't have two sick peoples here today. You go sit down so's I can help this baby. Mr. Dandridge be home soon. You need to be ready for him." Mim began her own silent prayers while she pulled Frances into a chair. "You a'most suffocated that little one, you did," Mim uttered to herself.

John Dandridge joined the men in an upstairs assembly room where there was a variety of liqueurs and wines. Smoke enveloped the room as pipes were lighted to further enhance the savory drinks. The men who indulged had discovered that a swallow of drink with a tobacco accompaniment was most refreshing. William Dandridge was encircled by five men who were in an intense discussion. As John approached the group, he heard a Mr. Howard say, "The French Canadians are moving into the Ohio River Valley. If King George wants manifest destiny, he must send the redcoats over to stop the infringement!"

"Now, now George, there will be a peaceful truce with the French, but the Algonquins may be another matter. The French are giving the Indians guns, so they could cause some trouble about who settles the Ohio," said Louis Schuyler, a Williamsburg lawyer.

"It is my belief that the colonies will be fighting the French right here on American soil before this conflict is settled. They have not given up on connecting their holdings in New Orleans with the Ohio Valley," replied George Howard.

William, upon seeing John, motioned him to join the group. He turned and said, "English immigration is moving into the fertile interior valleys. King George will never allow the French to start another war, especially here!"[14] It took John several minutes to catch up with the conversation. William whispered, "We're talking about the French Canadians moving south on the Ohio."

John Dandridge knew all the men in the conversation but one. He was a tall man with fair skin and blue eyes who stood as if he were standing at attention in the King of England's Company. John thrust out his hand to shake the hand of the stranger. "I'm John Dandridge, William's brother."

"Excuse me, John," said William. " This is Lawrence Washington, Adjutant General of the Virginia Militia.[15] General, this is my brother, John." The two men vigorously shook hands.

"Please continue your conversation, gentlemen. I'm anxious to hear the latest war news."

"We should be more concerned about the restrictions on trade with other countries. The English Board of Trade must allow other European countries to import our tobacco and rice."

"I hear that the rum from New England trade is gettin' mighty good into Guinea. We're gettin' bigger and stronger slaves and more molasses in trade from the West Indies," said Mr. Howard. "I believe the King and Parliament have the privilege to make sure our trade laws are fair and equitable for us."

"Gentlemen, the English have expanded their colonies and all their industry to make England more prosperous and to grow into a world power. You should certainly have no problem with their laws and tariffs, because a strong England means a strong Virginia. You can manage the

Navigation Laws as they are. It is a small inconvenience that all Virginia tobacco must pass through England before moving on to other parts. Who knows when Parliament might modify them to the colonies' disadvantage?" said Paul Fairchild, who had just joined the group.

Jonathan Milton stood across the room watching the enclave of the Dandridge brothers, Lawrence Washington and Louis Schuyler. He strolled across to an open window, hoping to inconspicuously eavesdrop on their conversation. Jonathan felt great inadequacy from never being accepted into the Williamsburg inner circles. As hard as he worked for respect and approval, he did not seem to achieve the recognition he desired. Although he remained Franklin Carter's attorney, he no longer had access to his land acquisitions or the selling or leasing of them. With the recent death of his sister Ann—Franklin Carter's wife—he was assured of a pending dismissal.

Sound sleep had eluded Jonathan for some time. His insomnolence was due to agonizing over all the business enterprises he tried to keep viable. He came to Virginia intending to develop an honest, trustworthy, and reliable reputation, knowing that almost without exception a Southern aristocrat was self-made.[16] "*One must must be smart and ruthless and exceptionally lucky to become wealthy in Virginia. I have the former, but it will be left to the celestial angels to determine the latter.*" Somehow, his need for legitimacy had been usurped by his unscrupulousness. The temptation to take advantage of corrupt deals was irresistible, especially when a sizeable profit seemed inevitable.

Jonathan and his brother Thomas planned carefully before deciding to leave England and booking passage to Virginia. The brothers did not want to apply for a charter of one hundred acres and begin new lives as tobacco planters. Fur trading looked like a more profitable business. Thomas agreed to investigate those possibilities. After long hours of study, the brothers agreed to work toward gaining legitimacy as respected businessmen. Their business plan meant patience and perseverance. Each one would work to be accepted by the Virginia aristocracy, gain the favor and confidence of the Royal Governor, and lead exemplary lives as loyal Virginians while remaining loyal to the British Crown.

Temptations seemed to be around every corner. Jonathan quickly realized his own weaknesses when Franklin Carter handed him all his accounts, giving Jonathan the opportunity to accumulate the deeds to acreages in the tidelands that once belonged to Franklin. Jonathan easily maneuvered titles into his own name because of his impeccable bookkeeping skills and schemes. The tidelands became prime pieces of property. Four rivers flowed into Chesapeake Bay, all of which were navigable by ships that also sailed the Atlantic. Plantation owners who built their own docks and warehouses were able to export and import their goods. Speculators bought up every available piece of tidelands because of the expected inflationary spiral. Jonathan could not resist the fraudulent manner of acquiring tidelands. Land grants given to increase western movement into the Alleghenies and the Shenandoah Valley were given by the Royal Governor of Virginia. Jonathan applied for a grant of two thousand acres, agreeing to pay the passage from England of forty immigrants to work the land. Never missing an opportunity to stretch his capacity to cheat, he added an extra zero to the figure, thus increasing his grant to twenty thousand acres. His double-dealing became an easy method for land acquisition, especially when the Governor could not locate his reading glasses and overlooked the extra numeral. Jonathan showed his appreciation by promising to share his windfall with the complaisant Governor. Jonathan also became involved as intermediary for factors selling tobacco in England. He discovered he could take a portion of the factors' commissions with little effort. He quoted a price to the planter, then raised the price to the factor and kept the difference.

Jonathan meandered around the room, catching a word or two among the five men. He ascertained the conversations were focusing on the conflict between France and England. He hoped that Mr. Washington might give some scuttlebutt pertaining to the skirmishes between the French and English over land holdings in the Ohio Valley. Jonathan was certain an all-out war was inevitable. His nose for finding adversity and taking advantage had made him a rich man. He hoped to hear a word dropped here or there that would lead him to a weak link that might bring financial gain in the looming crisis.

The festivities following the wedding continued in the ballroom of the Governor's Palace. Dorthea's family had carefully planned the celebration. The lavish food was mostly consumed, the ladies still looking fresh in their new gowns and the children ready for the music to begin. They waited for the bride and groom to be presented to the guests. The musicians were placed in front of two double doors opening onto the plush English garden. The spacious room looked and smelled as if all the millwork had been freshly painted for the occasion. Chairs lined the walls, mostly filled with the ladies waiting for the men to return from their upstairs retreat.

The pianoforte player was the mysterious man who had played the organ at the wedding. He was accompanied by a flutist, two violinists and a harpist. Their music, mostly written by the Italian composer, Vivaldi, was played for the enjoyment of the guests, still waiting for the men to come downstairs. All awaited the bride and groom to start the dancing.

Martha, keeping a watchful eye on her younger siblings, surveyed the adult guests. She was taking a mental inventory to see which guests attending the wedding were still present for the ball. She felt a shiver down her spine and her face flush at the thought of a man asking her to dance. Her strict dance teacher had told her that because of her small size, she would need to always dance on her toes, keep her back as straight as a board, her neck stretched high, and make sure her head never tilted. Martha had danced many times with Nate, who gave her the needed confidence to be a competent dancer. However, she knew she had trouble with time and rhythm.

Papa, and several other men entered the ballroom. They smelled of tobacco and liquor. "Here come the powdered wigs," John surreptitiously said to Martha. "They'll smell like old dried out whiskey barrels."

"Ask someone to open a window or two if you don't like the smell," Martha replied. "I like the smell myself. It always reminds me of harvest time when all the tobacco is ready for shipping." She turned quickly to walk toward her sister, and bumped into a small man only several inches taller than she was. "Excuse me. I'm so sorry to be so clumsy." Her right shoe slipped from her foot, causing her barely to keep her balance. She looked down and carefully made sure the shoe was back in place before she looked up and into the face of John Custis. Martha grabbed her bosom and turned crimson. "I didn't know you were behind me, Sir. Please forgive my ungracefulness. Are you all right? Did I hurt you?" She took her handkerchief and brushed his coat sleeve, nervously repeating, "Please, excuse me."

John Custis's face was deeply lined with what Mother called "sunshine lines." Martha observed they were from frowning morning to night. She had never been introduced to anyone in the Custis family, but she knew who he was from St. Peter's Church Sunday services. Papa called him the Indolent Patrician, whatever that meant. Papa said he owned over fifteen thousand acres of tobacco land and never lifted a finger during planting or harvesting time except to give orders to his son Daniel, the overseers, and his one hundred and fifty slaves. Daniel was over thirty years old and had never married. His father, John Custis, assumed the role of matchmaking by insisting Daniel's marriage to anyone of his choosing must first be approved by him. The objective? That he marry someone of equal social and monetary status. Daniel, who was as cunning as his father, always developed strategies to outmaneuver his father's choices.

Mr. Custis gave Martha a half smile. "I'm fine, my dear. Now you run along and play." Martha's embarrassment subsided but her flushed face turned scarlet with Mr. Custis' last remark. "*Does he think I'm still a child? Indeed, I'm nearly sixteen!*"

The bride and groom entered the room and all the guests stood clapping while the waiters passed trays of champagne. Dorthea's uncle, raising his glass, said, "To my beautiful niece and her husband—a wish for a common love which will last throughout your years together. May your passion and obsession for one another today develop into a love that embodies devotion, kindness, compassion, negotiation and compromise, friendship and affection." Holding the glass up, he tapped Dorthea's glass first, then Nate's.

"Hear, hear," said John Dandridge. The guests all repeated the "hear,

hear," as the musicians, on cue, began Jean Philippe Rameau's *Minuet.* The bride and groom stepped onto the polished wooden floor, joined hands, and lightly stepped into the rhythm of the music. The women and men lined the walls to allow them room to exercise their skill in the dance. Dorthea and Nate smiled in appreciation, their eyes bonded together as their proficiency dazzled the guests.

Frances Dandridge for the first time in her life faced the crisis she always knew one day would confront her. The baby's fever had steadily increased. The cold sponge bath and the wrapping in cold rags had made no difference in her temperature. Baby Frances continued to sleep, while whimpering, tossing and turning in her restlessness. Mother hung over her baby's head gently whispering into her ear, as if she might be wide awake listening to every word. "Mother is here to help make you feel better, so that tomorrow we can go to see Nathaniel and Dorthea. We'll ask Papa, Patcy, and Nancy to go with us."

Get ye' well my pretty baby,
Papa has gone to Tennessee.
He'll buy you a doll with lots of curls.
She'll be dressed in silk all trimmed in pearls.

Mother sang softly. "Where is John?" Frances' thoughts quickly shifted from her sick baby to the family wedding. "He'll know what to do. I wonder what time it is?" The thoughts meandering through her head made little sense. "Dear Lord, I will sacrifice anything to make my baby get better. Please give me the strength to see this through. Tell me what to do," she pleaded.

"The Lord is my shepherd; I shall not want.
He maketh me to lie down in green pastures."
Frances Dandridge was near incoherency.
"Hallowed be thy name; on earth as it is in Heaven."

The upstairs room was cast in twilight shadows. The burgundy drapes hung open, giving little daylight. The stillness wrapped the room in darkness and gloom. The malodorous air seemed to suck the breath out of Frances's lungs as she struggled to inhale and exhale so she could continue humming to her sick child.

"Mim, Mim—where are you?" Please go and make sassafras tea for Frances. Be sure and put extra honey in it. You know how she loves the sweetness . . . Mim? Do you hear me?"

Mim sat dozing in a corner in a small rocking chair. As the sun set, the corner was the first part of the room to be covered in complete darkness. Frances was unable to see her. Mim was startled as she awoke and looked at Mrs. Dandridge, the shadows crosshatching her face. "I'm here Mis Dandridge. I'm sure Mr. William's house cook will make the tea."

Frances Dandridge suddenly rose to her feet and quickly pulled at Mim's arm, jerking her from the rocking chair. "No! I want you to make the tea. Only you know how Frances likes sassafras tea! I do not want someone who hardly knows her name to make the tea. Now, get a move on. Hurry!"

Mim had trouble getting her legs to obey her need to hurry. The dizziness in her head when Frances Dandridge yanked her from the chair also caused her stomach to react to an almost retching feeling. "Yes 'um Mis Dandridge. I go as fast as I can."

"I *will* go as fast as I can," rebuked Frances.

Mim was sure she had never seen Mrs. Dandridge so hysterical. "*She all jumbled up, I never seen the like. I wish Mr. Dandridge get home soon.*" Mim descended slowly because she couldn't get her eyes to guide her feet where to step on the narrow, dark stairs. She entered the kitchen and found the fire burned down to embers. Mim knew that there would be trouble for letting the fire burn itself out. No house cook would ever let that happen.

Mim stepped to the door and looked out to see if Old Joe had returned to Francis Street. She clutched her apron, trying to wipe her sweaty hands, and then her brow. "Old Joe, you out there?" She knew she hadn't heard him come into the stable, but also knew that she had dozed in the upstairs rocking chair. Mim could not see or hear any familiar sounds of the Dandridge's house or barn help. "I guess I'll go get some kindlin' and try to build up the fire 'fore Mis Dandridge calls. Lordy, lordy—this been some day; what with Mis Dandridge nearly half out of her mind with that sick babin."

Just as Mim began to rekindle the fire, Frances called, "Mim, hurry up, the baby is stirring. I'm trying to get her to wake up so's she can swallow the sassafras . . . Mim, Mim, do you hear me?"

"Yes 'um, I hears ya," Mim said to herself. Then just as she heard Mrs. Dandridge's footsteps on the stairs. "Mis Dandridge, the fire done gone almost out. It be a while 'fore the water's hot."

As Frances Dandridge entered the kitchen, Mim turned around to see the face of a stranger. Frances's face was twisted, distorted into a grimace that frightened Mim. "There's enough flame in her eyes to light this here fire," thought Mim.

Frances stood over Mim looking into her maid's face with hollow eyes surrounded with dark circles that looked like the circles on a cut tree. Her pallor was ghost-like and her breath smelled like stale milk. "Please, help me. My little girl needs some liquid." Frances Dandridge spoke quietly. "Just bring up some cool water for her to drink. We'll try the tea as soon as you get the water boiling."

The musical ensemble's selections enchanted the wedding guests. There was an assortment of music, mostly familiar, but some heard for the first time in Williamsburg. The unknown organist from the wedding was apparently in charge of the musicians. Martha observed that he selected the order of the music and took requests from the guests.

John Dandridge approached his oldest daughter and asked her to dance a quadrille. Four couples were needed to complete a square. Young John and Nancy joined the group, as well as the bride and groom. There were four squares to begin the dance, with four sets, which meant exchanging partners at the end of each set. Martha had never danced with her father before and was delighted to discover his agility. She especially liked dancing with Nate, her first dance teacher before Mother hired Mr. Whatshisname. Young John had been taking lessons for several years with Martha and seemed light on his feet. Nancy was relatively new to the dance, but confident with the few lessons that had taught her rhythm and cadence.

The lead musician called for a brief intermission after the quadrille. The dancers, thirsty and sticky, hastened to the punch bowl or to the water barrel. The Dandridge children hurriedly filled their cups with water. A very tall young man joined the group at the water bucket and asked Martha if he could have the pleasure of dancing the next quadrille with her. Before she could answer, Bart butted into the conversation to tell her that Will was outside in a fight with Paul Howard and he was losing. "Go tell Papa. He can take care of it better than I can," Martha snapped.

"I already told Pa and he said to come get you, that you would take care of it," said Bart. His face was red, his hair full of sweat, his shirt hanging out, one sleeve torn, and his knee pants with mud and grass stains on his seater.

"Mother will be angry when she sees your clothes. Tomorrow is Church and just what will you wear?" Martha felt flustered. She had just been asked to dance for the very first time in her life, and her brothers had to pick this time for a fight. She turned back toward the tall man to give an answer, only to discover he had moved across the room toward another group of young people.

"Miss Dandridge? I'm Daniel Custis and I would like the pleasure of the next dance, if you please."

Martha grappled for words. "I . . . I well, yes . . . I would be pleased, but I'm not a very good dancer." Clearing her throat. "um. . .um. . .Sir," and reached down, trying to press her new dress with her hands as she looked into the dark brown eyes of a man only several inches taller than she was. His chin was small, angling into high cheekbones that gave him the appearance of a Romanesque sculpture. Engraved on his upper lip was a scar that his mustache couldn't cover. His nose was small and shaped to fit into the puzzle pieces that completed his face. Martha dropped her eyes away from Mr. Custis to discover that her sweaty hands, as she stroked her silk dress, had streaked the blue skirt with moisture. She quickly looked into Daniel's face to engage his eyes so he wouldn't notice the now-striped dress.

The music began again and Mr. Custis gently took Martha's left elbow and escorted her onto the floor for a minuet. He gracefully handled her hand and arm over her head as he stepped carefully, making sure there was agreement between his stride and hers. As an unseasoned dancer, Martha felt confident about herself as she danced with an experienced partner. The excellent musicians were harmonious in keeping perfect time, helping Martha follow the moves of Mr. Custis. Martha had been conscious of her new silk shoes since losing one as she lifted herself out of the carriage at the church. Her concentration now was on the Rameau and keeping a smile as she looked at Daniel's penetrating eyes. The dance was drawing to a close. The couple were walking side by side with hands overhead, when Martha lost her timing. As she struggled to regain her footing, her right shoe slipped off, planing across the floor where she had inadvertently kicked it. With consternation and embarrassment, she stopped, thanked Mr. Custis for the dance and excused herself. Her first inclination was to run out the French doors behind the musicians. Instead she walked to the punch bowl where her father was in parlance with two other men, and announced that it was time to go home.

"Yes, my dear, it is time we go. It is nearly dark. By the time we find the boys and walk to the carriages it will be dark," agreed Papa.

Many guests had already left the celebration and many were leaving with the Dandridge family. The vestibule was crowded with people, some waiting for their carriages to be delivered to the Governor's Palace. Papa told the children they were to walk back to the church where Old Joe would be waiting. Martha led her brothers and sister through the crush of people. Once outside, she could not contain the impatient tears any longer. "How can such a perfect day end so miserably?" Martha looked down at her stocking foot. "One shoe on and one shoe off and gone forever."

"Hurry up, boys," called Papa. "Your mother and Franny expected us a long time ago."

Martha dawdled behind her family, reliving her humiliation at

Nate's wedding. "If I could talk to him I know I would feel better. He always can put the right words in place to make sense out of things." Martha turned to look back. She thought she had heard someone call, "Miss Dandridge." A tall, lanky, young man worked his way through the guests to where Martha stood. He reached out and handed her a small, silk shoe, smiling gallantly as he said, "I believe this is yours."[17]

Papa, at the reins, was the first to pull into the yard. The windows of the Francis Street house were mostly dark, which startled Martha, Nancy, and Pa.

"Where are the house slaves? There is no light in the house and no one to take care of the carriage, Papa," Martha said. "Something is not right. Stop and let me out."

"Here, you hold the reins, Patcy," ordered Papa. "This horse has been spooked all day. John, walk him into the stable. Joe will need to handle his own rig."

Mim, hearing the arrival of the family, leaped up from the fire. She was bewildered by her light-headedness so she pulled off her bandanna and placed it in her pocket. "I've had it tied too tight," she thought as she hastened through the door to receive the family. "Mis'a Dandridge, I'm so glad you home. Mis Dandridge so worried about the babin, she still has the high fever. We be tryin' to get it down all day," Mim said breathlessly.

"Is she still upstairs with Franny?" John Dandridge asked incredulously.

"Yes, Sir. She ain't left that babin' side all day. She nearly jumbled up over her bein' so sick and all."

Martha, hearing Mim's conversation with Papa, bolted from the carriage and sprinted to Old Joe's wagon. "Joe, you must get some farm hands to help with the carriages and horses. Bring in wood for the fire and make sure there is plenty of water in the house. John, you and Will and Bart help Joe find the blacks so's they can help. On second thought, Joe, maybe you'd better keep one of the wagons hitched in case Papa wants Dr. Walters to come. You'll have to get him, if he does."

"I'll go and get him, if Pa wants me to," said an anxious John.

"Papa and Mother will want all of us to be here together, I'm sure. You can round up some of the help. This place is deserted. Where's the cook and barn man?" Martha had ridden home from the party immersed in deep disappointment at her failure at her first dance with another man other than her kin. The day had fulfilled all her expectations as her first grown-up outing, except for the shoe. "*I'll never dance again*!" she had told herself. She had wallowed in self-pity as her brother John and Nancy, knowing her misery, tried to cheer her by reviewing the day's events. She had given no thought to Mother, Frances or Mim all day. Her remorse deepened as she realized how they had endured the same day that, for her, had overflowed with gaiety, laughter, and happiness. "William and Bartholomew, go into the house, sit down in the parlor and do not make one sound until Papa tells you what to do next. Do you understand?" Both boys nodded in agreement.

John Dandridge had not expected this homecoming. His rational mind told him that the baby could not be seriously ill. "*There would have been mention today if any cases of typhoid or yellow fever were reported in Virginia.*" His head was trying to sort out the possibilities, such as smallpox. The Powhatan maladies often spread into plantations and cities, but there was no hint of any illnesses among the Indians. He was at the top of the stairs when Frances, hearing his footsteps, met him in the doorway. "Frances, darlin', tell me about Franny."

"John, I'm so glad you're home." Her arms wrapped around his neck; she kissed his cheeks and then his lips and held him tightly to her chest. "Her fever is high; she will take no liquid. She has slept all day but I've talked and sung to her so she wouldn't go into a deep sleep." Frances could not say coma, trying to keep John from hearing the word.

The one candle burning on the table beside the bed gave enough light for John to see Frances's face. The flickering light could not hide the ravishing toll this day had taken on his beloved wife. "My darling, how dreadful I feel to not have been here on this most distressing day." He stroked her hair. "Tell me, do you think we should send for Doc Walters?"

"Yes, I do. I feared he had gone to Nate and Dorthea's wedding, so I didn't send for him. Besides, I don't know where all the slaves are. The house, yard and barn are empty. I couldn't send Mim because I needed her here."

John tried to choose his words carefully because he was sure the blacks had left the premises when Mim had probably told the cook about Franny's temperature. The superstitious negroes had enormous fear about "The Fever," and they had probably left together to hide in the swamps. "Darlin', they may be holding a prayer meeting somewhere, knowin' all the family was goin' to the wedding today. I'll send Joe to get the doctor."

The clock chimed ten times and Joe had not returned with Dr. Walters. Mother, Papa, Martha, John, Nancy and Mim kept their vigil surrounding Franny's bed. The two younger boys were sleeping in the downstairs parlor. The cool rags wrapped around the baby's body made her look frail and withered. The evening was unusually warm depleting the small bedroom of much-needed fresh air. Too many bodies in a confining space swallowed up what air there was, choking the family.

"Mim, we need more cold cloths. These are already at room temperature," Papa said. He reached over to pat Mother's head, which was cupped between Papa's upper arm and elbow. "Please go into our bedroom and stretch out for awhile," he begged her.

Mother did not stir. Her exhaustion had climaxed into a cavernous sleep that only the cry of her baby could penetrate.

Martha saw that Mim was drained of energy, too. Her head was lying back on the corner rocking chair. She had not heard Papa's request for more rags. So Martha went downstairs to get replacements, letting Mim rest. Descending the dark stairs, Martha was sure she heard a wagon. Several candles were burning on the three-legged tea table in the passageway, so she hurriedly picked up one and opened the door just as Old Joe and Dr. Walters turned into the front drive.

"Hurry, Dr. Walters, the baby is upstairs," said Martha. "Joe, let me have the lantern. Come, follow me upstairs."

Papa was at the top of the stairs waiting, looking dishevelled as he greeted the doctor. "She's in here, Doc."

"How long has she been comatose?" The doctor asked.

Mother was on her feet immediately. "She is not in a coma! I have not allowed her to go completely asleep. I've talked and sung to her all day."

"Could be that she is just worn out from no sleep.Young children need rest, especially if they don't feel well," retorted the doctor.

"Dr.Walters, my baby has had a high fever since early morning. We have kept her swaddled in cold rags to try and bring it down. She is raging with fever; she has had no liquids, and I have worked myself into exhaustion to keep her alive. I do not want you to even think about bleeding her or blistering her with a hot poultice!" Frances Dandridge fell into her husband's arms weeping uncontrollably. "John, I know our baby is dying."

"Sshh, sshh—You don't want Franny to hear you say that," Papa consoled. "She will give up if she thinks we have given up. She is such a fighter, with so much get up and go. We should be telling her how things will be when she gets better."

Dr. Walters observed the fetid air that hung over the small room. The drapes were pulled back and the window open but still no fresh air circulated. High fevers have an undefinable odor that is the residue of inhaling and exhaling. After examining Franny, Dr. Walters declared her a very sick child. "She does not have the symptoms of yellow fever. Her skin would be a yellowish color and her liver would be swollen. Has she been drinking water from any place other than the well?"

Mother, answering quickly, said she didn't think so. The Dandridge family had been in Williamsburg for over ten days and she couldn't account for all that time. "Why, Doctor, would the water make a difference?" Her question puzzled John. He knew what Dr. Walters was alluding to and knew that Frances should too. Typhoid fever could be transmitted through diseased water.

"Doctor, may I speak with you downstairs for a moment?" asked John. "Frances, please excuse us. I need some air and would like to talk to the good doctor outside. Patcy, please go and down and get fresh water and bring it upstairs."

The two men were shoulder to shoulder walking away from the

house. John made sure that Frances would not overhear their conversation. "Are you trying to tell us that Franny might have typhoid?" John's emotions were about to break through. He hadn't been prepared to come home and find his wife in near hysteria or his baby near death. He needed to have a word with the Lord but he couldn't begin to find the appropriate words. The Dandridge family counted their blessings every night and were scrupulous about thanking God for their good health and fortune.

The doctor spoke carefully. "John, she does have the early symptoms of typhoid, but it takes maybe two or three weeks to know for sure. For one so young, it may not take that long, however. I want to isolate her because this sickness can be transmitted. Frances has done the right thing by keeping her sponged with cool water. She needs liquids, too, and I know this is difficult. It will take two people to make sure she's getting enough water. Take a small clean rag and roll it up, soak it in cold water. Have someone hold Franny's head back just to a tilt; she'll choke otherwise. Have someone take the rag, wring it out then let it drip into her mouth. I would like this to continue until she passes water. Her fever could break at any time. But if she continues in this state, it could mean the typhoid. Do the liquid every hour after she urinates the first time. You need to take turns during the night to keep her cool. I'll call tomorrow to see how she is. Send Joe for me if things look worse before I get here."

John Dandridge went numb. He needed to organize the long night ahead. Frances and Mim needed to be put to bed. Franny needed to be quarantined. He decided that the youngest children would sleep downstairs until this crisis ended. Patcy would take the night watch with him. He would plan tomorrow's schedule tomorrow. Before going into the house, John walked toward the large magnolia tree between the house and the stable. "I can hardly remember Psalm Twenty-five; Mama made sure I had it memorized word for word by the time I was nine years old, but it's been awhile. *Unto thee, O Lord, do I lift up my soul. O my God, I trust in thee. Lead me to thy truth and teach me. God of my salvation. Look upon my affliction and my pain; and forgive my sins.*" John struggled to continue, when he realized he was on his knees, weeping, not for himself, but for Frances, his beloved wife. And for his baby. And Martha and the rest of the family.

Martha and Papa followed Dr. Walter's instructions. By midnight, Franny had released a small amount of fluid from her bladder. "We'll have to rely on the downstairs clock chime to keep track of when to give her the next water," said Papa. Papa held the baby in his strong arms each hour while Martha dripped the water into the tiny mouth. Three hours passed, and each time Franny passed urine. Papa was afraid to think that might be a good sign. By four o'clock, Franny felt somewhat cooler and seemed to be sleeping more comfortably.

Martha and Papa tried to sleep between each treatment. Martha propped herself in the corner rocking chair and Pa laid his head down beside the baby. The chimes rang five times; the whole house remained motionless. The half-past chime rang out once; the morning sun responded by peeping through the east windows. The chimes began again, this time on the new hour; ringing one . . . two . . . three times while Martha sat up grappling with how many chimes she had counted . . . four . . . five . . . six. Papa lay with his cramped body still seated on the straight back chair, his head on the bed next to Franny. He placed his hand on her forehead. Baby Frances, making an effort to open her eyes, put her tiny hand against Papa's cheek, and, raising her head and turning toward him, asked, "Papa, did you bring me a doll with curls, dressed in silk all trimmed in pearls?"

CHAPTER NOTES

Fictional characters are introduced in this narrative to epitomize the human condition of colonial times. Jonathan Milton, a man with no connections, typifies the drive to achieve wealth and recognition without ancestry or inheritance. The name Carter was appended to Franklin because the Carter name is synonomous with colonial Virginia. No disrespect is meant to the name. Robert Carter, astute in business, politics, and land speculation, earned the name "King" Carter. His significant holdings included over three hundred thousand acres, one thousand slaves and considerable cash.

George Whitefield and numerous other revivalists arrived in the colonies bringing a message of God to listeners concerned about going to hell. "The Great Awakening," as the period was called, "brought evangelists preaching an old and conservative doctrine of God's sovereignty and the depravity of man," says Lloyd B. Wright in *The Cultural Life of the American Colonies, 1607–1763.* From this situation came the church segment with Martha's brother, Bartholomew, and Elizabeth Brown.

CHAPTER TWO

OLD JOE

1696-1747

1747 The John Dandridge plantation had increased in size by nearly fifty acres. John planned to manage and supervise the planting and harvesting himself. He contemplated employing a new overseer, but each time he looked over the possible candidates he realized the risk of getting many promises but little work. Old Joe seemed like the most reliable and trustworthy to be put in charge. John spent several weeks weighing his decision, knowing there were no other black overseers in the tidewaters of the Pamunkey. Joe labored as a responsible slave driver for the Chesnut Grove plantation. As a driver, the other field hands set great store in Joe, giving him respect and obedience. John was never drawn into the disciplining or chastising, and doubted there was little of either. Old Joe spoke with authority and with his heart as he prepared the hands for field work. John Dandridge dragged himself out of bed one morning and announced to Frances that he had decided to send Joe to the new farm.

Old Joe, as the head man, took his personal possessions and

moved on site. This meant leaving Mim behind. She had not been feeling well for some time, which caused Joe great uncertainty. His loyalty was to Mr. Dandridge, his owner, but his love for Mim remained the anchor in his life. Since leaving in April, Joe had not returned to Chestnut Grove. Word was passed to him that Mim was all right, but Joe still worried she might have the headaches and dizziness which she said were from too much sun. Joe knew better, because she worked inside the Dandridge home. The August harvest was about complete and the hanging shed for drying was almost filled. Joe planned to go to Chestnut Grove as soon as the curing began, after all his responsibilities were in place.

Brick and Cotton Buel were hired by John Dandridge to build a drying shed for the tobacco raised on the new acreage. The two white men were contracted to the Wellman farm, with two years left of a seven-year indenture. For a small fee, Mr. Wellman agreed that Brick and Cotton could work as carpenters on other farms. John knew the men to be skillful with hammers and saws, but their reputation also included a love for rum. Since they were available immediately, John enlisted them, even though rumors persisted they had difficulty meeting a deadline. He wanted the leaves hung as soon as they were picked, so he agreed to retain the men and pay a bonus if the job was completed on time. The men told John they had lumber left over from a previous shed and would be glad to bring the extra wood to start the project. When the men arrived, two days late, there was no lumber and no equipment for cutting and planing trees.

Joe, his wide smile displaying his large white teeth, greeted Brick and Cotton upon their arrival. He reached out his large hand to the men but was rebuked by both of them.

"Who's in charge?" Brick asked angrily. "Where's Mr. Dandridge?"

Sensing their animosity toward a black man, Joe replied, "Mr. Dandridge is not here. He is at Chestnut Grove today. He was here day 'fore yesterday waitin' for you . Left yesterday 'fore noon when you didn't come. We was very worried 'bout you," said Joe, lifting his straw hat and wiping his forehead. He looked up into the blazing sun, struggling to see the faces of Brick and Cotton where they sat on a crumbling utility wagon.

"We had trouble on the ways here," Brick explained, spewing a wad of spit between his teeth. "Wagon here, full of lumber, got stole by four of them Iroquois." The spit landed between Joe's feet.

"Are you sure? Don't know about any Indians in these parts for long time," answered Joe, covering the spit with dried dirt using the toe of his boot.

Cotton Buel, jumping from the buckboard to the ground, grabbed Joe's shirt front and screamed, "You callin' us liars? No black man has the right for that! We was robbed by them pirates and that is that."

"Mr. Buel, take your hands off 'n me," Joe said, taking his hands and removing Brick's hands from his shirt. "Mr. Dandridge put me in charge here and I 'spect any white or black man who is working on this farm who fails to agree better pack up and leave. I'll make sure ya get some water and supper, if ya want it. You can think over how things are here and let me know if ya want to stay." Joe left his footprints in the dry dust as he walked away from the Buel brothers.

"Let's get some grub and talk about leavin'. I can't think workin' for a black man would be right. What you think, Cotton?"

"Don' know if'n any place be safe without white folks, or if there be any white folks here. You're the one that makes the decisions. You s'pose only black folks?" asked Cotton.

Shortly after the discussion with Old Joe, the men told him they would be heading on back to the Wellman farm. "Don' think we can get the shed built in time for the pickin'," Brick told Joe.

Old Joe hid his disappointment, knowing his own carpenter skills allowed as how he could build it himself. "Sorry about your fixen not to stay," Joe told the men. "Make sure you take food and water enough to get back to Mr. Wellman. Iris'll fix ya up. Just go on over to the kitchen, she'll give ya some bacon and bread."

"Don' see no kitchen," a hungry Cotton said.

"See the smoke risin'?" Joe replied. "Over there you'll find Iris."

Brick and Cotton, following the smoke, found an open campfire. Iris, a young black girl, was stooped over pulling a pan of fresh bread up from the smokey fire. She turned and jumped when the two grimy, slovenly men approached. "My lordy, where'd you come from?"

"That put-on overseer sent us to get some grub and water 'fore we start back to Wellman's place," said Brick, working up another wad of spit. "You Iris?" Brick nudged Cotton with his elbow and said, "Ain't Iris name of a flower, just waitin' to be picked?"

Clenching his fist, Cotton punched Brick on his upper arm as he bent over in laughter, pretending this was the first time he had heard those words.

"You mean Old Joe sen' ya?" Iris asked with eyes wide.

"Did'n get his name. Ol' Joe, ya say?" as Brick's spit hit the dirt.

"I didn' ask ya to put out the fire, mister," Iris said, eyeing Brick's continued spitting. "If'n Old Joe said fer me to give ya grub, well 'round here, whatever Joe says goes." She looked directly into Brick's eyes, her hands on her hips, and asked, "What's you'en's name?" Pointing to Brick, she said, "You look like someone that's always acting tough on the outside when on the inside you scared to death. I bet your name is Pansy." Shaking her finger at Cotton, she said, "You're as yellow as a buttercup. Yes Sir, I bet your name is Buttercup."

"Why, you smart ass blacky. How you get off talkin' to us like that. This here farm run crazy by uppity black mens," shouted Cotton. "My brother's name is Brick Buel and I'm Cotton Buel. Ar' mama named us!"

"Just what I thought, your mama musta wanted you to be as hard as a brick when you're nothin' but a pansy," Iris said to Brick. Looking toward Cotton, she said, "You look like a rolled up cotton ball still on the branch, white on the outside and yeller as a buttercup on the inside. If'n Joe says to give ya food, well, here is some hot bread and bacon. Now git!"

The weary horse tugged the wagon forward as the two men gobbled up their provisions. Cotton reached under the seat and pulled up an object wrapped in cloth. "No water fer me, I'm gonna have a swallow of this," as he uncovered a full bottle of rum, shaking from laughter as he popped the cork. "This'll keep us warm tonight. I was sure looking forward to a night with a roof over us."

"S'pose we shou'd stayed and built the dang thing for Mr. Dandridge?" Brick asked.

"Mr. Wellman'll ask us where we been so long if'n we go back tomorrow. I say we go back and do the job and pay no mind to that black man. We'd 'preciate a cover to sleep under." Cotton took a lingering swallow of rum, some of which washed off his chin. Brick, at the reins, turned the wagon around and headed back to the Dandridge acreage.

Brick and Cotton were at the farm nearly a week before they realized there were no sleeping quarters for blacks or whites. All workers camped out in the open, including Iris and Dandy, who also worked the fields and cooked. Joe explained that the drying shed would provide cover if a summer storm came up. That was why it was important to get the roof on as soon as possible.

Joe was pleased with the tobacco plants. The seeds had been in the ground for nearly eight weeks and already they were six and seven inches high. Catastrophe was always around the corner in tobacco fields, however: chilling winds, roundworms, hungry insects, and the incessant weeds. The warm sunshine had nourished the plants, and the soil seemed fertile and of good tilth and drainage.[1] Joe left the two carpenters to manage their tasks during the daytime. At night he slept close to Iris and Dandy because he feared the brothers might try to take advantage.

The construction seemed to be moving slowly, the Buels making the excuse that the tools they were using were unsatisfactory. Joe had supplied the men with a chisel and mallet to take off unwanted branches, a saw to cut the trees, and a froe to shape the logs. Both men grumbled about the Indians who had taken their best tools. When time allowed, Joe offered to help fell the trees and ready them for construction to expedite the building. Cotton always seemed to like the idea of extra help, but Brick never accepted Joe's offer. He thought Joe, an unassuming man, had too much confidence in himself.

Three people had molded Joe's aptitude to be forgiving, merciful, and compassionate—his Gran'papa O'Quash, his mother Oney, and James Welch, his second owner. Old Joe thanked the Lord every night for the way his life had unfolded.

Mid-August came and the plants were healthy and ready for harvest. Brick and Cotton were nearly finished with the drying shed when Joe informed the two that he and several field hands would help complete the job. "The tobacco will be picked in two days. Six more hands will complete the shed," Joe explained to Brick.

"We don' need six more black hands. This is white man's work," shouted Brick, getting ready to spit. "We'll be done by morning, long before you start pickin'."

"Mr. Buel, we've managed to get along just fine for the past weeks. There's been no trouble with the field folks, no accidents or sickness with any of us. We have a good crop of tobacco to bring us good receipts. We managed to live together, each of us doin' our own jobs pitchin' in to help each other if need be." Joe paused, trying to carefully choose his words. "I prayed we could get through this here season man to man, not black man, white man. I've learned lots from you, way you cut trees, skin the branches and plane the wood into lumber. Mr. Dandridge tol' me you and Cotton have two more years of indenture. I don' know what your plans after that, but if'n you get your own plot and want to grow tobacco, I would sure be willin' to help you get started. Mr. Dandridge is gonna let me 'speriment next season with growing seeds into seedlings and then transplanting them to see if'n they grow better. Those first weeks the worms sure eat their hearts out on them babyroots. Maybe the seedlings be more healthy."[2]

Brick and Cotton stopped working and both men stared at Joe in disbelief. "You think we'd ask a black man for help of any kind? We tell you what to do, not you tell us what to do," Brick said, curling up his tongue and pressing it against his teeth. "We both decided not to bother your business and you haven't bothered ours. That's the way we want it." He spit between Joe's feet. Joe took his boot and kicked the dust over the spit and put his footprints in the soil as he walked away. Joe stopped and turned toward the brothers, "You men be out of here by sunup tomorrow, finished or not finished, you hear me? By sunup."

The first crop of tobacco hung in the brand new shed. Joe leaned against one of the support posts and surveyed the drying leaves. All elements had worked in favor of the excellence of this virgin crop. The plants had grown four to five feet high, each plant growing ten to twelve leaves. Joe and the field hands had carefully topped the suckers after the flowering to increase leaf development. The crew maintained the plants by cutting away each new sucker to allow the leaves to multiply and stay healthy. Now curing the plants would take about six weeks, before the leaves were stripped and packed into the barrels for shipping.[3]

Mr. Dandridge was sending a cooper to teach Joe how to construct the barrels. Joe was not sure when the man would arrive. The cooper was circuiting the plantations on the Pamunkey without a time schedule. Joe was anxious to return to Chestnut Grove to visit Mim, but he knew the four-hour ride each way meant it would take a whole day, without incident. Joe wished Lee was here to put in charge, but Mr. Dandridge had moved him into Joe's job as slave driver. Joe surveyed his options before he realized that the most reliable and capable helper was Iris. "Lord above, I need your help," prayed Joe to himself. "I need to see my woman in the worstest way. Maybe you can do some Divine intervention and send someone to take over whilst I'm gone to see her. Mr. Dandridge won't like it if'n I go to Chestnut Grove without leavin' someone in charge."

Later that day, a wagon pulled into the farm loaded with staves, heads, hoops, and bunges for barrel making. The cooper was a large, heavy chested, talkative man. "How are ya?" he greeted Joe. "I 'spect ya'll been waitin' fer me." He climbed down from the wagon and shook Joe's hand. "Mr. Dan'idge says you's a mighty friendly man and you'd be good help to put together these hogsheads. Joe, isn't it?" He continued to shake his hand. "My name is Gem," still pumping Joe's hand.

"Glad to meet ya, Gem," replied Joe, showing off his big white teeth. "We been looking for ya past couple days. How 'bout water and grub and some rest? Long day?"

"Yes Sir. Most long . . . too long," Gem said as he walked around to pat his horse's head. "Need some water fer Salty."

"Come on, I'll show ya where." Joe took the reins and led the horse to a trough full of springwater. "How long ya been on the circuit, Gem?"

"Left Will'msbur' mid-July. Been on the road ever since." Gem stopped to blow his nose and relieve himself on the side of the path. "My wife don' 'spect me home much before one October."

Just as Joe turned away from the water trough, he heard a horse running fast and hard. "Lordy, who that be, riding like fire?" He stepped into the drive and squinted his eyes through the shadows of the tall trees to determine the rider. "The horse is Mr. Dandridge's and I do think it might be either Princess or Fatima," Joe told himself. "My eyes ain't as good as they should be, but I do believe the rider is Mis Martha. No, it can't be. She'd never wear a horse down like that." The wind was strong enough to keep the dust blowing and hovering over the horse and rider.

"Joe, Joe!" shouted Martha as she started to slow Fatima. Powdery dust was in her hair, eyes, and mouth as she waved her arm at Joe.

"Mis Martha, what brings you here in such a hurry? Tell me you haven't run Fatima like this all the way from Chestnut Grove." Joe grabbed the reins and helped Martha climb off the horse.

Gem took the reins from Joe and said, "I'll cool her down. You two take care of your business."

"Joe, you've got to get ready to go back with me. Mim is sick and she keeps calling for you." Martha's face was flushed and she broke into a sob, "She's been good but this morning early she began to scream like a hyena. Mother was out of her bed and down to Mim's bed like a jackrabbit. Josie and Pansy were already trying to calm her. I jumped out of my bed quick to find out what was wrong. By the time I got to Mim, all I could hear was 'Joe, Joe. Where is Joe?' I told Mother I was coming to get you. I was saddled up and on Fatima before Mother or Papa could stop me," cried Martha.

"What's you think's wrong? Is she gonna die?" Joe's eyes gave away his terror.

"Joe, saddle up, take a lantern and get started. You might get to Chestnut Grove before dark if you hurry. I'll stay here tonight and take care of things. Tell Papa to send Lee tomorrow to take over your duties. Fatima will be rested and I'll ride her home then," Martha said with authority.

"No, no, you can't stay here tonight. Your papa would skin me inside out if'n I left you here by you'self. We be goin' together, Mis Martha. I got two fresh horses ready for a fast trip."

Martha felt her face with both hands and could feel the radiating heat. Her hair was dripping with sweat, her arms ached, and her legs were beginning to cramp. "I can't ride back tonight. I'm just too worn out. I'll sleep with Iris and Dandy. We'll be all right. You go."

Gem was standing apart, listening to the conversation between Martha and Old Joe. He strode over and encouraged Joe to get started. "I have a daughter just about this young lady's age. I'll make sure she is well cared for. Her horse is pretty tired, so I'll make sure she is taken care of, too. You get on now, ya hear?"

When the Dandridge family returned to Chestnut Grove from Nate and Dorthea's wedding in the spring of 1747, Mim knew she was sick. She labored to ignore fatigue, lightheadness, and the relentless headache. After baby Frances recovered from her sickness, Mim gave excuses to herself that she had the same affliction. So much had happened so fast after the wedding; that alone made her head reel. Mr. Dandridge bought more planting ground, bringing visitors aplenty as he examined possible overseers, coopers and carpenters. Young Frances was in Mim's care while the older children took their lessons each day. Franny had become a spoiled child whose demands were impossible to meet. Martha was acting out as a grown-up girl with the temperament of a child. Mim found her own energy waning each day as she tended the family garden, cooked, washed clothes, managed the children, and listened to the daily ramblings of the older Dandridge children.

Mim's most grievous blow came when Old Joe announced he was going to oversee the new tobacco field. She assumed she would go as field hand and cook, but Joe said, "Iris and Dandy will take those duties."

"Why would he send those young, skinny, lazy women when I can do the work of bof 'um? Dandy ain't but twelve, thirteen!" sobbed Mim. "Mister Dandridge thinks I'm sick," Mim thought to herself. "That's why he's keeping me here." Mim and Joe were in the barn yard, walking carefully between a flock of young, fluffy, yellow chicks feeding on bits of corn. Joe reached for Mim's elbow as he led her into their slave quarters. The hot summer morning was boiling over with humidity after a rain shower the night before. "Hon, listen to me. Mr. Dan'ridge is not takin you, because you're needed to keep the big house goin' and taken' care of that addled babin. Stop and think 'bout the Dan'ridge thinkin'. "

The two walked hand in hand into their bleak, dark cabin. Mim's tears rolled down each cheek. She picked up her pinafore and dabbed her eyes with the bottom corner. "I know, I know." Mim laid down on a pallet to think over what Joe had just told her. She reviewed the number of times she was unable to do her work because of feeling sickly in recent weeks. The crying began again, and didn't subside until she lapsed into a deep sleep.

The caller walking through Mim and Old Joe's quarters sounded the cow horn. Mim felt Joe's burly arm around her waist as she grappled to get up from the dirt floor. The deafening bell interrupted Mim's depthless sleep. She quickly sat up, trying to determine where she was in the darkened room. The sunrise was yet to appear as she shook her head, working to organize her bearings and what daily duties lay ahead. "Lay back down, hon," Joe whispered. "Don' worry, that wake-up wasn't for us."

"Do Mis Dan'ridge know I'm out here with ya?" Mim asked. "I s'pose I'd better git inside 'fore that babin wake up, huh?" Mim got to her unsteady feet and walked outside to the pail of water to splash the cold against her warm face. The upper sky was still a midnight blue, with a faint stripe of pink peeking through the trees standing in the east. The temperature was already rising, giving hints of what the high would reach before day's end.

Mim took off her shoes to let her feet breathe for awhile. She was fully dressed, including her turban. During her exhausted sleep, her body didn't once remind her to get up and return to the house. Footsteps came up behind Mim which she promptly recognized as Joe's. He wrapped his arms around her and gently kissed the nape of her neck. Mim put her arms up over her head and locked them around Joe's neck. "Mim hon, how will I gets along without ya? I prob'ly be gone six or so months." Joe's face was buried on the back of Mim's neck and shoulder.

"Maybe Mr. Dandridge let me come home on Sundays, I'll ask him."

Mim turned to face Joe and took his face in her hands, "We been together long time, Old Joe. Bran' new farm. Mister Dan'ridge gonna want ya stay put to make sure things go good." She kissed Joe on each ear and lovingly looked into his eyes. "Maybe Lee bring me to see ya on a Sunday. Ya go and do your best job and be proud," she said, rubbing her hands over his short cropped hair. "Mr. Dan'ridge might give us some piece of the new field, so's we can be free s'pose?"

"Mim, I want us to find the Reverend and pledge ourselves to be together forever, ya'll know, a weddin', like the white folks have . . . before I go. If'n Mr. Dan'ridge will give us permission." Joe rubbed his nose against Mim's cheek affectionately. "I'll speak to Mr. Dan'ridge this morning."

John Dandridge climbed out of his bed before sunup. The wagons were packed with planting tools, seeds, candles, tinder box, cooking pots and utensils, blankets, and other necessary items to set up a temporary home for Joe, Iris, Dandy and the other field hands. John assured himself that Joe was the right man to oversee the new farm. He was anxious to start plowing so the seeds could be placed by mid-April.

The day started like most late spring days. A slight wind, gently moving the trees, to let sunrise climb down through the leaves all the way to the ground, the birds singing love songs to one another as they readied nests, and the smells of rich, newly plowed soil waiting to accept seeds. Two wagons filled with supplies and farm hands would leave the Dandridge plantation at eight o'clock for the long trip. John asked young John to accompany the crew driving one of the wagons. He planned to leave one wagon on site along with one extra horse.

"Mornin', Mr. Dan'ridge," said Lee. "Looks like ya gettin' ready for to take leave."

"Where's Old Joe?" John Dandridge asked. "He's going with me and we need to get started. Will you go round up the others?"

"Joe not sure he leaving today. I'll go tell him ya'll waitin', Sir."

Mim and Joe were still discussing Joe's departure and the prospect of marriage when Lee found them. "If we gets a ceremony, Mr. Dandridge will never separate us, hon. I just knows that." Joe's convincing plan sounded good enough, but Mim knew in her bones that Joe would be swept away before the arrangements could be carried out.

"Com'on Joe, Mr. Dan'ridge ready to go," hollered Lee. "He been lookin' fer ya."

Joe turned to Mim and said, "Lee can't wait for me to be gone so's he can take my job. Mr. Dan'ridge tol' me we won't leave for a couple days." Joe quickly left Mim standing over the water bucket while he went to find Mr. Dandridge and ask when they were leaving.

A tarp lay over the goods in the wagon as John Dandridge worked to pull a rope through a hook pounded into the side of the wooden wagon, to hold the supplies in place. "We're leaving this morning. It'll take us a good bit of the day to get the supplies hauled over. Then we have to set up camp when we get there. Come on and help us finish loading. Young John will drive one of the wagons," John directed.

"Mr. Dandridge, I didn't know we was going so soon. I wanted to ask something before we left," Old Joe said with disappointment.

"Joe, we'll be late getting the plantings in the ground if we don't get going. You drive and I'll ride with you. We can talk on the way over. Now, get yourself something to eat so's we can get started."

Joe looked down at the ground and worked the toe of his boot into the dust. He dreaded telling Mim that Lee was right, they were leaving at eight o'clock. "Why does all the people that mean so much always seem to end somewhere else?" Joe stepped slowly, kicking the dry dust as he walked to Mim to give her the bad news. Mim still hovered over the water bucket, sprinkling her face before wiping her hands on her apron. She threw her head backwards toward the sky and looked as though she was talking to someone, then splashed her face again. Joe's face divulged the message before he spoke, "Mim, hon, Lee was right. We's leaving right away."

"Did ya as' Mr. Dan'ridge 'bout us?" Mim asked. "Can I go, too?"

Old Joe held Mim in his arms as she crushed her face into his chest. "No, he took no questions. He's ridin' wit me and says we can talk then," Joe answered dolefully. "Ya take ya'self to Mis Dandridge, now. She'll be need'n ya. I'll ask to come back as soon as I can."

"Mim, will you please go and get Frances and take her to the wash house with you. She needs to be outside this morning. She had a restless night and came to us looking for comfort. I guess you were so tired, you didn't hear her," Mrs. Dandridge said.

" I guess I didn't hear her. I sleepin' hard these days," replied Mim.

"I am concerned about your not feeling well, Mim. We need to make sure you are taking good care of yourself. Do you want for more food?" asked Frances, with deep concern.

"Mis Dan'ridge, I can eat and eat! I always seem to be hungry these days. I just gettin' old and fat," Mim said. I can't work as hard as I used to."

"Do you have any idea how old you are? We have never discussed your age in the long years you have been with us."

"Mis Dan'ridge, I 'spect I'm somewhere over forty. Never knew where I was born or when," answered Mim, sorrowfully. Old Joe, he's lucky. He knows his mama and papa, always thought his daddy was white man."

"That is preposterous, Mim! Where did you get that silly notion?" Frances asked indignantly.

"From Joe, hisself. He tol' me his gran'papa tol' him long time ago. O'Quash full of stories, so I never knew if that be true or not. Ol' Joe always thought his daddy was his first owner, cause he was a tall man and Joe a big man, too. Joe and his mama Oney left that farm when Joe was little boy, but Joe always remembered how big his owner was, can never remember his name."

"Mim, I will move either Iris or Dandy into the house as soon as they return from the new farm. You will be able to rest better with your people. Frances is three years old and she still doesn't sleep through the night, and I know that is hard on you. I'll make arrangements with Mr. Dandridge to bring one of them back on his next trip," Frances explained.

"Mis Dan'ridge, does that mean I can change places with one of 'em and go be with Joe?" Mim asked.

"We'll see. I have a tonic I want you to start taking. It is made with sassafras tea and you are to take it three times a day," Frances said as she held up three fingers for Mim to see. "You will start feeling stronger right away, I'm sure. A little calomet might help, also."

Every day was a struggle for Mim. Her legs were wobbly and ached, she shook the wooziness out of her head each morning and her back could hardly lift Franny or keep from aching as she stood over the wash tub. The three-times-a-day regimen of taking the tonic had not helped her feel better. "I's gettin' old and this ol' body is lettin' me know it," Mim told herself.

Joe had been gone nearly two months, but to Mim, it seemed like two years. She still had all the house chores and care for Franny. Neither Iris nor Dandy had returned to the Dandridge plantation as promised. Mim's salvation was nighttime, when she could lie down beside Franny's bed to rest and then fall asleep. The backache would wake Mim enough to know it was throbbing, but she always slipped back to sleep, sometimes without completely waking up. Mim usually slept curled up, never moving a muscle. She found such discomfort that she discovered sleeping on her back on the hard floor brought more rest.

One morning before dawn, Mim awoke screaming, "Mis Dan'ridge, Mis Dan'ridge!" Franny climbed out of her bed and leaned over Mim trying to help as she wailed

"I'm dying. I know I'm dying. Tell the Lord I'm comin'."

Mrs. and Mr. Dandridge entered the room briskly, trying to focus on Mim's shrill crying. "What is it, Mim?" Mrs. Dandridge asked calmly.

"I don't know, but I got worms crawling around inside my stomach. They moving back and forth scaring me out of my skin." Mim continued to roll back and forth from one side to another, shrieking loudly.

"John, please take Franny and go back to bed in our room. I'll try to see what is the matter here." Martha came into the room to offer help and Mother asked her to go for water and rags. Mim was dripping with sweat and Frances thought she had had a nightmare the magnitude of which she had never seen. "Mim, listen to me. Tell me what happened. Did you have a bad dream?"

"No, Mis Dan'ridge . . . I got something wrong with me. The Lord mad to me."

"The Lord *is* mad at me," corrected Frances. "Tell me again what happened."

"Well, I was trying to get my back to stop hurting so I rolled over on it and something started crawlin' inside," Mim said choking out each word.

"You get into Franny's bed and get yourself settled. I'll be right back." Frances Dandridge went into her bedroom and sat down on the edge of the bed to talk to John. "John, I think Mim might be with child. She keeps saying something is crawling inside her stomach, and a baby's movement sometimes feels that way."

John sat upright, propping his pillows, careful not to disturb Franny. "I do not believe she could be expecting a baby after all these years. She has been with us nearly twenty years and she is barren. Besides, Joe has been gone for only two months. It is not possible!"

"Yes, it is, John. I'm thinking back to when we were in Williamsburg when our baby was so sick; Mim did not feel well then. We have paid no mind to her weight gain along with her complaints of fatigue. I have had enough babies to recognize the symptoms." Frances, ever vigilant, looked at John, who had confidence in her powers of observation.

"Will she be able to survive the labor of childbirth at her age?"

"Many women have given birth in later age, but most have had babies before. Each labor gets easier. I do not know about first babies coming after forty, John. I'm going back to see how she is. I fear I will need help if she is in labor."

"Frances, I want you to take Mim out into the slave quarters and let her people take care of her. They know more about birthin' than you do, besides, you'll have extra work with Mim gone." John reached up and patted Frances on her cheek as his eyes communicated his deep love for her.

Mim was resting quietly while Martha brushed her face with a damp, cool cloth. Frances entered the room across the hall. "Mother, I believe she is sleeping now," Martha said quietly.

"Yes, let's leave her to sleep," Frances replied. "She will need the rest."

Mim refused to believe she might have a baby growing inside her belly. She had good days when she worked doing the Dandridge chores. The bad days were the times she pined for Old Joe to come home and be with her. She asked Mrs. Dandridge how long she'd have to wait to learn if there was really a babin. "Every child born is a gift of God, Mim," Frances replied. "Your time will come, and when the baby leaves your body, your heart will fill with so much love that you can not imagine life before."

Several months passed before the bearing-down pain of childbirth began. Mim awoke early one morning in unbearable pain. The reality of her immense fear of delivering a child at her age had started. She had resigned herself to motherhood, but blissfully ignored the early hints her body gave her, like a sleeping volcano stirring and moving before the large eruption. Josie and Pansy were experienced mid-wives and stayed with Mim, directing the push and rest between each pain. Weakness and fatigue were replaced by lethargy and faintness as the hours drifted into first one day, then a second.

Old Joe arrived at the Dandridge farm the second day of her labor. He vigilantly sat beside Mim, trying to keep her conscious. "Mim, hon, remember the first time I met ya'? Ya were 'most twelve and ya thought I was old enough to be yer daddy." Joe, watching Mim's eyelids rise and fall, knew she could hear his words. "Mr. Dandridge has gone to fetch his preacher. He's goin' to marry us, just like the white folks, and like I promised we would. Mim, can you hear me?" Josie and Pansy stood behind Joe, watching Mim as she underwent another contraction. Mim began to heave and pitch as she worked feverishly to wake up and push.

"Old Joe, ya need to step outside whilst we take a look," ordered Josie. "This may be the last of pain before that babin gets borned." Joe reluctantly left Mim's side, wishing the preacher would hurry. He paced back and forth. Joe's steady pace changed into a rhythmical beat to O'Quash's prayer to Nkuwu. "*Utopia, Utopia . . . Wah, wah . . . ta, ta . . . rah, rah. We've come home to be with you . . .* Dear Lord, if ya care to hear my prayer, please give Mim your blessing for havin' a strong babin. Help her to bring her strength to bear the pain. She so strong."

Pansy shook Joe's arm, disturbing his meditating conversation with Nkuwu. "Hurry, Joe, the baby girl's here. Josie breathing into her mouth so's she can cry." A squall sounded as Joe stepped inside to look at his daughter. Pansy gently rubbed the fully formed baby with a wet cloth. "What ya doin' to my girl?" Joe asked, as he observed the ritual.

"Just washin' away the birthin' leavin's. Babin gets mighty messy sometimes when tryin' to come into the worl'," Pansy replied.

Josie leaned over Mim, wiping her forehead with a damp rag and said, "It's all over, honey. Ya got a big, strong, baby girl. Look, Joe here. He been waitin' and waitin for ya'll to talk to him."

Mim struggled to lift her eyelids and raise her head. She whispered, "Joe," as she worked to move her arms to reach out to him. "Joe, I been waitin a long time for ya. . . ." Her head fell back on the pillow, her eyes closed and with breath heaving, she peacefully fell asleep.

"She so light-skinned, not black," Joe said scornfully. "She not my baby girl. How could Mim do that to me?" Joe began to rock and sway back and forth, his emotions breaking out into tears and sobs.

"Joe, what's the matter wit you?" Pansy retorted. "All babin look light-skinned when first born, besides Mim tol' me long time ago ya might have white blood inside yer skin. Now here, hold your babin and be thinkin' 'bout a name."

Josie let out a wail and screamed, "Joe! Joe! Get over here quick and talk to Mim. I think she limpen'. She mighty weak, but ya gotta help keep her 'wake for awhile. She need sleep bad to git her strength back."

Overwhelmed with emotion, Joe sat down beside his cherished Mim and rubbed her hand and face. He worked to wipe away the beads of sweat resting on her forehead with his oversized hands. His kisses melted on her still-warm skin. "Mim, hon. It's Joe. Can ya hear me talkin' ta ya?" Joe sat patiently waiting for a response.

Frances Dandridge entered the dark, damp cabin where Mim lay, Joe hovering over her while Josie and Pansy tended to the baby. Martha followed her mother, carrying a pot of steaming broth. Word had reached the Dandridge home that Mim had given birth to a baby girl, but no word had come about Mim's condition. Frances recognized Old Joe with a nod of her head, then asked to examine Mim.

"She mighty tired, Mis Dandridge." Joe stood at the foot of Mim's straw bed. "She had a hard time bringin' that babin in the worl'."

Mim's stillness gave Frances a start as she leaned her head over Mim's breast to listen to her heart. "Joe," Frances called. " Joe." Frances was frozen in place as the color disappeared from her face. "Joe, I believe Mim has passed on. I can't be sure, but she lies motionless and I can't hear a heartbeat." Frances, in her usual inability to face reality, could not force herself to say the word dead.

Joe kneeled down beside Mim and leaned over to try and find a sign of life somewhere inside her chest. "Mis Dan'ridge, the Lord wouldn' take my Mim away, would he? She gotta still be in there."

"Let me take another look." Frances felt Mim's forehead, still moist from the labor. She laid her ear close to Mim's heart, knowing there was little chance to find any sign of life. "I'm sorry, Joe." Martha gave out a cry of shock and disbelief at her mother's announcement. "John will be here soon with Reverend Mossum. Do you want me to send for your preacher? Mim would want her last rites to be done by someone of her own kind."

"The only service I want is for the Reverend to marry us!" Joe said. "I promised Mim we would be married with a preacher, like the white folks, and that will still happen." Joe's throat tightened with emotion as he swallowed hard to keep the tears inside.

Joe could not look forward to the decisions he needed to make. With Mim dead, how could the baby live? By law, the baby belonged to the Dandridges, but Joe promised Mim they would never be separated, and this also meant any children born to them. Joe decided the baby's name would be Oney, like his mother. He knew Mim would give her approval.

Frances Dandridge made the decision that Oney would be moved to the William Dandridge farm, because there were no nursing mothers at Chestnut Grove. She was sure there were two women available at Chestnut Creek to wet-nurse the healthy baby.

John Dandridge, with Reverend Mossum, arrived late in the day to discover there was to be a wedding but there would also be a funeral. Work stopped on the Dandridge farm as soon as word reached the field hands and the house slaves. Mim and Old Joe were considered the chieftains of the slave population at Chestnut Grove, and the loss of Mim left a void and uncertainty about their future. Martha was inconsolable. She left the slave quarters and walked to the barn where her favorite horse stood quietly. Martha stroked Fatima's mane, trying to shake the despair that overwhelmed her.

Arrangements were quickly made to allow all the slave community and the Dandridge family to squeeze into Mim and Joe's cabin for the marriage ceremony. Joe stood next to Mim where she lay on her pallet. Pansy had clipped daisies from the garden and pinned them in her hair. Her long and beautiful lashes rested on her cheekbones, which Martha had colored with powder and rouge. Joe held the sleeping Oney in his arms. Lee stood next to Joe; Josie, Pansy, and Martha knelt beside Mim. Each woman held a small bouquet of fresh daisies. Joe took Mim's hand in his as the ceremony began.

Reverend Mossum had difficulty beginning. He cleared his throat several times, trying to carefully choose words appropriate to this unusual situation. "We are gathered here today to join together Mim and Joe in holy matrimony. Your love for one another has stood the test of time and no obstacle has diminished that love and honor. No rain too heavy, wind too strong, clouds too gray, labors too fatiguing, or sickness too grave has broken your commitment of loving, honoring, and obeying each other. You were born together and together you shall be today, tomorrow, and forever. I now pronounce you man and wife."

The ambivalent tears, some of joy and most of sadness, flowed. Lee tugged on Joe's arm as he whispered something into his ear.

"Reverend, Reverend, I have a ring to put on Mim's finger. I would like to do that now," Joe said. Lee had scavenged the barnyard to find something to make a ring for Mim. Time was limited, but he found a piece of iron left over from a recent horseshoeing and was able to heat it and reshape it into a crudely made ring. Joe took the ring and placed it on Mim's limp finger. "I's loved ya from the first time I met ya. I've always been true to ya and ya to me. We's always wanted a white folks weddin'. I always had faith we'd have one someday. I never knew it'd be like this. I promise to take care of our baby girl forever." Joe leaned down and kissed Mim's forehead for the last time.

August 22,1747 Dear God, Please help me to unerstand your ways. My bes frend is gon an I cant begin to xplane this lost feelin in mi bode. I seem to hav no purpose or want to leav my bed. Who will put flowrs in mi hare and fix mi shews so they fit Franny wil hav no one to tak her to the barn an plaa wit the animals. Her pet bunne will be lonsome. Mother will hav to mov jose into the hous but papa says she is lazy an not trusted. Oh DEAR LORD what wil we all do wit out Mim? She lookd peacful wit her new ring. an the flours in her hare. Who will go wit me to Willumsbur? Jose cant pac mi things lik Mim Mim nos how to talk to folks an git things don. The boys wil mis all her storys abut the daes she was wit the Hughs famly an the other slave famly. Mother an me took babe Oney to Chestnut Creek todae. The folks over ther just sold a house boy to anoter famly on the james river. Nate tol me the boys mother trid to cut herself wit a nife becaus she was so sad bout her boy leaving Chestnut Creek. She quit eating to. I was sur Nate made that up about the nife. Most nigra dont have that kinda thoughts.

Mother an me made sur to met the two nursing mamas. We made them promis to luv Oney as there own. Mi hart is so hevy. Old Joe is so sad that papa sed he wud not send him bac to the new farm so he cud be near Mim. Pleas LORD help me feel beter soon maybe I hav a fevr coming on. Blessed be to yur ways Amen and GOD bles us all. Martha Jones Dandridge

Joe prostrated himself over Mim's grave before dawn every day. Only a large rock distinguished her burial site. Joe was still laboring on the carved cross he was making out of a piece of hardwood. His plans were to plane the wood until it had a satiny sheen before he replaced the rock with it. John Dandridge had cordoned off a piece of the Chestnut Grove plantation for the farmworkers' final resting place. Only five graves there had markers, and most of them were weathered and worn. Joe worked feverishly to make sure that Mim would always be remembered with the cross.

Joe's head was imbued with the last hour of Mim's life. Every night he relived her debilitating labor, her strong will to live, then her waning strength. She was two days with pain.. then anticipation . . . sharp pain . . . then waiting . . . excruciating pain . . . then one last effort . . . then deep despair as Mim's life ebbed away. "The Lord giveth and the Lord taketh away," Joe repeated to himself, trying to understand why God would take her away.

Joe regretted that little Oney was living at the Chestnut Creek plantation. She came into the world sturdy and strong-voiced, even though she struggled to take a first breath. Joe had promised Mim he would care for their child and raise her. Every morning during his visits to Mim's gravesite he promised to go and fetch her as soon as she was weaned. He also promised there would be no more family separations and that Oney would learn where she came from, even though her mama knew nothing about her roots.

1685 Joe's earliest memories began the day he and his mama were sold to the William Welch family. His mother Oney begged Mr. Welch not to separate the two from her family. "Please, Mas'er Welch, don' take us witout O'Quash. He be my papa an' he need me. We be together since day I was borned," Oney pleaded, reaching out and pulling on his sleeve.

William Welch recoiled from Oney's hand. "Consider yourself lucky that I am taking your son Joe. He is only five years old and hardly ready for farm work. I have a four-year-old son with only older sisters. He needs a companion and Joe can help him with his daily duties," Mr. Welch responded.

Oney was on her gnarled knees, threatening, "I run away . . . I take my boy and run far away. I find O' Quash; we live in the swamps so's I take care of him." Oney was rocking back and forth on her kneecaps, sobbing, "Please, please don' sen us away. My papa die witout me and Joe."

"Your father is very old. He has done his life's work. Besides you're Big Joe's woman and that is why I'm taking you."

"I'm not Big Joe's woman!" Oney screamed. "My man done pass on long time ago."

"Joe told me you were his and Little Joe was his son," replied Mr. Welch.

Oney raised herself up from the drenched ground, grimacing and wiping her forehead, her eyes slitted, and said "Ya go as' Mister Wellman who planted the seed of my boy," looking eye to eye with Mr. Welch. "O'Quash is the only papa my boy ever had."

The sky was a slate gray. The spring rain clouds emptied themselves while the wind blew the saplings parallel with the saturated earth. Little Joe needed his mama to wrap her warm arms around his body and comfort his soul. He was bewildered by the outcry from Oney and wasn't sure who the strange man was that caused his mama to be so crazed. Joe was unable to hear the exchange between Oney and the stranger because he was trying to keep himself hidden and dry behind an old oak tree. Little Joe heard the thunder getting closer. He felt shivers up and down his backbone. "Mama, come get me," he whispered to himself. Joe stuck his small forefinger into his left nostril, a habit O'Quash taught him, which he'd started recently when his stomach began to toss and heave. The finger seemed to push away the need to throw up, but today he pressured his nose too hard and blood began spilling down his bare chest and onto his cotton pants. Giving a mighty yell, "Mama, Mama! Help me," he ran to her side.

"Sshh . . . sshh. You get on back to our place. I be there in a minute," Oney said as she pushed Little Joe aside. A flash of lightning illuminated the dark clouds and was followed by a clap of deafening thunder. Little Joe screamed, putting his hands over his ears, crying, "Mama, help me! Please come with me back to our place." Copious blood continued to drip from Little Joe's nose. He worked to wipe it with the back of his hand, but between the rain and the nosebleed his small hands couldn't stop the flow. Reaching up to grab a piece of Oney's dress, Little Joe cried, "My nose's got somethin' wrong, Mama."

Oney still was face to face with Mr. Welch, but their words were swept away by the wind. Little Joe tugged on his mama's leg, begging her to pick him up into the safety of her arms. "Stop it!" Oney shouted to Little Joe.

"Go home now, else I skin you alive." She drew up her hand to strike him across the face, when she unlocked her gaze with Mr. Welch and looked down to discover blood running down Joe's face, chest, legs, and feet. She picked up her boy and swept him into her arms, sobbing into his little chest. "My Gawd, what has happened to my baby?" She fell to the ground, clinging to Joe while he buried his face in her shoulder, his arms wrapped around her neck. "Oh, my baby boy, what have I done?" she moaned as she rubbed the back of his head with her wet hand.

"Mama, Mama," Little Joe sobbed, with a catch like a hiccup between each breath.

Oney balanced herself and carefully got on her feet, still embracing Little Joe. "Tell me, my little patty cake man, what happened." She put Joe at her feet while she tried to swab his nose with her apron. Looking toward the clouds and sky, Oney saw the lightning in the distance and the sounds of the thunder that seemed to have moved on with it. The wind and rain continued, but she was sure it would soon follow the storm to the east.

Little Joe, quiet now, said, "I was 'fraid that man might hurt you, mama. I was scared." Oney stroked Joe's cheek as she looked around and discovered that Mr. Welch had gone.

The poorly built wooden wagon bumped along the dry road. Oney sat on the seat next to the driver who was a bulky black man with no interest in conversation. Little Joe ran alongside the wagon, full of questions about their new home. His excitement grew as he discovered miles of fields planted with tobacco and rice. The boy's confinement to the Wellman farm had limited his exposure to an outside world that he was anxious to explore. All Joe knew were the stories O'Quash told about his home in faraway Gambia, across a big water where his mama and papa lived, and that he was stole from his people. Little Joe felt his heart tug when he thought of his gran'papa. Mama told Joe that they might never see O'Quash again and that they'd never forget him and he'd never forget them. "We'll just have to keep him in our hearts until we find him again in Heaven," Mama said.

"Little Joe, you keep up with this here wagon or you'll have to git in and ride with me," Oney warned. Her new straw hat sat stiffly on her head, like an eagle's nest in a tree top. Mr. Welch had sent a new dress, shoes, and hat for Oney. Little Joe had new shoes, britches, and a white shirt. The shirt felt strange against his brown skin. Sometimes when the weather got chilly Mama put an old cotton jerkin on Little Joe; otherwise he was always shirtless. He had a rousing feeling in his stomach; he just knew somethin' good was ahead. Just looking around at a new world, having new clothes and soon a new home, made him excited. Big Joe had gone to the Welch plantation on Sunday last. Little Joe didn't know why his mama and himself were left behind to follow a week later. The man driving the wagon refused to answer the questions he asked about the Welch farm. He either nodded yes or no or just shrugged his shoulders. Mama tried to coax him into talking, but he continued to ignore her.

The Welch plantation was much larger than the Wellman farm. The elongated, tree-lined drive to the main house seemed endless. The afternoon sun had begun its drop into the western sky, leaving a hue of bright yellow on the horizon, stratified with changing colors of oranges and pinks. Oney felt relieved when it became obvious there was no field work because of the Sabbath Day. Children were playing on the brilliant green rolling lawn. Little Joe was riding in the wagon, wide-eyed at the pastoral sight of the white-columned home, tall trees swaying in the light breeze and numerous outbuildings surrounding the manor house. Three well-dressed white children and two bare-chested black children ran to meet the wagon. The oldest girl directed the wagon to the left drive. "Papa wants you to take Little Joe and Oney right to the slave quarters."

"She knows our names," said Joe. "Mama, look at the house. Do ya think ya might work inside?"

"Don't know, son," Oney answered. "If we's lucky we might both be sleepin' inside. If'n Mister Welch keeps his promise that ya be with his boy every day. Big Joe will know the arrangements by now, I 'spect."

There were six log houses in a row, each with a brick chimney. The houses were situated close to the fields so the workers had a short walk to work. The mute driver motioned Oney toward the door with a big painted "A" next to it. Oney unloaded her meager belongings, then picked up Joe and carried him inside. The house had wooden floors and a big fireplace. There were no people inside except a boy about Joe's age, curled up and sleeping on a pallet in front of the fire. "Sshh," whispered Oney. "He may be sick or he may be playing possum." The two tiptoed outside to take the opportunity to look around their new home.

"Mama, this a bigger farm than Mr. Wellman's. S'pose we have to work harder?" Joe asked, looking into his mama's eyes.

"Don't know what's in store for us. Let's sit down on the stoop and wait for somebody to come." Oney reached out and pulled Joe down on her lap.

A shiny black horse with a well-dressed man in the saddle came galloping up to the porch where Oney and Joe sat waiting. William Welch swung down from his horse saying, "Welcome to Willow Place. I hope your trip was not too tiring. Your people are still celebrating the Sabbath and haven't returned yet."

"We was wondering where everyone is, 'cept for a sleepin' chile inside," Oney said.

"I'll have the two of you follow me to the big house. I want the boy here to meet my son, James. You may have seen him when you came up the drive," Mr. Welch said to Joe. "Come along, now." He put his foot in the stirrup and swung back up on to the horse, then cantered toward the white-columned house.

James Welch and Little Joe grew to be best friends. Mr. Welch kept his word, making Joe a companion to his young son while Oney was placed as a house slave in charge of James's older sister, Anne. The tasks of Joe and Oney were many, extending most days into fifteen and sixteen hours. When the Welch family entertained guests, their days were sometimes eighteen to twenty hours. Neither one complained, because being house slaves meant sleeping on pallets on the floor next to the beds of their charges. The inside also included getting much of the leftover food, to be shared among the house slaves.

James was a small-boned, underweight boy with tendencies to chest ailments, a runny nose, and earaches. Joe was a year older than James, outweighed him by twenty pounds, and stood a head taller. Joe, who loved to probe the outdoors, spent long hours inside with James, who was often confined to bed. Mr. Knoblauch, James's live-in German tutor, refused to work with his charge if he was ill, so Joe sat and listened to James read aloud, for "enlightenment," while recovering.

Joe couldn't make out the "A" on the first dwelling of the slave quarters when he arrived at the Welch plantation, but he soon learned. His educational apprenticeship began with James reading aloud to him. Joe patiently listened to the rhythmical poems and rhyming riddles written for children. Both boys loved *The House That Jack Built*, and would create their own verses with different titles, most of which bordered on the disgusting. Mr. Knoblauch soon promoted James to *Assemblies of Aesopic Tales*, a collection of over two hundred fables. He required James to utilize his skills and develop five fables of his own creation. Little Joe, who had listened to his gran'papa's folklore about his homeland, offered ideas and stories to James. James, mesmerized by Little Joe's tales, pressed for more accounts of slaves being kidnapped, living in squalor in the ships bringing them to the New World, and then being sold into the harsh life of a slave. In disbelief, James always asked for the true story of how Joe's gran'papa got to Virginia. "Them's the true stories, honest, James," Joe tried to explain.

James became a proficient and prolific writer. Little Joe was responsible for keeping James's lap desk full of paper, quill pens, and powder for mixing ink. Mr. Knoblauch gave James numerous writing assignments, which he easily mastered. Joe began to recognize certain letters and soon put them together into words. While understanding that reading and writing were exclusive to white people, he often looked over the papers that James read aloud, as if to read them himself before putting the work away.

"Joe, do you want me to teach you the letters and numbers and perhaps to spell your name?" James asked nonchalantly.

"If it please you to do so, yes, I would like that." Reluctantly, Joe asked, "Will you need to ask your father?"

"No need to do that. He doesn't often come into my room when you are here."

Thus began Joe's matriculation into formal education. He quickly mastered the alphabet and numerical configurations. James's ability to be patient and composed as a tutor gave Joe opportunity to learn at his own pace. The boys planned the lessons carefully, because James knew his father would not approve. Repeatedly he told Joe not to worry if their collaboration was discovered. Learning to write his name made Joe ecstatic. He loved the feel of the soft quill between his fingers and the scent of the ink. James taught Joe how to add two marbles with two marbles, then take away two marbles from four marbles. This was a game to Little Joe, and he swiftly learned to add and subtract using larger and larger numbers.

Little Joe had limited contact with Mr. and Mrs. Welch or James's sisters, Anne and Lizabet. Oney, attending Anne, was able to keep up with the doings of the household. At thirteen, Anne was a talkative child and considered Oney her best friend. She revealed one day that her mother was suspicious about James teaching Joe to read. Anne said that Mrs. Welch mentioned this to Mr. Welch at the supper table. "James responded with the reddest face you ever did see," Anne prattled. "Father asked James if that was true, and James faked a cough and put his napkin over his mouth and left the table. I don't know what happened next, because Father followed James up to his room. All I heard was a loud slam of his bedroom door."

Oney confronted Joe about his learning and he told her it was true. "Mr. Welch'll put ya out of the house!" Oney shrieked. "Ya make sure this stops, 'cause he might get a notion to bargain ya to someone else. I couldn't stay alive if'n ya were taken away."

Joe tried to explain that the learnin' came about when he helped James write fables and such. "I just told him gran'papa's stories about the kidnappin', the ship, and bein' sold. He thought I made the stories up, so every time he had to write somethin' he always asked for my ideas. Mr. Knoblauch liked his stories so he kept havin' him write more. One day

James asked me if'n I would like to learn to read 'em 'cause I was so good at makin' 'em up. I told him, I would." Joe become somber as he looked into his mother's eyes and said, "I meant no trouble."

Several months later, Mr. Knoblauch asked Mrs. Welch if he could meet with both her and her husband as soon as possible to discuss James. The meeting was arranged for the following afternoon. Both Mr. and Mrs. Welch feared his request was to ask to be relieved from continuing to tutor James because of his consistent illnesses. Mrs. Welch fretted about the get-together, pacing while waiting for Mr. Knoblauch to arrive. She asked Mr. Welch, "What are we to do if he refuses James?"

"Sit down and calm yourself. James seems satisfied with him, so we'll have to listen carefully to what he has to say." Mr. Welch was a man whose exterior projected coldness and lack of feeling. The anticipated knock fell on the door and Mrs. Welch sprang from her chair. Mr. Welch motioned her to remain seated. "I'll invite him in."

"Please sit down, Mr. Knoblauch. My wife and I feel you are doing a splendid job with our children. We do hope that something has not happened to displease you with your stay with us."

Mr. Knoblauch, wearing gold-rimmed glasses hanging down on his nose, pushed them into place and replied, "No, no, on the contrary. I am content with this assignment. I am here to speak to you about James."

Mrs. Welch, relieved to hear the good news, asked, "Please, tell us. I hope he hasn't offended you in any way. We do worry about his frequent illnesses."

"Your son has an incredible talent for imagination and for transferring his talent to paper." Mr. Knoblauch sitting forward on his chair, pulled out several essays from his carpetbag. "I gave him an assignment which he has fulfilled beyond my expectation. Please look over his work." Mr. and Mrs. Welch examined the writings, both amazed at the originality. "I am here to suggest that James will soon surpass my ability to help him. He needs to be matriculated into an institution where he can receive the finest tutelage, one that can offer pedagogical direction and guidance."

"Mr. Knoblauch, our son is not well enough to send away. Mrs. Welch and I would not consider this. Perhaps you can recommend someone who will come here," pleaded Mr. Welch. "He is too young to be sent to a boarding school where independence is necessary. Our plan has always been to send him to England for higher education, but the cold and damp climate there would not benefit his ailments. Please help us find someone suitable to come here."

Oney called Little Joe and James her twin boys, different as day and night—one tall and muscular and the other short and bony. "Ya'll bof like lightnin' bugs, trying to light the way for each other, one light on, the otheren off. Back and forth. I do declare, sometimes I think ya boys joined at the hip."

When James was fourteen and Little Joe was fifteen, Oney was told by the chief house cook that she overheard Mr. and Mrs. Welch talking about sending James to London to finish his education. His health seemed much better now, although occasionally he still had chest congestion that put him to bed for several weeks. *"The Welch house chang'n all the time,"* Oney thought. *"Mis Anne and Mis Lizabet both married now. Mis Lizabet motherin' two of her own."* The Sabbath was a good time to catch up on the plantation gibber. Mr. Welch gave Sundays to his field hands if it was not planting or harvesting time. The house slaves rotated so that everyone had one Sunday off a month if there weren't guests. Oney heard that she might go live with the newly married Mis Anne whenever a babin might be comin'. During the ten years at Willow Place, she often felt overburdened, neglected, and lonely. O'Quash was dead. Little Joe was nearly a man, and she felt the changes in her body that could give way to old age. Joe was Oney's greatest worry. He had spent little time learning the fields. The companionship with James deprived Joe of important experience in cropping, animal breeding and care, pasturage, and soil preparation. Instead he was called uppity by the other slaves because he had book learnin', some travelin' with Mr. James, and he wore clean clothes most of the time. *"If'n James goes to England what's to become of my boy?"* Oney pondered.

Little Joe knew that James was going away to London eventually. James told Joe years back that Mr. Knoblauch wanted him to start preparing for a calling in the writing profession. James felt his health problems waning, and as they seemed to disappear completely, he prepared himself to leave. He promised Joe his first writings would be about their growing up together—two men, one black, one white. All the passages their young lives brought so far were shared together. James taught Joe the alphabet and numbers. Joe's revelation at realizing the letters on the slave quarters were part of a counting system giving identification to each dwelling brought him laughter and joy. The boys had journeyed together through books of travel, history, natural science and the classics. James always stopped to explain the passages Joe had difficulty understanding.

The last book James read to Joe was written by Samuel Sewall and titled *The Selling of Joseph.*[4] Mr. Welch bought the book for James in Baltimore, while on a business trip. He explained to James it was touted as one of the most read books in Maryland. At first, James decided he would not share the book with Joe, since it was the first book published in America protesting slavery. A week later James developed chest congestion and was confined to his bed. The opportune confinement helped him to decide to read the book to Joe. The boys laughed together and they cried together. Joe was left with a deep sense of apprehension, an almost forlorn feeling about his future. With James leaving, Joe's uncertainty grew into panic, as he pondered, *"What will be my next obligation, and to who?"*

1700 James did go to London. Oney went to live with Mis Anne. Little Joe was sold to a Mr. Robert Hughes when he was twenty years old.

After James left Willow Place, Joe went to live in the slave quarters. James was sure Joe would continue to take care of his personal needs and travel with him to London. Mr. Welch had made a decision some time ago to move Joe to the fields and start working him into plowing and planting. Joe was nearly six feet tall, with strong legs, shoulders stretching across his body like wheels to an axle, and stalwart arms capable of lifting a hogshead of tobacco without assistance.

Joe worked diligently on all the Welch crops. His love for working under the sun grew, even though the days in the growing season were from sunup to sundown.

Joe tried to establish contact with house slaves to get word about Mr. James. His contact with his mother had been daily, until she moved to Mis Anne's. Joe understood his status had changed considerably since James left. He did not feel the freedom to initiate conversation with the white folks—or the black house servants, for that matter. The first year after James left, Mr. Welch carried a message twice from him to Joe. Both times he was cordial and said he would tell James in his next letter that all was well. The second year there was one message, the third and fourth years, no word.

"Mister Joe, wake up. Mr. Welch wants you to come up to the house right away," Sam the house servant said, shaking Joe's arm to awaken him.

"What's wrong?" Joe demanded. Sam shrugged his shoulders. "You have no idea? Is it Oney? Is something wrong with her?"

"I know Mr. Welch got some terrible news. Mrs. Welch is nearly prostrate."

"It must be James. They've got word somethin' wrong there." Joe scrambled into his pants and slid his arms into the sleeves of his shirt as he ran to the big house, Sam right behind.

"Oh, Sam, I forgot my shoes. Will ya go back an' get em for me? Mis Welch don' wan' no black folks in the house without somethin' on the feet." Joe needed the time to think through what the possibilities might be for the call to the house. He was sure it was Oney or James, most likely James.

Joe slipped into his shoes and entered through the kitchen. "Mr. and Mrs. Welch is in the li'bary," the cook directed

Joe passed through the doorway. He saw Mrs. Welch first, sitting in a chair close to the big walnut desk, her head resting on the desktop, crying. Mr. Welch had his back to the doorway, standing in front of the window that looked out onto the long porch.

"Mr. Welch, Mrs. Welch. It's Joe."

William Welch turned and said, "Come in Joe. We have some very bad news. We have just received word that James is dead." He choked on his words, then cleared his throat and put his fist over his mouth. "A messenger brought us word early this morning. We wanted you to hear the news from us first."

"Thank you, Mr. Welch. Do you have any details?"

Clearing his throat again, Mr. Welch said, "All we know is, it was pneumonia."

"We should never have sent him to that horribly damp place," Mrs. Welch sobbed. "Why, William, did you insist he go there?"

"His things have been shipped home. They will arrive in about three days," Mr. Welch said to Joe. "The messenger rode ahead to give us this wretched news and to explain the arrival of his trunks."

Joe slipped quietly out of the big house, tears bursting from his eyes and tumbling down his brown cheeks. He jerked as a clap of thunder sounded in the western sky. "No rain yet, but it can't be far away," he thought. "Oh, I wish Mama was here. I feel so lonely. James, he's like my brother. Mama alway said we was like twins, one black, one white." Joe walked past the A, B, C, D, E shacks, smiling to himself. "If James hadn't taught the letters, I'd still never know what they meant."

The lightning stabbed downward out of the sky, touching the earth. Seconds later, a thunderous clap exploded. Joe did not hear it. He found himself walking toward the barn, deep in grief over James's death, and headed for an unknown destination. The horses stood patiently in their stalls, waiting for morning feed and fresh water. Leading one of the saddle horses outside, he jumped on without saddle or bridle and rode into the trees. The sky was still filled with lightning, the air was filled with the sounds of thunder, and the rain began to pour down. "It's raining harder in my eyes than the raining on top of my head," thought Joe. He pulled his handkerchief out of his pants pocket to wipe his eyes, and discovered that his nose was bleeding.

The Robert Hughes plantation contained but five hundred acres. Joe was downgraded to field hand. His treatment was rigid, the food ration slight, and the slave quarters poorly built and dilapidated. There were two buildings, identified with neither letters nor numbers. The floors were musty-smelling dirt, alive with vermin. There were no beds, just piles of straw for sleeping. The overseer was a white man assigned to keep the field hands laboring long hours. He had no compunction about flogging the slaves for laziness, disobedience, or insolence. Joe soon learned that the overseer had come from Barbados in the British West Indies, where the handling of slaves was brutal to the point of death from whipping, castration, or chopping off a foot or hand.[5] Mr. Hughes, however, abhorred such treatment, giving instructions that flogging would be allowed—but never more than five lashes to women or ten lashes for the men if for a first offense. The orders stated that no salt or other condiments were to be used on the wounds. Mr. Hardy, the overseer, had difficulty adhering to this ultimatum.

Disorientation settled quickly over Joe. He regularly thanked his Lord for the blessings he had received from his former owners. William Welch had explained to Joe the reason for his sale—a request from Mrs. Welch. "She says that your presence brings back memories of James and the laughter and happiness you two brought into our home. We both feel you should move on to another farm."

Since Mr. Hughes was the husband of James's sister, Lizabet, Joe had high expectations of the move. Oney was the servant of Anne Welch, and the sisters were very close. Joe was sure he would see his mother occasionally when Mis Anne came to visit.

The black hands were few. Mr. Hughes managed the cropping, planting, and harvesting. Three hundred acres were planted in tobacco and two hundred in rice and wheat. Joe worked the tobacco fields and quickly learned how the delicate plants needed individual care. Joe still relished working outside every day, even though Mr. Hardy gave him what seemed like the largest plot to weed and pull grubs. Joe knew he was being tested by Mr. Hardy, and felt he was waiting to find an excuse to lay the whip on his back. Joe also knew his size overwhelmed Mr.

Hardy, who had to look up to find his eyes. "Yes, Sir" and no, Sir," became the limit of Joe's dialogue with Mr. Hardy.

Poke and Jim became Joe's friends. The two black men shared the same woman, Sally. They all lived in building B, a name given shortly after Joe arrived to the Hughes farm. Sally had two children, a boy named Topper and a girl named Mim. Both children worked the fields every day. Topper looked like Poke, with long arms and legs, and probably was ten years old. Mim was tall and willowy, with short, frizzy, black hair. "How old you be?" asked Joe. "Let me guess—I bet you be somewhere 'bout fifteen or sixteen," grinned Joe.

"Ya think I'm that old?" asked Mim, embarrassed but accepting the compliment. She dug her hands in her pockets while she twisted her body back and forth smiling at Joe. "How old you be?"

"I'm past twenty, I 'spect. Hard sometimes to keep up with birthdays—they come and go 'round so fast."

"You be twenty?" the unbelieving Mim asked. "You be old enough to be my daddy!"

Joe was captivated with this young girl, whose eyes were the color of coal, with dense eyebrows and heavy lashes that weighed down her eyelids. "No, no, not that old," roared Joe with uncontrolled laughter.

"I be twelve and untouched," said Mim still swaying her hips and batting her eyelashes. "My mama tol' me no man could vi'late me 'til I was least fourteen. You be so old by that time ya be sittin' on the stoop tryin' to smoke yer pipe, watchin' hens lay eggs."

"Mim, I need to learn ya some numbers so's ya count properly."

"I don' need no numbers. Besides where did ya get yer learnin' if yer so smart?" Mim asked. "One thing I know fer sure is that ya be old—I think I'll call ya Old Joe."

Joe was struck by this young girl and dazed by her forthrightness and honesty. Her eyes contained a thousand stories and Joe knew he wanted to hear every one of them.

Christmastide was upon the Hughes plantation. Joe learned from Mim that the field hands were not expected to work on the day of Jesus' birth. "We have to wait for Mister Hughes to tell us if we get to wake up on our own or have the cow bell in our ear," Mim told Old Joe.

Joe, who had eyes like the beam in a lighthouse, observed lots of activity in the Hughes's house. Evergreen boughs were cut and carried into the house. The smells of baking breads and cakes floated across the farm. There seemed to be hustle and bustle everywhere. Joe prayed Oney might come with Mis Anne to the Hughes for the holiday. It had been nearly a year since they had been together. Joe had sent a message with Poke once, when he drove a wagon to the Welch plantation. He hoped the message had been transferred to someone going to Mis Anne.

Mr. Hughes, with Mr. Hardy by his side, announced to the slave community their holiday would run from sunup December 25 to sunup December 26. He gave every man a piece of beef or pork and a loaf of fruitcake. "This is a special gift from Mrs. Hughes. A year has gone by with no trouble from any of you and very little sickness. Merry Christmas!" Robert Hughes, holding a horse whip in his hand, struck his riding boot with the whip, turned toward the house, and walked away. Mr. Hardy, his flogging whip in his hand, followed Mr. Hughes.

"Hum-m-m, he always does that whenever he wants to talk to us," said Mim to Joe, whose watchful eyes noted the swipe with the horse whip.

"He's afraid of us," replied Joe. "He thinks we be restless and maybe do bad things to him and his family."

Mim was perplexed by Joe's words. "I always scared of him. I never thinked he be scared of us. His face look like it's made of rock or a piece of wood left in the rain too long."

"We would all be better for not making Mr. Hughes think we're untrustworthy. Kindness goes a long ways for both sides. If we are nice to him, he'll be nice back," Joe told Mim.

"Sometimes ya talk so funny I can hardly un'erstan' what ya sayin'," Mim replied.

Christmas morning the carriages started to arrive. Joe's watchful eyes recognized Mr. and Mrs. Welch's carriage, then Mis Anne, her husband, and—yes, there was Oney, giving her attention to the two children. Joe refrained from greeting his mother, knowing Mr. Hughes would come down hard on both of them. He hoped they planned to stay several days. However, he knew Christmas Day would be the only day he could visit with his mother. Joe sat on the porch of building B and waited. Mim joined in the suspense as the two maintained an appearance of calm. Her vitality always lifted Joe's spirits. She was full to the brim of questions about where he came from, how many owners he had, who was the best owner, did he know his family? Joe patiently answered her questions, telling her about O'Quash, Oney, the Wellmans, the Welches and James, and now the Hughes. "Ya know yer mama and gran'papa?" Mim asked in disbelief. "I know I was borned, but I don' know where or when."

"Ask your mama, she'll tell ya."

"Ya mean Sally? She's not my mama," Mim said. "I came here wit Poke, just a babin. He always says he found me in the bullrushes in a basket floatin' down the Pamunkey. Never knew what them bullrushes is. Poke, he's like my papa and Sally's like a mama. I call 'em that." Mim scooted herself close to Joe's side, looked into his eyes, and said, "Joe, yer so easy to talk to. I'm so glad ya came here. Sometimes I preten' yer my family." Joe wrapped his arm around Mim's shoulders; they both felt contentment in the contact of each other's warm body.

Oney made her way to Joe while the Christmas dinner was being served. The two embraced, kissed, and said how much they missed each other. "My baby boy's all grown so tall and big," Oney gushed. "I brought ya somethin' from Mister Welch. He said it was a book from Mister James, just special for you." The book was wrapped in tattered paper and tied with string. Joe ripped the paper off and immediately recognized the gold engraved *William James Welch.* "What is it, Joe?" Oney asked.

"I think it's a book written by James Welch. I'm havin' trouble makin' out the name of the book. It's *The* . . . somethin'. I know it starts with the C." Joe continued to page through the book. The title page had "James Welch" spelled out again, with "1718." On the next page he spelled out "Joe" and the word "friend." "Mama, I've forgotten everything James taught me. I can recognize some of the words but I can't get enough to make sense of what it says. Mr. Knoblauch taught James to keep readin' 'less ya forget how to do it. He sure right."

Joe kept rubbing the cover and spine of the book until Oney told him, "You'll rub the gold of'n those words if ya don' watch out."

"Mama, who'll read this book to me? James promised me he'd write a book about the two of us someday. I'll prob'ly die never knowing what it says," moaned Joe. "T'aint nobody around here that can read."

Oney wiped a tear from her son's eye. "We'll think of someone, don' ya worry none." Oney said sympathetically.

"Mama, James is in my dreams 'most every night. We playin', fishin', readin', or gettin' into some kind mischief. . .I guess I miss him every day."

"I know, I know." Oney patted Joe's shoulder, trying to comfort him.

"I hate bein' so ignoran'. "

Joe and Mim became closer as each day passed. At first, he played the role of father and teacher. Mim's lack of exposure to anything other than the grind of washing clothes, tending the family vegetable garden, and feeding and watering the planter's livestock limited her worldliness. Joe was concerned because the Hughes slave community was living in squalor. He had learned the habits of cleanliness and sanitation from the Welch plantation. The living quarters, damp and dirty, were in desperate need of cleaning and scrubbing. Old Joe decided he would put wooden floors in the cabins, somehow, to keep the field mice and rats out. The mosquitoes seemed double the numbers of those at the Welch farm. Joe set out to study the reason for their multiplied numbers.

Mim's lack of guidance showed in her use of language and inability to keep her clothes and herself clean. Joe worked to keep his English polished whenever he could. His lack of association with whites threw him back into slave lingo, but he took on the task of training Mim to improve her usage, which helped him retain his dialect learned from James Welch. "You'll be a house slave if you practice to talk like the white folks," Old Joe coaxed Mim. "House slaves live better, get more leftover food, and get to sleep inside the big house." Mim wrestled with "I will go" instead of "I be gone." Old Joe struggled to teach her to put endings on her words, such as "going" for "goin'," or "working" for "workin'." She practiced intensely, but told both Joe and herself that she couldn't change overnight.

Joe taught Mim to keep her hands and face clean. He suggested she bathe at least once a week, especially in her private parts such as under her armpits and between her legs. Old Joe showed her how to make a toothbrush by fraying the end of a twig and use salt poured on the twig for cleaning. But the salt supply allotted the slaves was limited, so Joe suggested sand or ground-up bricks.[6]

The metamorphosis of Mim began almost a year after Joe arrived. Her childlike mannerisms began to change and she progressively moved into womanhood. During the year between Mim's thirteenth and fourteenth birthdays, she and Joe became closer. Mim was the first to tell Joe of her abiding love for him. She fumbled for the words, but with his assistance she spilled her feelings into his head and heart.

"Mim, hon, I believe I have had more feelin's for ya than anyone I ever knowed. The first day here, I looked into your black eyes and just knew there was somethin' inside that I needed to know about. Ya were such a child and now you's a grown-up woman. You'll be my woman as long as we live. I make that pledge." Old Joe took Mim in his arms and gently kissed her on each cheek.

"You's can kiss me on the lips if'n ya want," Mim said, turning her face up to the sky to try to reach his.

Joe managed to rebuild the A and B cabins into weather- and vermin-tight houses. He salvaged wood from other building projects around the farm and used rejected firewood to piece and patch the floors into place. Then he built front doors to shut out the weather when the temperature dropped in the wintertime. Mr. Hughes offered no thanks to Joe for his extra labor. Mr. Hardy told Joe that he must not be working hard enough in the fields if he had time to work on the slave quarters. Joe just gave his usual "yes" and "no" answers to Hardy, to keep the peace. Old Joe worked on the Sabbath days and during the times when the harvesting was completed. He took out James Welch's book at every opportunity to try to make out some of the words on each page. Joe stroked the cover, front and back, hoping his memory would open up so he could read the pages himself.

One warm Sunday in March of the second year on the Hughes farm, Joe was sitting on the front stoop of cabin B. He had the book and was fingering it, tracing over the gilded letters on the cover. Mr. Hardy approached with his usual whip in hand and said, "Don' tell me you's is tryin' to read now! Where did ya get such a fancy book? Looks like one Mr. Hughes said was missin' from his lib'ary."

"This book is mine," replied Joe. "It was a gift from William Welch's son James."

"I hear tell James Welch be dead a long time. Did he send it from his grave?" Mr. Hardy said with malice and a sinister laugh. He snapped his whip and missed Joe's feet by inches. "I'll tell Mr. Hughes you are the one that stole his book! He'll fix ya good, probably cut off'n yer hand!"

Joe, controlling himself with difficulty, stood up to tower over Mr. Hardy. "You go ask Mr. Hughes—" Joe's sentence was broken by the sound of the whip as it snapped against his shoulder. Joe dropped the book and reached to his shoulder which was now dripping in blood. A big chuck hole filled with muddy water covered the book. Joe stepped from the porch and was bending over the mud hole when Hardy snapped the whip again, hitting his wrist. and laying it open to the bone.

"There, that will keep you from turning the pages on a book you can't even read," Mr. Hardy said with a sneer. Mr. Hardy reached down and picked up the book from the mud. "*The Crossing.* Now tell me, what's that all about, boy? Don' make much sense to me—Crossing who?"

Now Joe knew the title of the book. "*The Crossing.* Of course, James would pick that name. He told the story of O'Quash as he promised." Mr. Hardy threw the book on the porch, "Maybe the sun'll dry out that book. Mr. Hughes wouldn't want something lookin' like that back. Keep it!" He snapped the whip again, this time into the air.

Poke and Jim found a dazed Joe sitting on the porch. Underneath his torn shirt, he bled profusely. He was holding his right wrist, which was also bleeding, in his left hand. "Joe, Joe, what happened?" asked Poke.

"Mr. Hardy came with his whip and wrapped it around my shoulder and wrist. I'm settin' and tryin' to feel better so's I can get me some fresh water to put on 'em," whispered Joe. "First time I ever went under the whip. Don' like it much."

"Why did he do that? Ya always mind yer own business," said Jim.

"He been waitin' fer excuse to whip me for 'long time. He find it t'day," answered Joe. "I guess he thinks I'm just another dumb darky. He pro'bly right," Joe sighed.

Several other field hands gathered around Joe to see what the commotion was about. Mim was the last to arrive, and became hysterical when she saw Joe, now lying on a pallet inside the cabin. "Who did this? Was it that rat, Hardy?" she raved.

"Mim, hon, calm yerself down," Joe said. "I's okay."

"I'm okay," she corrected. "Remember, no slave talk no more," she said as she put her head against Joe's.

"Remember, no slave talk anymore," Joe responded.

Old Joe missed nearly a week of field work. His shoulder locked into place so he couldn't raise his arm above his waist. The wrist seemed to heal quickly but was of no use because of the shoulder. Mim applied a concoction of eringo root with sassafras directly on the wounds. Three days after the flogging Mr. Hughes came to see Joe. His usual stone face didn't indicate any emotion. Joe, at first, thought he had come because of concern for his health, but when it became apparent he was not even mentioning the wounds, Joe knew he had another purpose. The book was standing upright in front of the fire drying out. After a few minutes of silence, Joe broke first. "Thank you for coming to see me," Joe whispered. "The book, over there by the fire. . .the one you thought was taken from your library . . . It is my book. James Welch gave it to me."

"I have no concern for the book," Mr. Hughes said, clearing his throat. "I have come to tell you that I will be posting you for sale as soon as possible."

"But, Mr. Hughes, why?" Joe tried to raise up and touch Mr. Hughes's coat sleeve.

"There will be an auction in two weeks.You be well and fit so's I can get top price, you hear?" Mr. Hughes said, clearing his throat again. "Do you need my wife to come out and help with your recovery? She has a salve that treats wounds and brings quick healing."

"Mim has been treating me and I'm healing just fine. No need for Mis Lizabeth."

"I beg your pardon!" Mr. Hughes said loudly. "She is Mrs. Hughes to you!"

Joe realized he had erred in calling Mrs. Hughes, Mis Lizabeth. "I'm sorry."

"Is there anything else we can do to speed your recovery?" Mr. Hughes asked painfully.

The realization why Joe was being sold settled into his head. "Yes, there is," Joe said confidently. "I want Mim to go with me."

Clearing his throat for the third time, Mr. Hughes said, "It will be arranged."

Sale posters appeared on most available Pamunkey tree trunks. Mr. Hughes had passed them from farm to farm advertising the sale of Old Joe and his woman, Mim.

TO BE SOLD & LET
BY PUBLIC AUCTION
On Tuesday the 12th of April 1718
Under the trees
SLAVES

Old Joe, about 22 Years old, strong field hand
Mim, free with purchase of Joe, about 14 years old, field hand
English horse for sale
1:00 O'clock[7]

Joe's shoulder was still giving pain when he carried heavy loads. The gash on the wrist healed quickly, but it ached at night. Mim and Joe prepared themselves for the auction. Mr. Hughes allowed each slave to take personal items, but all Joe carried away was the James Welch book *The Crossing*. Mim stuffed her toothbrush, old comb with broken teeth, and tattered shawl into a rag that was a remnant of a bedsheet. She tied the rag into a knot to enclose her possessions. Mr. Hughes refused to supply Mim and Joe with new clothes, but requested they wear their best old garments for the sale. They were told to leave all other clothes behind. The night before the auction Old Joe, Mim, Sally, Poke, and Jim gathered together for one last time. Joe promised to send a message to those left behind telling them about the new owners, living conditions, and treatment. Sally, Mim's surrogate mother, gave her a piece of a mirror that Lizabet had thrown away. "Ever'time you look at yerself in the mirror, think of how much I'll miss not bein' yer mama no more," Sally said as tears tumbled down her cheeks. "When ya look at yerself, you'll see me standin' behind ya hopin' and prayin' you's got good owners that don' beat on ya or try to vi'late ya'. I pray you and Joe are never torn apart." The two stood with arms wrapped each other, crying and wiping one another's tears.

"You'll always be my mama and I'll never forget ya," Mim said through her tears. "Me an' Joe might to be free someday, and if'n we do we'll be back to see ya."

Poke and Jim were having difficulty too, saying good-by to Old Joe. "You've learned us lots, Joe," said Poke.

"Remember what I tol' ya, if'n ya be good and do what you're told, Mr. Hughes will treat ya good. Don' talk back to Mr. Hardy 'cept yes or no," Joe reminded Poke and Jim.

"First time ya get in trouble wit Mr. Hardy, Mr. Hughes's is sellin' ya!" retorted Jim.

"Ya know why Mr. Hughes is sellin' us," Joe answered. "He's 'fraid we'll hurt him or his family for Mr. Hardy's meanness to us. Watch out for that whip; it don' take much fer him to use it. Yer best prayer is that somethin' happen to Mr. Hardy."

The five slaves stood in a circle in the middle of cabin B with their hands clasped, chanting an old negro prayer that Joe had taught them.

O'Quash had taught it to Joe when he first learned to talk and Joe had repeated it every night of his life.

Bring us home Nkuwu
We'll come home to be with you
Take us home Mvemba
Utopia, Utopia
Wah, wah, ta, la, rah, rah
Utopia, Utopia

The five people stamped their feet in rhythm as they moved around in a circle, clapping their hands to *Utopia, Utopia.*

John Dandridge stood observing the auction sale of Mim and Joe. Mr. Hardy had told prospective buyers that Joe was steady, didn't talk much, liked to work from sunup to sundown, and was strong as two oxen put together. Mim was described as a young girl ready to bring babies into the world. "She is cheap," hollered Hardy. " She goes with Old Joe and costs nothin'. She cooks, washes clothes, and works the fields."

Two men were bidding against each other and the bid was up to twenty pounds for both Mim and Joe. John Dandridge did not know either man bidding, but felt the bids were rising past his limit. The man who seemed to be the most aggressive bidder said, "Twenty-four pounds, and that is my last bid!"

"Twenty-four and five shillings!" shouted the opposing bidder.

Mr. Dandridge could not hear the words being exchanged between Mim and Joe. He realized the girl was anguished by the sale, but Joe's words seemed to calm her. He was promising they would not be separated.

Joe saw an elderly man with a familiar face and soon recognized Mr. Wellman. Joe knew the rumors that had circulated at the Welch plantation about Oney and Mr. Wellman, about his frequently having his pleasure with her and that he was probably Old Joe's papa. Joe kept his eyes planted on the wooden platform constructed to hold him and Mim above the people coming to bid. Mr. Wellman stepped closer to Joe to observe his bulk and brawniness. "How old are you, boy?" asked Mr. Wellman.

"Twenty-five pounds," a new voice resounded.

Joe swiftly looked up to see who had made the bid, but his eyes met Mr. Wellman's. Mr. Hardy called the sale finished, saying, "Sold to the man with the three-sided hat."

Mr. Wellman backed away without asking Joe the question again, while his new owner came forward to pay Mr. Hughes for Mim and Joe.

Mim sat shivering in the wagon driven by John Dandridge. The sky was an inverted bowl, blue from rim to rim. The sun was burning all things on the earth, except Mim. Her heart was beating so fast, she thought it would jump out of her skin. Her backbone quivered so, she felt the shaking in her toes. Her skin felt damp and clammy as she rubbed her hands together and across her brow. Joe sat erect on the buckboard next to Mr. Dandridge. His anxieties were not evident to Mim's watchful eyes. This, her first move from one farm to another and to an unknown owner, gave her such distress she expected to lose her dinner at any moment. "Joe, can ya come set beside me? I'm not feelin' too good right now," Mim asked weakly.

Joe turned to answer Mim but before he spoke he looked into her face and saw a washed-out, pallid, almost colorless mask, so unlike Mim. "Mim, honey, ya gonna be sick?" Joe asked.

"Ya, I've tried to let it be, but it keeps coming back to remin' me. Please come sit with me," she pleaded. Joe asked Mr. Dandridge if it would be all right to move into the back of the wagon with Mim.

Mr. Dandridge wasn't a talkative man, but in the short time of their acquaintance, he seemed like a gentle man with concern about both Joe and Mim. Underlying Joe's concern was his worry that Mr. Dandridge might fear for his own safety. Old Joe observed that there had been no conversation with either Mr. Hughes or Mr. Hardy about the conduct of Joe or Mim. Mr. Dandridge was a slight young man, barely five feet six inches, whom the slave community would best describe as scrawny. Joe's size didn't outwardly seem to overwhelm Mr. Dandridge. He knew that he could overpower John with little effort, take the wagon away, and he and Mim could head west to freedom.

"Yes, go ahead and tend to her," John Dandridge replied.

Old Joe clutched Mim in his arms until the wagon pulled into Chestnut Grove on the Pamunkey. He listened to her worries about a new home and consoled her fears as best he could. He reminded her about his first move from the Wellman farm to the Welch plantation. "It was about the best thing that ever happened to me," he said. "Let's pray we be half as happy at the new place."

John Dandridge was only sixteen years old the day his father sent him to the auction on the Robert Hughes plantation with an explicit directive to succeed in the purchase of Joe and Mim. John's father suffered with recurring bouts of gout that came more and more frequently. He sipped brandy in the morning and always had several jiggers before bedtime. Recently, the sipping started upon rising in the morning, continued throughout the daytime, and finished only when he retired at night. This regimen thrust young John into the role of planter, overseer, and caretaker of the Dandridge farm.

Old Joe and Mim were pleased with their new home, primarily because of John Dandridge. He was a mature, kindly, and tolerant young man given a great deal of responsibility. There was only one other farmworker; he, young John and his father, managed the farm between them. Old Joe would replace the senior Dandridge, bringing years of planting and harvesting experience. Mim worked the fields, weeding and pulling grubs, as well as handling the chores of cooking and washing.

The years passed quickly as Joe and John, working side by side, developed a dependency upon one another. The senior Dandridge died when young John was twenty. During the years of living at the Dandridge farm, Old Joe and Mim became part of the family—trusted, dependable, and loyal. Old Joe's capabilities exceeded John's in arithmetic, fractions, and geometrics. Joe could look at a tree and estimate into board feet without any measuring devices. He could study a garden plot and tell how many pounds of potatoes it would produce. Mim was extending her education into learning how to nurture the family garden, weave, and tailor clothing. Joe taught her how to measure, add, and subtract. His greatest disappointment was losing his ability to read. He did teach Mim the letters; still, without the sounds, putting the letters into words became impossible.

Joe clung to the hope that one day he would find someone to read James Welch's book to him. The book was wrapped in a rag hidden in the rafters of his cabin. Every night before retiring, he made sure the book was still in place. Joe dreamed that one day he would feel comfortable asking John Dandridge to read the book to him. He had been close to asking several times, but the conversation somehow drifted in another direction.

There would always be a line drawn between Old Joe and John because of their color and status. Joe intuitively knew his place and always backed away from crossing the line. James Welch had given Joe a sample of the human condition of white folks lifestyle. Joe knew about man's inhumanity from the teachings of his gran'papa. He learned from his mama a universal life force of the flesh and blood of family. James Welch, as his tutor, taught him about humankind, nature, creation, birds and beasts, fish of the sea, flora and fauna, and the importance of education. Mr. Knoblauch repeatedly had reminded James of the old proverb, "*Soon learned, soon forgotton*," as he insisted James keep reading to learn.

Joe could still feel the pain of the day James left for England. The departure put him into a void that left him feeling abandoned, destitute, and empty. John Dandridge had helped fill that vacuum. Yet, there were differences between John and James Welch. Old Joe and James began their lives as youngsters and grew into manhood together. The twist of fate of James's illnesses brought the two into a close relationship. They communicated without words. John Dandridge and Old Joe had both reached maturity, not by numbers of birthdays but by their individual responsibilities, when they first met. Old Joe learned quickly that John's apprenticeship as a farmer was one of drudgery, toil, and diligence. The parallels between the two were striking.

Frances and John Dandridge married in mid-1730. Frances's grandfather was a Rector of Bruton Parish in Williamsburg. Her father, also a minister, performed their ceremony.[8] The first Dandridge child was expected the following June and the expectant parents were ecstatic—especially John, whose braggadocio was heard around Kent County by any listener who took the time to heed his words.

In late January, John and Old Joe began clearing a stand of trees on Chestnut Grove to increase ground for planting. The trees were mostly scrubby, so the job was easy for the two men, who worked well as a team. The biggest job was the removal of the stumps, which took the help of several horses. John always handled the reins as Joe shouted the directions, "Heave right," or "Pull left." The obedient horses followed John's lead and wrestled the stumps with little effort. The job was nearly finished on a day that was unusually warm. A stubborn stump was causing all the workers, both man and beast, undue exertion. It was then that John broke his left leg below the knee. Joe was giving directions to "Pull left" as the horse stepped into a concealed hole full of soft soil. John dropped the reins and ran up around the horse to make sure the animal would not break a leg. The horse reared, kicking John and breaking his leg. The break was clean but painful. Old Joe lashed branches together by using rope and cloth from his shirt. He made a primitive sledge to be pulled by the horse and carried John home.

Frances and Joe managed to get John into the house and into bed so they could confine the leg as best they could. John was a restless patient with this, his first accident. He was determined to stay in bed only as long as he thought necessary, but Frances became very aggressive and sent for a doctor who lived several miles away.

Dr. Perkins helped deliver babies, cows, and horses; he pulled decayed teeth, treated bullet wounds, gave shaves and haircuts, and set broken bones. He examined John and the boards used to stabilize his leg, then ordered him to stay put for six weeks. "Come on, Doc," pleaded John. "That means my soil won't be ready when planting time comes."

"You will just have to find some extra help someplace until you're ready for farming again," the doctor answered. "I'll be back to see you in a week."

Joe, lying in his bed, reviewed how the accident happened and blamed himself for John's broken leg. "I should'a told him not to fuss with a strugglin' horse." Joe rolled over on his back and put his hands under his head, staring at the ceiling. "Sleep sure is a long time comin' tonight," Joe thought. His wide eyes bounced from rafter to rafter until he spotted his book. Quickly sitting upright, Joe said, "Oh, Lordy, my Lord! Suppose Mr. Dan'ridge might read my book?"

"What?" Mim asked, as she turned over and met Joe face to face. Joe explained his reason for insomnia and Mim told him, "Just quit yer worrin' 'bout Mister Dan'ridge. Sleep is the best medicine for bof ya. Ask him when he's feelin' better. Maybe he read yer story after all."

"But I want him to read it to me."

Old Joe planned his maneuver to offer his book to Mr. Dandridge very carefully.

The Crossing had never been mentioned to anyone at Chestnut Grove. Joe cherished the book too much to risk an incident such as Mr. Hardy had caused at the Hughes farm.

Three weeks after the accident, Mr. Dandridge began to feel better and was giving directions and orders to everyone passing his room. Frances became impatient and irritable, mostly because her pregnancy was progressing rapidly and she needed more rest.

She shared with Mim her anxiety about John's restless days, and Mim told Mrs. Dandridge about the book and suggested Mr. Dandridge read it.

Mim, feeling proud that she made the first move, told Old Joe that she was sure Mrs. Dandridge liked the idea of giving the book to Mr. Dandridge.

"Hon, I guess that's why I love ya so much. You're never afraid to speak up." Joe pecked Mim on the cheek, then climbed up and retrieved *The Crossing.*

It took John Dandridge nearly a week to read the book. The Dandridge home was peaceful and quiet during that time, for which Frances was grateful. "Frances," John shouted one day. "Find Joe and tell him I want him to come see me as soon as possible."

Joe had not visited John while he read the book. Mim reported every day that Mr. Dandridge was still reading, and she heard no comment from him about his pleasure or displeasure. Then Frances told Mim to ask Old Joe to see John as soon as possible. The message reached Joe's ears after he and Mim retired. "Do ya suppose he liked the book?" Joe asked Mim.

"Don't know. I din't hear him say much about it," Mim replied. "Are ya goin' to ask him to read it to you?"

"We's never talked about my years at the Welch plantation. Don't know if he'd much care hearin' about those years, anyways."

"Joe, ya worry yerself to your deathbed; most things ya worry about never happen. Get yer sleepin, ya'll need it for tomorrow," Mim directed.

The next morning Old Joe nervously entered the Dandridge house by the back door. Mim stood in the parlor dusting the three-legged teatable. "Hon, does Mr. Dandridge want me to come to his room?" Joe asked plaintively.

"Go ahead on in, he be waitin' for ya," answered Mim. Joe tiptoed into John Dandridge's room, where he found his owner sitting up, propped with pillows, sleeping. John's leg, stretched out on a stool, looked uncomfortable. Joe quietly sat down, trying not to disturb him. John's mouth was wide open with a faint snore blowing out with each breath. Old Joe patiently waited for John to awaken, counting the snores. When he reached number thirty, he paused, arose from his chair and tiptoed carefully across the wooden floor. When he hit a joist, a loud squeak caused John to sit upright. "Oh, Joe, you are here. I've been waiting all morning for you. Sit down. I want to talk to you about the book."

"Yes Sir, Mr. Dandridge," Joe answered deferentially. "I'm anxious to know if it helped makin' your days shorter." Joe settled himself into the chair once again.

"I do not think I have ever read a story as compelling. Tell me where you heard these stories. I cannot believe your imagination. William James Welch has written an intriguing story about your family. Of course, I realize that the barbarism of the treatment of your grandfather is greatly exaggerated."

" S-s-Sir, Mr. Dandridge," Joe stammered. "I have no way of knowin' James's words. I can't read, Sir. We talked lots 'bout my grandfather's crossing. And how he was stole from his family and got here from Africa."

"Are you trying to tell me these stories are true, Joe?" asked John Dandridge, with disbelief.

"Sir, I can't answer that 'cause I don't know what Mr. James wrote."

"Joe, if there is any veracity to this story, every God-fearing man in Virginia should read it! I am going to read this story to you and I want you to tell me the falsehoods, and then, tell me factually what your grandfather told you. You have never deceived me in all the years you have been with me. I would trust you with my life, but this powerful tale needs to be told if it, indeed, is true."

CHAPTER NOTES

Mim and Old Joe represent the enslavement of blacks in the Southern Colonies. Robbed of their identity, dignity, culture, and heritage, uncertainty was the horror of the average slave. Fear of mistreatment or of being sold or bartered separately haunted most slave families. All progeny born into slavery became property of the plantation owners. The owners provided their slaves with lodging, food, and clothing; the amount and quality varying widely. Slaves had no legal rights to marry, own property, or earn freedom. The more fortunate slaves lived inside the manor house, working fewer hours and receiving other privileges. The field worker slaved from sunup to sundown. This tale is an endeavor to write a composite account of the good, the bad, and the ugly of this dreadful institution.

DANIEL CUSTIS

1747-1750

The three-day trip from Arlington to Williamsburg twice a year for the Assembly meetings became a nuisance for Colonel John Custis, a member of the General Council. He owned a home in Williamsburg and one on the Pamunkey River. Four years earlier, he had decided to move across the Chesapeake Bay to Arlington, on the Eastern Shore of Virginia, for reasons only he knew.[1] The winter trips were never easy, since crossing the water from the finger of land to the mainland depended on wind conditions which made the timing for the ferry trip uncertain. Allowing only three days in November to reach Williamsburg was risky because roadways could be hazardous. John Custis had had to order a new carriage when the inclement weather during the return trip from Williamsburg the previous November destroyed his carriage. That trip took seven days to get back to Arlington. Wind and rain had caused the roadways to be full of furrows filled with muddy waters, which broke an axle and injured two horses.

The new chariot was an engineering marvel. It had stronger

steel springs and gave a more comfortable ride. The Colonel anticipated an uneventful trip this year because of the new carriage's reliability.

The trip began with perfect conditions which made crossing the Cheaspeake effortless. However, late afternoon brought ominous clouds, which meant rain wasn't far behind. The drivers encouraged Mr. Custis to find shelter and spend the night as daylight faded and threatened danger to the horses. Mr. Custis's orders were to press on. The lead horse proceeded to step into a rut several inches deep and broke a leg. Mr. Custis, an impatient man, ordered the liverymen to put the horse down immediately. "We'll never make it to Yorktown tonight if you don't hurry!"

Mr. Custis's mind had survived his sixty-eight years much better than his body. He complained of stiff feet and knees, raging pain in his hips, swollen ankles, a tearing in his jaw, dizziness, dull headaches, and nosebleeds. His search for cures had taken him into the latest studies of English and French medicine. He heard reports about the work of a man named Rene Descartes who believed the body was a machine, and that any kind of sickness meant a mechanical breakdown.[2] Mr. Custis read about his philosophies and, making his own interpretation, decided the Descartes declaration was that the mind could overpower the body. Mr. Custis lived by that code and refused any further medical attention, especially bloodletting—which any so-called doctor would prescribe for various illnesses.

Mr. Custis's travel companion was a young, light-skinned black boy named Jack. His mother Alice was a longtime house servant for the Custis home.[3] She was a trusted and loyal woman who had cared for the two Custis children. Jack exhibited circumspection regarding Mr. Custis's needs. In his stewardship, he managed all correspondence, all social obligations, and most receipts; supervised dietary needs and all his personal needs. Recently it had been rumored that Jack was named to receive all of the Custis estate.[4]

The travel wore on until darkness. The persistent Mr. Custis was still giving orders to the intimidated drivers. Jack had long ago lost his patience. "Mister Custis, I do believe we should stop anytime soon so's ya can get yerself some rest. I'm looking for some light so's we can find a farm to put us up for the night. Okay, Mister Custis?" Jack asked. "Those animals got to have rest pretty soon if they are going to make it to Williamsburg tomorrow," an exasperated Jack said, trying to use diplomacy. The first day's journey was planned to end in Yorktown. However, when the rain reached monsoon proportions, Colonel Custis finally ordered the drivers to locate a farm house.

The next morning the dark clouds still hovered over the terrain. The wind was diminishing but the rain continued, filling the puddles and cracks in the road. The two liverymen took turns leading the horses through the water, careful to monitor their steps. Mr. Custis, with his head protruding from the window, shouted to the men, "Watch for the wheels to stay in the ruts. Don't let the horses slow down too much. Billy, use your whip to keep 'em moving. I'll get up there myself if I have to, and show you how to handle those creeters."

Little progress was made on the second day of the three-day journey. Tempers raged, and, by all accounts, the weather won the battle over man and beast. Before nightfall the wind returned, and the rain maintained its course, wet and cold. John Custis tried to remember something his mother had told him about Mother Nature. "You can drive her away with a pitchfork, but she'll always return."

"Let's find us another farmhouse, boys," a weary John Custis conceded. "We need food, water, and rest. So do the horses. We'll see Williamsburg when we get there," Colonel Custis told Jack and the liverymen.

The Canada geese were resting on the James River after their long flight from the north. Their homing instincts bringing them south always meant that winter had, indeed, arrived. The trees had shed their spring and summer foliage long before; leaving the afternoon sun hanging low in the cloudless sky, casting only the shadows of barren trunks and branches.

The Custis chariot arrived in Williamsburg one day later than the planned three-day trip from Arlington. It was midday when the carriage turned into the rocky drive of the House of Six Chimneys.[5] John Custis had the home built after his wife Frances died. She had begged John to leave Queen's Creek Plantation and move into Williamsburg where they could be closer to the all social gatherings. The mulish John began planning for a Williamsburg home shortly after Frances died. His inexorable mind wouldn't allow the changing of location to look like anyone's idea but his own.

John had considered selling the manor house, but his son Daniel pleaded with him to keep it for the sake of his garden. Mr. Custis was a talented horticulturist whose reputation was known as far away as London.[6] His Williamsburg garden had hundreds of visitors each year. Since moving to Arlington he had turned over its maintenance to an Englishman named Thomas Milton. Mr. Milton was a brother of Jonathan Milton, the Williamsburg attorney who had earned his way onto the General Council. Upon Jonathan's recommendation, John Custis had paid Thomas's passage from London, to bring him to Williamsburg to manage the English-style garden.

John Custis was consumed with exhaustion. The journey had been long and tedious, causing his head and neck to throb, his eyes to twitch and his back to spasm. He put his head out the carriage window to peruse his cherished garden. Popping his head back inside like a jack-in-the-box, he thrust his cane upward and poked the ceiling of the carriage, shouting, "Stop this wagon now! Billy, Lee, do you hear me?"

Billy firmly pulled back on the reins to stop the three horses. Lee sprang from his seat and leaped onto the ground to take command of the jittery animals. Billy descended swiftly, reaching for the door to assist Mr. Custis before he tried to leave the carriage by himself. "Billy, I want you to go and find Mr. Milton. Tell him he is to meet me forthwith—in the north garden! I don't care what he is doing. He is to see me without delay!"

"Yes, Mister Custis." Billy reached up for an elbow to guide Mr. Custis down the narrow step. Billy was much taller than the old man, but Mr. Custis, with his strong will, insisted on helping himself. The heel of his boot landed on a small stone that set him off balance, turning his left ankle. He was on the ground before Billy could break the fall, landing on his right hip and writhing in pain.

"Get me up from here, Billy. I'll be fine in a minute."

"You best rest for awhile 'fore you try and get up, Mister Custis." But the old man had rolled over on his stomach. Using his arms, he lifted himself up. Mr. Milton and Lee came from the back of the house, and, seeing Mr. Custis's struggle, hastened to help Billy. The three men, Lee on one arm and Mr. Milton on the other, with Billy tugging on the skirt of his coat, tried to lift him off the ground. Mr. Custis recognized Mr. Milton's voice and turned his head to look directly into his eyes. Pulling away, he said, "This is all your fault, Milton! Have you paid any attention to the responsibilities I gave you? I'm flabbergasted with your lack of care for my garden!"

"Mr. Custis, don't you think you should be concerned with yourself first? We can discuss the garden once you're inside the house where it is warm," Thomas Milton replied.

"House, mouse! Get me on my feet, boys, then hand me my cane! I'm gonna let Mr. Milton know how it feels on his outsides the way I'm feeling on my inside right now."

Jack had quietly left the chariot to go inside the house for more help. The house servant, the cook, and a liveryman arrived with Jack, just as Billy handed over the cane to the irate Mr. Custis. Jack, horrified to see him raise the stick, quickly snatched it from his shaky hand. "Mister Custis, please stop; you'll hurt yourself more than anyone if you use that."

"My Lord above, Jack, have you seen what this man has done to my garden?" Mr. Custis's emotions betrayed his cold exterior, as he began to weep softly. Pathetically, he said, "Help me, Jack."

Jack crept up the stairs, carrying a breakfast tray for Mr. Custis. The old man was lying awake in his bed, grumbling that his whole body ached. "Mister Custis, can I help you sit up so's you can eat something?" Setting down the tray, Jack pulled apart the window coverings. "Mister Custis, do you mind if I open the window a bit?" Jack asked. "The room here smells like fresh air would be apprec'ated."

The second floor of The House of Six Chimneys was seldom inhabited. Most activity took place downstairs in the north parlor and the bedchamber used by Daniel, when he was in Williamsburg. John Custis's upstairs bedchamber included a small parlor that connected to a library. Double French doors separated the other rooms from the bedchamber. The enclosed sleeping room reeked of an odor of sickness and high fever with uncontrolled body waste. Jack knew that Mr.Custis was always very outspoken about cleanliness, especially when he was in a strange bed. His expectations for his own homes included clean bed linen, spotless floors, polished furniture, and dishes washed and rinsed in boiling water. Jack told himself, "Mr. Custis's fall from the carriage is more serious than I first thought."

"Jack, I want you to fetch Thomas Milton and send him to see me. I'll need your help to get me out of this most untidy bed, but I want to be dressed and sitting in the chair over there." He pointed to a blue brocade high-back chair by the now-open window.

"Mister Custis, your son Daniel is here and he wants to have a word with you right away."

"Now, what in heavens's name does he want? More money, I suppose! You tell him I'll see him when I'm good and ready and that may not be until after the Council meetings are over," Colonel Custis replied with disdain. "And if I'm lucky, I'll be back on the road to Arlington before those meetin's are over," he added to himself.

Jack turned away from Mr. Custis. He did not want to be a wedge between Mr. Custis and his son. Alice, his mother, had told him that Mr. Custis might change his will against his son, Daniel, leaving all his holdings to Jack. Jack tried to understand the meaning of this action. He worked hard to please the senior Custis, but the harder he worked the more displeased Mr. Custis seemed to be. Mr. Custis seldom spoke kindly to anyone. Jack's early recollections of their relationship were of disapproval, intimidation, and outright tyranny. Deep down inside Jack feared the old man.

"I'll go and give Mister Daniel the message, Sir." Jack obediently left the room, thinking that John Custis ought to be pleased to see his son.

Daniel Custis sat in the north parlor, sipped a mug of hot tea and scanned the latest Virginia Gazette, looking for the names of families visiting Williamsburg during Publick Times. Daniel's permanent home was a plantation named the White House at Poplar Grove located on the Pamunkey River.[7] John Custis assigned Daniel's duties, reluctant to give him full management of the farm. John still considered his son, at thirty-five, to be an inexperienced incompetent, which Daniel benignly accepted.

A poor decision had been made by John Custis when he placed a family to manage Poplar Grove that had no interest in maintaining the property. When John Custis assigned its operation to Daniel, three decisions needed immediate attention to keep the two thousand acre farm productive. First, Daniel needed to hire an experienced overseer, with expertise handling black workers in the field and keeping the daily duties of the plantation churning. Second, he needed to search for a new English factor to market the Custis tobacco. The third decision was to manage the rebuilding of the house which was suffering from neglect.

Upon his arrival in Williamsburg, Daniel scheduled an appointment between himself and Jonathan Milton to discuss the enlistment of a new factor. Jonathan's London connections were numerous and his reputation impeccable, or so his referring parties said.

Jack entered the north parlor inconspicuously, hating to interrupt Daniel. "Mister Daniel, your father is unable to see you this morning."

"Is he ill?" Daniel asked, as he looked over his reading glasses.

"Yes, Sir . . . I mean, no Sir," Jack stammered.

"Well, is he or isn't he?" a skeptical Daniel asked.

Jack was not sure if Daniel had heard about Mr. Custis's fall from the carriage and was concerned that the old man had broken his hip. "Have you heard about the fall your father took yesterday?"

"No, I have not. Has Doctor Walters been here to see him. Or is this just one of his usual complaints he always seems to have after a trip from Arlington? Only the Lord knows why he moved himself so far away from his precious flowers. It's probably that Mrs. Moody!" Daniel exclaimed.

"Mr. Custis fell as he stepped from the carriage yesterday. I think he may have broken his leg. You know he will not allow a doctor in his house, but he is unable to get out of bed, Sir." Jack cleared his throat with embarrassment and looked down at the floor. "He has soiled his bed . . . Sir," he said quietly.

Daniel bolted out of his chair. "What? Jack, we must get him immediate attention. Send someone to get Doctor Walters. I will handle my father and tell him he has no choice but to see a doctor. You get him cleaned up for the doctor."

The tall, lean, swarthy-looking man poked in his pocket to find the key to his office. His had been a tedious and frustrating day, and he wished to go home rather than discuss business with Daniel Custis. Jonathan Milton sat down in his tall leather chair, leaned back, propped his legs on the desk, and began to clean his overlong fingernails with his pocket knife, a habit developed from the childhood experience of nail-biting. His grandmother had many remedies to help break him from the discomfort of bleeding cuticles, the worst of which were rags soaked in vinegar tied like mittens over his hands. She made him wear them during lessons, when he was most likely to chew until the bleeding began. When she threatened to pull his front teeth so he couldn't bite anymore, he gave serious consideration to stopping. He let his nails grow several inches to prove he could overcome the biting. As a man, not one known for his fastidiousness, he took undue pleasure from letting dirt and filth accumulate so he could pick it away with his pocket knife.

Daniel Custis was always a prompt man, usually early, never late. It was half past four, according to Jonathan's gold pocket watch. He told himself he would wait fifteen minutes more, but assured himself there had to be good reason for Daniel's missing their meeting. Jonathan was on his feet, buttoning his jacket, as the door opened and Daniel entered. "I'm so glad you are still here, Jonathan," said Daniel, offering his hand for a friendly shake. "We have a number of things to discuss. Thank you for waiting."

"I knew there would be good reason if you missed the meeting, Daniel."

"My father fell yesterday, and Doc Walters says there is a deep bruise to his hip, perhaps a cracked rib or two. Not a broken bone, thank heavens, but for his advanced age, this can be serious if he doesn't rest for a week or so. You know my father, obstinate and unyielding. He will not take care of himself."

"Yes, yes, of course. What can I do to help? Other than your father's stubbornness, he has been in fairly good health."

Daniel sat down in the dark-grained Windsor chair in front of Jonathan's desk. "Jonathan, where is your brother Thomas? Father is very upset that he has not been available today to talk about his duties at House of Six Chimneys. Thomas was at the house yesterday when Father had his untimely accident, but today he is gone. Jack, Father's houseboy, says it looks like Thomas has packed his things and left."

Jonathan's eyes lowered as he picked up his knife and began working over his nails again. "I haven't seen or talked to Thomas in some days now. Are you sure about his clothes?"

"I have not checked his quarters myself, if that is what you ask. Jack is a reliable young man. Please let me know if you see or hear from your brother. Father is most anxious to talk with him."

"How long do you plan to be in Williamsburg?" asked Jonathan.

"I plan to be here during the Assembly, and I hope we can settle the commission of a new factor before I leave. Have you arranged for someone yet?" Daniel asked, knowing the answer even before Jonathan said, "No."

Daniel stood up to take his leave and reluctantly offered his hand to Jonathan. As the two shook rather inconsequentially, Jonathan whispered slyly, "Has your father spoken to you about his will?"

Daniel rode back to the House of Six Chimneys, mystified about the conversation with Jonathan Milton, and especially his last remark. Daniel sensed Jonathan's deceit about both his brother's whereabouts and the engaging of a new English agent. He was most troubled about the mention of the will. John Custis, in his demanding way, consistently menaced Daniel if he didn't do what he wanted. Frequently, he would threaten to change his will, especially, if their arguments were about Daniel's choices versus his father's choices for a wife.

Daniel made preparations to attend the Assembly Ball at the Governor's Palace. He loved dancing and socializing. This was the main reason he had ridden two days to visit Williamsburg. "My father be damned! If I could fix his broken-down body, I would. If I could find Thomas Milton, I would. But he won't even allow me into his bedroom! I'm looking for festivity and conviviality tonight!"

Elizabeth Milton, Jonathan's wife, was in the front parlor reading to her three-year-old daughter Betty. Mary, age twelve, was playing the spinet. She sat on the edge of the bench with her back straight and her arms held extended as her hands moved up and down the keyboard with refinement and grace. She stopped in mid-song and turned to her mother to say, "I think Papa just came up the drive." Mary jumped up and went to the window and saw her father on the front step. Fleeing to the door, Mary rushed to greet her Papa, with Betty and Mother close behind. He picked up Betty and swung her around once, then threw his arm around Mary and hugged her tightly. Elizabeth waited patiently for Jonathan's greeting, which was always a touch of his warm lips on each of her cheeks.

Jonathan removed his coat and hung it on the hook in the passageway, his nightly ritual upon returning home. "Papa, you're so late tonight," said Mary. "It is nearly dark and almost time for Betty to go to bed."

"I had a meeting late this afternoon. I'm so sorry I missed your sonata tonight, pet. Maybe you will play it tomorrow?"

"The best part of the day is when you come home and I can play for you," Mary said.

"Me too, Papa," mirrored Betty.

"Girls, I need to talk to your mother privately. Do you mind if I ask you both to go ahead with your supper? I'm sure Sally won't mind serving an early meal for the two of you." Jonathan smiled and lovingly stroked the cheeks of each girl.

Once the girls were gone, Elizabeth's calm changed into alarm. "Jon, what is it?"

"Beth, have you seen or heard from Thomas in the past two days?" asked Jon.

"I haven't seen him since church on Sunday, why?"

"John Custis is in Williamsburg for the General Council. He arrived yesterday and is more than displeased with the care that Thomas has given that abominable garden. Mr. Custis had some kind of accident and injured his hip and ribs, making him even more cantankerous than usual. This morning the old man, still feisty, asked to see Thomas, but he was gone, clothes and all."

"Oh, Jon, you don't suppose he boarded the *Marysville* that set sail early this morning, do you?" Beth said.

"I've had the same concern. I've begged him to educate himself on horticultural matters, but he just laughs and says anyone can take care of a garden; you need no books for that. I was worried he would come here and expect us to take him in." Jon said, furrowing his brow.

"Thomas has been so untrustworthy all of his life. That is why it is easy to expect the worst in him."

"Beth, darling, Thomas is my brother and we both love him, don't we?" said Jon, as he twisted slightly on her wrist in reminder of what her answer should be. "Don't forget he has rendered himself up to our every whim."

"Yes, Jon." She pulled away from his grip.

The *Marysville* had left the Yorktown Harbor at dawn flying the English flag. She was a comely, vintage English galleon built as a warship but now used for cargo. She carried a foremast and mainmast, each with three sails, and mizzenmast with two. The high sterncastle housed three decks of once-elaborate living quarters. The upper two decks now housed overloads of cargo, leaving the bottom deck as the captain's quarters.

The captain was an unkempt, middle-aged man that the crew called Cap'n Lester. He was an experienced seaman, but arrogant, rude, and bad-tempered. He frequently overloaded the ship with mismarked goods. The ship's manifest was often incorrect, listing items not on board or cargo mislabeled.

The ship headed northeast on a direct route to Bristol, England. Captain Lester was at the helm surveying the night sky. He was grateful the celestial bodies were in unison with the westerly winds. The perfect sailing weather assured the Captain his estimated time for heading southeast was two o'clock. Thomas Milton stood watch with the Captain. "It's a good time to bring down the King's flag, don't you think, Captain?" asked Mr. Milton.

"I'll have someone take it down before sunup, Mr. Milton," the captain answered. "The water's settled so's we can head for the West Indies in 'bout an hour. What brings ya on board this trip, anyway? Sure surprised to see ya."

"Yours was the first ship heading out from Virginia. When I heard the *Marysville* was loaded and ready to ship, I rode hard to get there before you left port. I was worried you'd already be gone. What goods do you have in cargo?" asked Mr. Milton.

"Fish, lumber, and other provisions. Lots of goods come from New England. The *Marysville* been doing lots of tradin' in Martinique and Guadeloupe. The French pay in real specie and there's no four-and-one-half percent export duty like in the West Indies.[8] The King gettin' grabby. He don't want trade with no one but himself and his uppity Lords of Trade. Don't ya work for John Custis, or should I say . . . did you work for the most bad-tempered man in Williamsburg? Are ya in some kind of trouble?"

"I guess I could be. Not taking any chances so I'm going to take a trip for awhile, just to get away from Colonel Custis. He fell and broke a hip, I think, so I don't know what'll happen to him. He'll probably meet his Maker," answered Thomas Milton.

"Your brother the land lawyer?" asked Lester, knowing the answer before he asked the question.

"Do you mean Jonathan Milton? Yes, he's my brother but why did you call him the land lawyer?" asked Thomas, somewhat incensed.

"Oh, tavern talk, I guess. Word has it he got himself rich and on the General Council buying land out west." Captain Lester strained to see Thomas's face in the darkness. He knew there were no secrets in Williamsburg, for it was whispered everywhere about Jonathan's corrupt negotiations.

Thomas cleared his throat. "Where did you hear that? Gossip, I suppose. My brother serves many of the grandees in Virginia. He does very well for himself. Now, if you will excuse me, I believe I will try and get some sleep. Good night."

As he readied himself for the Assembly Ball, Daniel Custis stood before his mirror deciding whether to give approval or disapproval to his new coat and knee britches. He felt the coat was a mite large, with sleeves a little long. He did like the color, which was a chestnut brown, with wide lapels piped in buff. Being at the mercy of the English tailors made sizing difficult, so he often had Alice shorten the sleeves on his jackets. Daniel turned in front of the mirror, tugging on the bottom of his coat and drawing his shoulders upward. His backside faced the mirror as he judged himself as needing more height and less circumference around his waist.

Frustration marked Daniel's face as he reviewed the visit with Mr. Milton that afternoon. He needed desperately to talk with his father since Jonathan had failed to offer names of agents in London or Bristol that were trustworthy. Under his father's control, the burgeoning Custis assets had prospered, and Daniel wanted approval from his father to try and further aggrandize their holdings on his own.

John Custis was adamant in making all decisions since Daniel's early years. He was an untouchable father who gave the commands and then expected someone else to carry them out. Daniel couldn't recall one time his father had personally taken part in his upbringing. There were the many schoolmasters who lived in, hired to educate the children. There was extensive turnover among them because of John's interference with the pedagogy. There were three different educators in one month when Daniel was ten years old. He pleaded to keep a Mr. Wells, who was kind, gentle, and understood Daniel's fear of his father, but the colonel thought he was unclean and a rowdy; he said even the farm animals didn't like to be in his company.

John Custis made a practice of belittling Daniel, especially in front of others. It was a relief to Daniel when he turned fifteen and was sent to a boarding school in Maryland. His father told Daniel he would be on restriction for one year and if he exhibited talent for higher learning, he would go to Cambridge in England the following year. Daniel was euphoric with this prospect, and promised his father he would be proud of a son bringing home an enviable credential from Cambridge. John Custis was considered a well-educated Virginian. He was a member of the House of Burgesses, held a position at William and Mary, and later became a member of the General Council. He expected his son to follow him and join in the notoriety and politics of becoming a Burgess.[9]

After one year in Maryland and one year at Cambridge, Daniel returned to the House of Six Chimneys in Williamsburg.[10] John promptly informed Daniel, "I have made the decision it is time for you to marry. I know several women with creditable prospects."

Daniel realized his years away from home had changed him, but his father remained an obstinate and reprehensible miscreant. "Please tell me with whom I am supposed to spend the rest of my 'until death us do part' life, Father?" Daniel's experiences in England had taken a youthful boy and reconstructed him into a polished and vigorous man with grit and backbone. Daniel sighed and crossed his arms while he studied his father's face, alert to the anticipated rising of color in his neck and cheeks.

"Dammit, Daniel. You are not going to return to my house and speak to me in your usual condescending manner. I strongly suggest you review the meaning of the sixth commandment, 'Honor thy father and mother.'" John slammed the upper drawer of his desk as he fixed his eyes on Daniels. "I can see the English pedagogues had little success in teaching you the meaning of the word respect!"

Daniel turned and walked toward the door, "Respect is honor, appreciation, and consideration, something a person earns, Father!" Forcefully, he pushed the door into its jamb, making the windows rattle on both floors of the house.

John Custis's own marriage began as a romantic attraction to Frances Parke, an eighteen-year-old beauty whose father, Daniel Parke II, was Governor of the Leeward Islands and owned numerous land holdings in both England and Virginia. The accumulated Custis wealth combined with Frances's made a marriage between the families seem a practical and wise merger. However, the ardour between Frances and John soon cooled and turned into violent disagreements, distrust, and temper, drawing the tenuous marriage into a shambles. Family and friends begged Frances and John to draw up a legal agreement delineating rules of conduct for them both; divorce was an unacceptable solution—or resolution. However, the problem ended when Daniel was five and his sister was six years old. Frances contracted smallpox and died, leaving the young children in John's care.[11]

John took pride in his children at first. He said, "My children are all the comfort I have in the world, for whose sake I kept myself single and am determined so to do as long as it shall please God to continue them to me."[12] John chose not to marry again, probably because of the failure of his marriage to Frances. He spent his days in Williamsburg planting, transplanting, pruning, grafting, and ordering the latest seeds and horticulture magazines. His garden at the House of Six Chimneys filled his days and gave him pride and fullfilment. The boxwood hedges wove around the carefully planted flower beds, giving color all year. Magnolia trees centered many of the beds, which were planted with spring bulbs: crocus, daffodils and tulips. Summertime brought roses, heliotrope, oriental poppies, foxglove, violets, marigolds and flowering herbs.

Daniel's reverie was interrupted as the clock on the fireplace mantel rang eight times. He pulled his reliable gold watch from his pocket to verify that the two timepieces gave the same time. Daniel was checking his reflection one more time before leaving for the Governor's Palace when the bedroom door burst open. "Father, what are you doing out of bed? Dr. Walters will be angry if you fall again and do more injury to yourself. Where is Jack? He is supposed to see that you stay in bed."

"Never mind, never mind—you can see I do quite well with a cane. Daniel, I expect you to be at our dinner table promptly at three o'clock tomorrow. William Byrd is here for the Assembly, and his two daughters will be with him, as well as his new wife. You have not seen your cousins and uncle in some time, so you will be seated in your mother's place at the head of the table!" John Custis spit his words abruptly, emphasizing, "You *will* be seated!"

"I look forward to dining with Evelyn and Anne, Father. I will bring a guest also," Daniel declared with confidence. "Alice will easily set another place at the table."

"That will be seven at the table rather than six. You know how uncomfortable I am with uneven numbers, Daniel."

"I can manage another guest, in that case," Daniel replied, watching his father's face turn color.

"Would it be appropriate to ask who the guests may be? If you are planning to bring another of your common lady friends into this house, I will not allow it!" John's face was now a brilliant crimson.

"My answer to your question is another question, Father . . . Pray tell me, which cousin are you going to push upon me to marry?"

John's long forefinger was shaking at Daniel. "You have rejected Evelyn time and again. Anne may be better suited for you. She is not nearly as pretty and her conversation is not as quick as Evelyn's. The two of you have a great deal in common."

"I enjoy Evelyn and Anne, Father. I will be on time and in place tomorrow, without guests." Daniel excused himself and left his father standing alone in his bedroom.

Daniel Custis and Evelyn Byrd were very fond of each other, drawn together by the similar dispositions of their fathers. Both men married Parke sisters, Frances and Lucy. The marriages brought expanded properties and financial gain for both couples. And the similarities did not stop there. Lucy and William Byrd suffered the same fate as Frances and John Custis—hostility and rancor that proliferated into hatred. The men were both domineering, short-tempered, and contentious. However, the redeeming characteristics they shared were ambition, generosity, and friendliness to those outside the family. The sisters mirrored one another in semblance, attitude, and fortune. Ironically, the Parke sisters also met the same fate. Within two years of one another, they both died from smallpox. William Byrd declared that his wife, Lucy, had died of the same distemper that destroyed her sister Frances.[13]

The dinner party was cordial, with John leading the discussion about his "unfortunate" accident. Daniel was left with the two sisters when their fathers retired upstairs for brandy and tobacco. The three cousins took deep breaths, all in unison, after the retreat of the men to the library. Laughter broke out as Evelyn spoke in a guttural tone, imitating her father, "I wonder when the King is going to learn to speak English?"

Picking up on the question, Anne replied in a high soprano voice, "Whenever the pope learns German." The girls doubled up with laughter as Maria Byrd, the girl's stepmother, entered the room. After four children, she was very plump, and excused herself frequently because of her overactive bladder. Anne surreptitiously asked Maria if she was feeling all right. She promptly replied with a timid, "Yes . . . why do you ask?"

Anne's glance to her sister needed no words. William Byrd loved women . . . all women. Maria and William were never quiet in their bedroom encounters. The upstairs bedroom walls did little to absorb the sounds of their lovemaking. The lust between them often did not make it to the bedroom. Whispers around their home in Richmond talked about William's bragging about his success on the pool table.[14]

"Daniel, please pour me another glass of that beautiful burgundy," asked Evelyn. "Then teach me the toast you gave at the table. Where did you learn it?"

"Cambridge students resurrect toasts you have never heard before. I think this came from an Irishman, but I'm not sure. It is probably at least one hundred years old."

All love at first, like generous wine
Ferments and frets until it's fine,
But when 'tis settled on the Lee
And from th' impurer matter free,
Becomes the richer still the older,
And proves the pleasanter the colder.[15]

NOVEMBER 15, 1747 The next morning John Custis descended the stairs and stormed into the parlor. Daniel knew as soon as he heard his footsteps and his cane hammering the floor that his father was in a confrontational mood. "Good morning, Father," Daniel said over the top of his glasses. "I hope you had a restful night."

"If I could disown a son, I would do it this morning. Why did you insult Maria Byrd last night? Daniel, so help me, I will disinherit you yet!"

Daniel was speechless. "I am sorry, but I have no idea what you mean."

"Yes, you do! Innuendo floated through the air like feathers from a pillow." John Custis tried to keep his anger in control. "I received a message this morning from William, saying Maria felt displaced and insulted at the conversation that took place in our parlor last night. You will write an apology this morning and deliver it yourself."

"It will be difficult to write an apology for something I do not understand." Daniel's agitation began to grow into anger. "We all had a wonderful time. The laughter was as effervescent as our overflowing wine glasses."

"I know you so well! You are a master at manipulating any situation. You did not want to attend this dinner and you made sure it would be a disastrous evening." John's face flushed beet-red.

"There is no amount of money in the world that would pay enough to the teacher I had, Father."

DECEMBER 12, 1747 The Custis family crest was placed at the top of the stationery. Daniel was sitting at his father's desk, writing a note on John's stationery—to John, about a planned trip to Antigua. Daniel's penmanship was not his best because of his haste to complete the letter before John's return.

Four weeks had gone by since the dinner with the Byrd family, and John was still nagging Daniel about his ill-mannered behavior. Daniel practiced expediency by sending an apology, but felt guilty about the fragmented note because he still did not know for what he was apologizing. This latest set-back with John gave Daniel impetus to visit his grandfather's grave in the Leeward Islands in the Caribbean.[16] When Daniel heard a carriage pull up in the drive, he looked out of the window to see who was coming. "Damn!" He crumpled the letter and buried it in his pocket, waiting for his father to arrive.

"What, pray tell, are you doing in my library?" John asked, as he limped through the door with Jack firmly latched to his arm. "Who have you managed to offend now?"

"No one, Father. I have come to tell you I am leaving tomorrow for Antigua. I have always wanted to visit Grandfather Parke's burial plot, and there is a cargo ship sailing on which I have booked passage."

"Booked passage? Is the ship licensed for the West Indies or is it one that deals in illicit trading? Do you know the captain?" John was incredulous.

"I can assure you it is not a pirate ship with freebooters, buccaneers, and a peg-legged captain," smiled Daniel.

"How long will you be gone? I have plans for you to return to the Pamunkey, but I suppose I will have to look for someone else to take over the plantation." John thrust his chin toward Daniel and folded his arms across his chest.

"I am going to Antigua. I regret your decision because I have waited a long time to be accepted into your business." Daniel knew his father was working to control him. "I will see you when I return."

Daniel was drawn to the West Indies because of a portrait hanging in his parent's front parlor at Six Chimneys. The picture dominated the wall by its size, opulent colors, and ornate gilded frame. The subject was Daniel Parke II, Frances Parke Custis's father and Daniel's grandfather. As a child, Daniel often studied the portrait, mesmerized by his grandfather's brilliant velvet crimson-colored long-coat. The artist had captured rays of light beaming on his right shoulder, giving the velvet a brushed sheen. The vest was a heavy silk brocade in sky blue that matched the trousers. Around his neck and hips were silk sashes in russet hues from burnt orange to an almost-burgundy, all wrapped and tied with perfection. Pinned on the lapel was a miniature framed picture of Queen

Anne, a gift from the queen to Colonel Parke.[17]

Upon Daniel's return from Europe, he studied the picture not so much for its beauty as for the depth of character in his grandfather's pensive yet earnest face. The portrait spoke to Daniel, seeming to tell him that strength, honesty, and courage were virtues his grandfather wanted him to have.

DECEMBER 13, 1747 Daniel left his bed at three the next morning. He wanted to be out of he house before the cook came in to light the fires. Quietly, he picked up his satchel, unlatched the door, and walked to the edge of the drive where a liveryman was waiting with two horses, one for Daniel and one for himself. The two men guided the horses carefully to the outskirts of town before running them at full speed. Without incident, the ride to the bay would take more than an hour. The ship was scheduled to leave at five and he wanted to be there early. A fine mist was blowing in from the Chesapeake, making visibility difficult. Dawn was an hour away.

However assured he appeared in front of his father, Daniel felt apprehensive about the trip. He had engaged the passage with a man who called himself Robbie. He had met him at Moody's Ordinary already filled with ale and bragging that the captain had made at least twenty trips to the West Indies and knew the seaway by memory, needing neither charts nor compass. He promised that the ship was clean and that no sickness had been reported. Daniel paid the man one-half of the fare in the tavern and promised to pay the other half before boarding.

Disappointment settled in when Daniel saw the size and shabbiness of the ship. The men were finishing the loading as he approached. He asked a coxswain where Robbie might be. "There ain't nobody 'ere name Robbie," his voice crackled. "The Cap'n's in the for'ard cabin if you want 'a talk to 'im." Daniel picked up his satchel and carefully walked up the wet gangplank.

There were barrels lying haphazardly on the deck that Daniel recognized as hogsheads of tobacco. He was under the impression that food stuffs were going to the West Indies, but did not dare question the cargo. The narrow steps leading him below creaked and groaned with every step. Using his hand against the wall to guide him down the dimly lighted stairway, he was jolted by a stench of rot and refuse. He tapped lightly on the door of what he thought would be the captain's quarters. A scratchy voice hollered, "Come in, door's open."

Daniel opened the door and poked his head inside, saying, "Captain, my name is Daniel Parke Custis. I'm looking for a crew member named Robbie."

"Yeh, yeh, what do you want with him?"

"Last week I bought passage from him to Antigua on this ship, Sir," said Daniel.

"Ain't nobody named Robbie on this ship. How much did you give 'im?" the captain asked wrinkling the skin around his eyes and mouth as he laughed, which brought on a deep and raspy cough. "I bet he hornswoggled you out of plenty."

"I paid him one half of twenty shillings. The other half was to be paid after I boarded," Daniel said with remorse.

"We never take no passengers on this trip. You, Sir, lost yerself ten shillings for stupidity. This boat ain't even goin' to the West Indies. We're going straight to the Gold Coast to get us some of that Black Gold, then we're goin' to the West Indies to sell that Black Gold, if you know what I mean." Again the captain began the hacking, this time choking, barely able to get his breath. After clearing his throat several times, he said,

"I lost one of me best hands yes'erday. He caught himself in a running rig and rumpled 'is arm a bit—the ninnyhammered jacky.You can sign on to take his place, I reckon, if ya please."

Daniel paused for a minute to ponder the captain's offer. He wanted to leave Virginia immediately, but the African coast was not the destination he wanted. It became clear that the half-empty lower deck was to be filled with slaves on the return trip to Antigua. "I find myself unable to stay on board for this trip. My plans are to go to the Indies and from there book passage on a French ship sailing for France. Thank you for the kind offer, but maybe you can be so kind as to tell me if you know when such a ship might be going east." Daniel wanted to leave the captain's quarters as quickly as he could without offending the surly man.

"If I was you, I'd git meself to London, Bristol, or Liverpool to make the trip across the Channel to git to France. The English Admiralty is mighty hard to deal with these days. They don' want nobody from here to sail on ships not English. The Parleemen's always making laws that don't seem right. Trade shud be for everyone that's got a ship, I say. If you've got reason to go to the Indies, there's plenty ships goin' from the King's palace to Antigua. I can't think why anybody'd want to go them hot islands."

Daniel offered his hand to the captain and thanked him for his help and advice. He crawled back up the crumbling stairs to the upper deck just as the gangplank was being untied. "Please wait," Daniel called to the deck hands. "I won't be sailing with you this morning after all."

ONE YEAR LATER

NOVEMBER 12, 1748 The change in November weather was a predictor of the attendance at the General Assembly. November 1748 brought becalmed winds and mild temperatures that filled Williamsburg with the hurry-scurry and hurly-burly of legislators, wives, and busy townfolks—much like the springtime Assembly.

Martha Dandridge arrived in Williamsburg to visit her cousins Nathaniel and Dorthea. She came to see her namesake, three-month-old Martha Spotswood Dandridge, and be in attendance for her christening. Nate and Dorthea's first-born delighted Martha with her dark Dandridge eyes. "How are we going to know which Martha is which when she gets older?" asked Martha.

"You'll be Martha One and the baby will be Martha Two," Nate replied, with his infectious laugh.

"How about Big Martha and Little Martha?" suggested Dorthea.

"I would love to be called Big Martha for a change," agreed Martha. "But how about just calling me Patcy. Papa gave me that name and everyone at home calls me that, anyway."

"We've always called you Patcy, until just recently, when you asked us to call you Martha. Now that you're such a fully developed young lady . . . Patcy doesn't project refinement or polish," Nate said. "Perhaps we need to address you as 'Madame Martha'—such sophisticated alliteration, don't you think?"

"Dorthea, I hope you have changed your mind about going to the ball tonight. I'm afraid I'll have to dance with Nate all the evening and listen to his nonsensical drivel. Besides you and Nate dance so smoothly together and my clumsiness is such an embarrassment."

"Don't worry, there'll be lots of young men waiting for the chance to dance with you. When they see your face and new dress your dance card will be full," Nate interrupted. "Besides, I'm planning a game of cards with the Carter brothers tonight. I love taking their money."

"I jump every time I hear the name Carter," Martha said to herself. She handed the baby to her mother before climbing stairs to prepare for the evening.

Martha Dandridge patted her stomach to control the fluttering of the butterflies inside. She measured her image in the cheval glass and rated herself as a possible candidate for Belle of the Ball. Dress? New rose-colored silk damask, decolletage very wide and deep. Martha turned to admire the back of the dress with its full lengths of silk, shoulder to hem. Her waist, tightly laced, exaggerated the fullness and beauty of the dress front and back. Hair? Hanging loosely around her face with the the back swept up into a roll and pinned with dried rosebuds that matched her dress. Face? Ivory skin with a nose dotted with sun freckles, and cheeks with a touch of pink rouge, the color of her dress. "*I guess I will have to do. I wish my five feet would stretch a bit more with the two-inch heels of my shoes. I'll never look like that tall Sally Cary who dances every dance at the Assembly Ball. But I guess I'll do!*"

Nate and Martha's carriage pulled into the oak-lined drive of the Governor's Palace. Large lanterns blazed to greet and to light the way for the guests as they arrived. Martha continued to pat her stomach, sending a message to settle down. "The powdered wigs and cinched waists are all waiting to greet the Governor, I see," said Nate. "No one will need a snuff box tonight. There will be enough powder floating through the air to fill a hogshead."

"I sneeze every time I try to wear to wear a wig," Martha replied. "I hope I'm not going to feel out of place without one. At least I won't have to be concerned about it falling off my head when I curtsy to the Governor."

"Don't worry. When the men standing against the wall are choosing their next partner, their eyes will light on you because of your dazzling hair, not your missing wig."

Music filled the room, a prelude to the dancing, which was due to start shortly. Guests enjoyed the harp, flute, violins, and other strings that were led by the spinet player. Protocol had the husbands dance two dances with their wives before retiring upstairs for tobacco and libations. The forsaken wives would then gather in a circle for chit-chat, gossip, and sweet punch.

The first dance was traditionally a minuet, and the second was an allemande. As the General Councillors, Burgesses, and their partners filled the floor, Martha carefully scrutinized the young men banked against the wall as well as those standing around the punch bowl. Nate kissed the hands of each dowager, combining his winning smile with flattery and charm. He worked his way across the room to where Martha was standing, waiting to be asked to dance. "Come, my beautiful cousin. Let us find room on the floor and show off a bit for the old folks."

Nate, Martha's first dance teacher, was a patient partner. Martha was not a relaxed dancer since losing her shoe at Nate and Dorthea's wedding. "Please forgive me if I miss a step, Nate. I work hard to be a noble dancer."

"You are such a pessimist; I'm just putting you on display. All the young men need to see how beautiful you look tonight," Nate said. "I'll be going upstairs to cozy with the powdered wigs after this dance, but you need to catch the eyes of all the young men before I go."

"I feel disappointed with the number of men here. I hardly recognize anyone. They all look to be my brother John's age. I feel marvellous, and

I know my dress is beautiful and my hair is in place, but there are no interesting men!"

"What you need is a beau, Patcy darling," Nate said. "Be patient. Someone will sweep you away all too soon."

Nate climbed the stairs looking for a partner to play cards. The smoke-filled room was full of men grouped together in deep discussion. The card players sitting in front of the open window gambled seriously, concentrating on each hand. Nate waited for a place at the card table. When he noticed Jonathan Milton, Paul Fairchild, and George Howard, he asked, "Do you mind if I join you?"

"Do you know everyone?" Jonathan asked as he invited Nate to participate in their conversation.

"I don't believe I know this man," Nate said, reaching his hand to George Howard.

"My wife is Sarah Wills Howard, Dorthea's cousin. We attended your wedding last year and enjoyed your hospitality immensely," Mr. Howard said, offering his hand.

"Yes, yes, of course," Nate replied. "I apologize for not recognizing you. It was, indeed a very happy but hectic day; but please don't let me interrupt you. Continue your discussion."

"We were debating the advantage or disadvantage of asking the General Council for a proprietary charter in the western frontier," Jonathan responded. "The French, from all reports, are working toward an alliance with the Algonquins and are staking out land claims in the Ohio Valley. I think it might be wise to form a company and colonize the Ohio River Valley ourselves."

"How many men have you told about this plan, and how will it benefit the colonists?" asked Paul Fairchild. "I am sure my father would be interested."

"You, my friends, are the first to hear about this. If we can form the company with twenty or twenty-five men, we can settle on a charter which will be administered by the company. We first would commission a survey, then deposit the plat at the proprietor's office where a patent would be issued granting the land to us. Our company charter would then be formed; allowing us to fix the rents to our own standard. We would all share equally in the monetary reward from the rents."

Nate listened carefully to Jonathan Milton's plan. "What about the French? My information says the fighting is spreading and a treaty will be a long time in coming."

"The French Canadians are working south to the Mississippi," George Howard contributed. "They will fight until they reach New Orleans."

"How many acres are you considering?" Nate asked.

"Two hundred thousand to five hundred thousand acres," answered Jonathan. He raised his forefinger and shook it to signal the men to drop their conversation. Jonathan turned to recognize the finely dressed Daniel. "Good evening," Jonathan said brightly, as Daniel Custis approached the group. "It is always good to see you. I hope things on the Pamunkey are going well."

Daniel warmly acknowledged all the men. "My pleasure, gentlemen, and yes, life is good on the Pamunkey, Mr. Milton. I trust you are all well?"

"Gentlemen, if you will excuse me. I see an available chair at the card table," said Nate. Paul Fairchild and George Howard also walked away, leaving Jonathan and Daniel alone.

"I hear your father is getting around much better these days." said Jonathan. "He is a marvel. There are not too many men his age able to recover so expeditiously."

"It has been over a year since his accident. He still has pain, but if he uses his cane for assistance, he manages quite well. Of course, Jack is his savior. He administers to his needs, giving back rubs and massaging his hips and legs with hot oils. My father has a very strong will and firmly believes he can control his body with meditation and hot oil."

"There is an English factor in Williamsburg whom I would like you to meet, Daniel. He sailed into the Chesapeake a week ago. He is consulting with several planters about handling exports to England," Jonathan said. "Time has passed quickly. Hasn't it been nearly a year since you located a Mr. Tyler? I feel you have not been pleased with him, so you may want to meet this fellow. His commission is reasonable."

"Yes, if you will arrange a meeting, I will be most pleased to talk to him."

Daniel Custis entered the ballroom during the intermission. The French doors were open and many dancers had stepped outside for air. The night was cool. Brilliant stars hung so close that one felt two long legs attached to a long arm could reach up and pluck the sparkling diamonds from the sky. Martha was straining to find the Little Dipper, when an unfamiliar voice from behind asked her if she knew Genesis 1:16 from the Bible. "No, I don't remember it but I am sure I have heard it," Martha answered.

"And God made two great lights: the greater light to rule the day, and the lesser light to rule the night; he made the stars also," the rich male voice recited.

Martha still strained to count the stars. "No, I have not heard that passage. My great-grandfather and grandfather were both ministers, but I do not know the passage from their teachings. It is truly beautiful. I have always believed that my grandfather is the last star on the handle of the Big Dipper. It always twinkles the brightest whenever I'm looking at it."

"Are you looking at it now?"

"No, I've been looking for the Little Dipper. Where is the Big Dipper?" Martha asked. "Oh, there it is. Look at it sparkle!"

"It just started to twinkle when your eyes gazed upon it," said the man. Martha looked around to see with whom she was conversing. The man stepped forward but the shadows hid his face.

"I'm Martha Dandridge," she said, holding out her hand.

"I know who you are, but you probably don't remember me. I am Daniel Custis." He grasped her extended hand in return as he stepped into the light.

"Yes, of course I do," Martha said, color rising in her cheeks.

"May I have the pleasure of the next dance?" Daniel asked. "The music will be starting soon." Martha's heart raced as she remembered the last dance with Daniel and the cataclysmic loss of her shoe.

"Yes, of course, but I am a novice dancer, so don't expect too much."

"I have observed your mastery on the floor," Daniel grinned. "You are a graceful and attentive dancer. Your tutor was English-born?"

"Mister Custis, you are a very clever man and very observant," Martha smiled, with an air of flirtation.

Martha's only partner the rest of the evening was Daniel. He gently held her elbow as the two walked to the punch bowl together. She was mesmerized with the tiny scar on his upper lip, and was drawn to the way it moved up and down when he spoke. His teeth were milk-white, straight, and aligned perfectly in his mouth. A shiver raced up and then down her back, which surprised Martha because she did not feel chilled. There was an aura about Daniel that captivated her.

"I have our carriage waiting in the drive, Patcy," Nate said to Martha. "It is nearly midnight and Dorthea will wonder what has kept us so long." Nate nodded his greeting to Daniel. "I hope you have enjoyed the company of my cousin tonight, Daniel."

"Yes, we have had a splendid evening. It has passed much too quickly," Daniel said, without taking his eyes from Martha. "Goodnight, Martha, and thank you."

Silence accompanied them on the ride back to the Francis Street house. Martha tried to organize the whirling inside her head. She began to sort out the evening: visiting with friends, punch bowl talk, dancing with Nate, studying the stars, and then Daniel. He had been a grown man as far back as she could remember, seeing him at St. Peter's Church, at Bruton Parish in Williamsburg, and during Publick Times. His family was frequently discussed at the dining table. At last she broke the silence. "Nate, do you know how old Daniel Custis is?"

"Not for sure, Patcy, but I know he is much older than I am," he answered cheerfully. His thoughts about that were ambivalent, because his eyes told him that Patcy and Daniel were drawn together like flies to honey. "*Patcy is ready to find a beau, and yes, he is a bit older. Daniel Custis has searched for a wife a long time. His eyes were fastened to hers,*" he thought. "*This may be an unforgettable evening for Madame Martha. Her eyes danced and sparkled. Hmm-mm, could Daniel Custis be the one to steal her heart?*"

Martha lay still in her bed, unable to fall asleep. Her body was exhausted but her stimulated brain was wide awake. She had never had another person look at her with such intensity. "*How can I describe Daniel's eyes?" she thought. "Papa has always looked at Mother with the same affection in his eyes. Dorthea looks at Nate like his existence is hers only. What is this that exists between two pairs of eyes communicating wordlessly?*" Waiting for the sleep that did not come, Martha sat up and opened the journal her mother insisted she write in every day. "This will help you learn to write," Mother had said. "When you are married and move away from Chestnut Grove, you will be expected to keep in touch with your family." Martha labored each time she began this daily chore.

November 16, 1748. I had a happy but perplexing dae todae and tonite. My new dress fits well and color is just rite for me. My hair staid in place during the asemble Ball and I think my breath staid sweet to. I talked with many frends. Elisbeth Milton told me her sister Amelia is going to hav a babe soon. Many of my frends alreade have one or two. I'm not redy for babes yet. Daniel custis dancet wit me many times. He seems to be a nice man wit dark brown eyes that tend to see things insid my hed. He is old. he has never marryd. I wonder why. I see him at cherch. He is wit evelyn Byrd sometimes. John custis wants him to marry her. Daniel mae think of me as a dauter. My shoos staid on. Sally Cary dancet every dance. Looked vere beatiful. Yours frankly, Patcy

Closing her journal, she laid it carefully inside the lap desk. The candle beside the bed was nearly burned to the holder, so she blew it out before settling herself under the covers for a peaceful sleep.

NOVEMBER 20, 1748 Jonathan Milton unlocked his office and opened the door to find the air dank and the temperature frigid. Jonathan had not been in his office for nearly a week because of the legislative meetings. The weather had turned cold and windy after the previous week of mild and pleasant days, so he lighted the fireplace before settling down to review the past week's events. The most encouraging news was that a treaty between England and France, settling the collision between the two countries contesting ownership of the Ohio Valley, was imminent. Jonathan was confident that a new treaty would not definitively declare ownership to either country, so his plan for formulating a company to colonize the Ohio Valley seemed like a sound business plan. As a councillor, his confidence in acquiring a proprietary was more than high. "It will be expedient to move quickly to formulate the company, move settlers into the valley, and start receiving rents for the land,"[18] he told himself.

Just as Jonathan's fire began to blaze, the door opened, allowing the outside chill to enter. Jonathan looked up to recognize his visitor as Daniel Custis. "Come in, Daniel. Shut the door."

Daniel rubbed his hands together as he stood in front of the fireplace. "The weather has surprised us all. I planned to return to the Pamunkey tomorrow, but I may wait until the weather warms a bit."

"That might not be until February or March, Daniel," Jonathan laughed. "What can I help you with today?"

"You mentioned an English factor visiting in Williamsburg. Is he still in the area?" Daniel asked.

"Yes, I expect him in my office sometime today. Are you interested in meeting with him?" Jonathan replied. "I will be most pleased to act as your intermediary."

"Yes, I'm sure you would. May I sit down, Jonathan?" Daniel looked down to the floor as he lodged himself in a cold, wooden chair. The discomforting stare on his face gave Jonathan a hint of the serious nature of Daniel's visit. "Yes, I would like to speak with your factor, but may we discuss that later? There is another matter of greater consequence that I need to address. Some time ago you spoke to me about my father's will. My impression at the time was that you had information about his beneficiaries . . . in fact, may have drawn up his will. Is that right, Jonathan?" Daniel drew up his left eyebrow, waiting for an answer.

"No, I did not, but I know the associate who witnessed the last will and testament. And that should be beneficiary," Jonathan corrected.

"Is the will on record with you his most recent will or could he have enlisted another legal advisor to file a new one?" Daniel asked.

Jonathan's razor-sharp eyes could detect Daniel's pensiveness. "It is possible. You must know your father better than anyone in Virginia. His unpredictability is perplexing, and now that he has marooned himself across the Chesapeake, it is difficult to communicate with him."

"He is difficult to communicate with under the best of situations." Grimacing, Daniel asked, "Is it a breach of attorney-client privilege to tell me about the declaration of the will?"

"Yes, it is. However, your father has vacillated several times. Depending upon his mood, he has changed the will three times that I know of since the untimely death of your mother. Naturally, the expection would be that his estate would be bequeathed to you as his son.[19] However, given his right to change the will, Mr. Custis originally drew up a will giving his complete estate to Jack, his houseboy.

"You must understand that with the status of your father and his extensive holdings, a document of this nature could hardly be kept secret."

Jonathan began to feel ambivalent about giving Daniel this news. Reaching into his pocket, he searched for his knife so he could scrape his fingernails. "I'm sure this is distressing information, but I must tell you, the second time he drew up his will, he reversed himself and named you as his only beneficiary." Looking intently into Daniel's face, he thought, *"You rich, undeserving, worthless bastard! You've never labored a day in your life."* Engaging Daniel's cold stare, he tugged at the stock wrapped tightly around his neck and said, "Sometime later, he changed the beneficiary back to Jack, as it presently stands."

Daniel sat with his head propped in his hands. "The rumor has passed to me that Jack was engendered by my father and that he was named the beneficiary of his estate. Each time I displeased my father, he threatened to change his will. I did not believe he would do such a thing. Thank you for breaking a confidence to give me such news."

"I have debated this very conversation many times, Daniel. Have you plans for your future?"

"I have managed Poplar Grove for some time and my wish is to make it profitable. Father thinks I am a pleasure seeker with an impotency toward the work ethic. I choose to be a useful and productive entrepreneur instead of an ornamental prig," Daniel said. "Thank you, again, for the information. I will keep this conversation confidential, and I trust you will do the same."

As Daniel opened the door, he turned and asked, "Jonathan, have you had word from Thomas? My father frequently inquires as to his whereabouts."

Jonathan shook his head and shrugged his shoulders as he watched Daniel delicately close the door behind himself. Of course, he knew every move his brother had taken since leaving on the *Marysville* some time ago. The two brothers had engaged in the fur-trading business in the frontier for several years. It had become a thriving and lucrative business, giving Jonathan great interest in the French Canadian move into the Ohio Valley.

Daniel Parke Custis mounted his horse and slowly rode back to the House of Six Chimneys. His father had recently announced that he didn't plan to return to Arlington until the weather improved, so Daniel was sure the Colonel would be home. A chill settled over Daniel as his horse cantered up Duke of Gloucester Street. The wind bit into his cheeks as he debated a discussion with John Custis. "*My first question to him will be to ask him to explain Jack's claim as a recipient of the Custis estate. I want him to tell me if the rumors are true about his patrimony. My parents had a loveless marriage, but would their distaste for one another drive my father into Alice's bed?*"

Daniel was now pacing the passageway and the north parlor, trying to sort out the information given by Jonathan Milton. "*The next question for my father will be concerning the will. If Jack becomes the recipient of the Custis estate, do I have to relinquish Poplar Grove?*" Daniel continued to walk back and forth nervously, thrusting his left fist into his right palm. "*Does he realize the public outcry there would be in the colony of Virginia about a black heir to such a vast fortune, and what the moral and legal ramifications might be? I will not marry Evelyn or Anne Byrd and spend the rest of my life in misery and despondency! I must have a discussion with John Parke Custis immediately!*" Daniel took the stairs to the Colonel's library two at a time, then burst into his father's upstairs sanctuary without bothering to knock.

"It seems I spend all winter anticipating spring. When the wait is over, I marvel at how swiftly the months passed by," Martha said to Daniel as they rode their horses side by side, ambling through the budding trees and wildflowers.

"My favorite time of year," replied Daniel. "I am so glad I rode to Chesnut Grove today. It was a pleasure to see your father, and your mother also. She looks well. Your brother John is a man! And so handsome. He must dazzle the young ladies when he goes to Williamsburg."

"Young John is so like my father. Sometimes I see them in the fields and I can hardly tell them apart," Martha answered. "I feel blessed having all my family at home every day."

"You are indeed lucky to have your family together, happy and healthy. Each one unique in their own way."

"Tell me about your family. I know little about your sister, mother, and father," Martha requested.

"My mother is dead, as you know. She was a tenacious woman, which she had to be to cope with my father. She was unyielding in her love for her children, but my parents had a very unhappy marriage. It was a marriage arranged to strengthen the Custis and Parke estates.[20] Let me tell you the story of my grandfather Parke. He was as stiff-necked as my father. He insisted that every family member must have the name Parke. After my parents married, Grandfather insisted my father add Parke as a middle name. If your name did not include Parke, you would not receive a legacy! He was quite a rogue! My sister and I, I'm sorry to say, are not very close. She was forced into an unhappy marriage for the same reason as my parents.[21] Seems my father had the last say with her also."

"I remember seeing you at St. Peter's Church with your father and Evelyn Byrd sometimes. Nate and I always waited to see how late you would be." Martha was laughing as she confessed to observing that usually the Custis family was seated by the end of the first hymn. "We waited for you to move to the back of the church, but we didn't know why."

"My father insisted I marry Evelyn. She didn't want to marry me, either. I didn't want the church gossip to think we were a betrothed couple, so I moved," Daniel explained. "Did you know that Evelyn died last December, shortly after Publick Times?"

"Yes, I did. The fever, I understand."

"She was a very lovely lady. We had many conversations about the conniving of our fathers. Evelyn fell in love with a brilliant young man with a title while she was in England. Uncle William Byrd, who, by the way, is one of my godfathers, gave his approval for the marriage. Evelyn and her beloved were ecstatic and began to make their plans, when her intended announced he was Catholic. Her father, upon hearing about his devout Church of England daughter marrying a Catholic, brought her straight back to Virginia.[22] I do not believe she completely recovered from that disappointment," Daniel said. He took his small chained-watch from his breast pocket, clicking it open. "We should probably turn back and return you home before your mother sends one of your brothers looking for you."

Martha watched and listened to Daniel carefully. She was taken with the way his nose fit between his cheekbones, so perfectly sculpturing his profile. He rode erect in his saddle as he gracefully handled the horse's reins. "Will you stay and have supper with us? Mother is always anxious to set another plate on the table."

Frances Dandridge begged Daniel to spend the night at Chestnut Grove. After supper, John and Daniel exchanged views about the conflict with the French on the western frontier and the pending treaties with the Iroquois. The discussion then moved to the lack of safety of ocean travel, because of pirates sailing from Africa to the West and East Indies, then back and forth to the colonies. Then Daniel gallantly thanked the Dandridge family for their hospitality, but excused himself. He carried a lantern to give light on the well-travelled road between their two plantations, so he bid his farewells and invited the Dandridges to be his guests soon.

Daniel rode back to Poplar Grove cautiously. He reviewed the evening and thought how much he enjoyed the dining table at the Dandridge home; the children well-mannered and respectful of one another, and the deep affection that John and Frances had for each other. Reflecting on his own home, he could not remember a peaceful meal unless there were guests to impress. Daniel wanted a family like the Dandridges, and he had finally found the woman with whom he wanted to share his life—Martha Dandridge! "I will speak to John Dandridge about courtship soon. However, it troubles me to think of my father's reaction and his persistent and illogical reason for changing his will," he told himself.

March 4, 1749. Daniel Custis came to call todae. We rode sevral ours together unsaperoned. I'm saprised mother and papa let me go wit him. We talkt a lot about his famly. I know Daniel was not happy at home. I like to lisen to him talk. I like to look at his nose and the side of his face. He rides well. He makes me smile and feel happy inside. Yours honestly Patcy

The meeting began at four o'clock in Jonathan Milton's office. Six men sat around Jonathan's desk, waiting for Paul Fairchild and George Howard, debating the cause of a livery stable fire on Francis Street earlier that day. "Gentlemen, please help yourself to the rum and brandy. I have sherry, if anyone wants a drink of that." Jonathan felt apprehensive about this get-together. His plan was well laid-out in his head, but he didn't want to forget any important issues.

Arriving together, Paul and George poured their drinks and joined the group. Jonathan took control and began laying out his plan. "Thank you all for coming." He looked around at each face, their eyes on his, and began to speak. "I think I have spoken with all of you about an investment possibility that will benefit us all."

Paul Fairchild spoke up. "Is this the subject we talked about at the last Assembly?"

"Yes, indeed it is," Jonathan replied. "I have studied the situation across the Alleghenies and into the Ohio Valley very cautiously—very carefully. The Canadian French are beginning to move southward into the Ohio

River Valley; their intention is definitely to link up with their trading bases in New Orleans and St. Louis.[23] Many English settlers have moved into the frontier, where there is an enormous amount of fertile farmland. As British subjects with allegiance to our King, it is our duty to protect the families moving west and drive the French out of North America!"

"I think we all agree the French are becoming aggressive. So tell us, without guns and fighting, how can we stop them?" asked Paul. "The recent treaty between France and England has not solved anything, but only laid the groundwork for another all-out war."

"Is not possession nine-tenths of ownership?" asked Jonathan. "Let me lay my plan before you to see what you think. First we form a company, of which we are all partners. Then we apply for a charter with the Governor's Council asking for at least two hundred thousand acres, preferably on the Ohio River. File the plat, then set the rents and find the leaseholders to move west. We, of course, will be the investors and partners, sharing equally in the profits."

"Have you considered that the Governor's Council may reject our request for the two hundred thousand acres?" asked Paul Fairchild.

"My question is: would we settle for less, if, say, we are allowed only one hundred thousand acres?"commented George Howard.

"We will appeal directly to London if our charter is blocked in Williamsburg," retorted Jonathan. "Building the Empire is the only interest the Crown has in the colonies. They will never refuse expansion in the west. Our only problem would be the inconvenience of the wait to hear from the King. We must be prepared to build roads for the farm workers and fur traders to bring their goods into Virginia. It will be prudent to plan bringing indentured workers from England by offering ship's passage. They will work to clear trees, build roads, and build company trading posts. After their seven-year obligation, they will become leaseholders. It will be our privilege, gentlemen, to raise rents, and each year charge higher base rents to new leaseholders." Johathan sat back in his chair, put his hands behind his head and waited for comments.

"Who will manage the company?" asked one of the potential company owners.

"I am prepared to do that, Sir," replied Jonathan. "Of course, a bookkeeper will be needed to assist me, and there will be expenses to hire a surveyor and several chainmen."

"What amount of investment will we initially need to begin, and will we be considered stockholders, or does that depend on how much we each agree to invest?"

"We are pioneering this approach here in the New World to increase our land ownership. This is not a new idea. If you all will pardon my choice of words, it is much like the feudal system in England. We will all have many questions, so why don't we retire to our homes, think over the idea and agree to meet again next week." Jonathan stood up and dismissed the group.

"Honestly, Daniel, I have dealt with your father for over twenty years. His disposition and moods are unpredictable, at best. When and why did John retain someone else to attend his will?" asked James Power. Mr. Power was a close and trusted friend to Daniel Custis, as well as one of John Custis's attorneys. He knew the family dynamics were volatile because of John's outrageous behavior. Daniel had confessed some time ago that he thought John had precipitated Frances Custis's untimely death. Her obituary read "smallpox," but Daniel believed it was exacerbated by a broken heart crushed by her insufferable husband.

Pacing restlessly across the wooden floor, Daniel lamented, "Evelyn, the woman my father insisted I marry, is dead. Mother, who may have been my greatest advocate, is dead. My father, my greatest adversary, might as well be dead. For me the Custis estate is dead. I've found the girl I want to marry, but I have nothing to offer her, so that situation is dead." Desolation covered Daniel's face. "James, give me advice and guidance. I am unable to cope with this. Martha has offered to move west with me where we can live our own lives. I love her for saying that. She is the first person in my life to turn darkness into daylight. Her eyes penetrate so deeply into me that I know she understands my deepest thoughts. How do I explain this, James?"

"The word is old and Biblical. I believe God would explain it as love,

Daniel." James offered to confer with Colonel Custis as soon as they could both agree on a time. "I will speak to him as lawyer to client. If he chooses to not see me, as his attorney, I will serve him with a legal document of some sort that will require him to report to my office."

The outburst from Colonel Custis, when Daniel told him of his plan to marry John Dandridge's daughter Martha, was heard by the housemaid downstairs, the cook in the outside kitchen and the liverymen outside in the stable. "You will not marry someone far beneath the level of the Parke and Custis families." John's bony forefinger was shaking in Daniel's face. "You used delaying tactics to stall the marriage to Evelyn Byrd and now she is dead!" shouted John. "If you please, Sir, it will be me who will decide when you may marry and who."

"It has taken me nearly forty years to find the woman I care for. As a matter of fact, the best word to describe my feelings for Miss Dandridge is a word you could not even comprehend. It is a word no one in this world has ever heard from your lips, Father. The word is love. I love her!" Daniel was leaning into the Colonel's face eye to eye.

"Poppycock! You do not know what the word means."

"No, you are wrong, Sir. It is you who does not have an acquaintance with the word. Your life is a void! You have lived as an emotionless, unfeeling, and unsympathetic man. You are as cold as the stones in your garden in wintertime. I can see by your frown you cannot understand my words. Granted, I was very young when my mother died, but I remember her as the one person in my life who taught me compassion, understanding, and feeling, and yes, love. That was my mother, your wife. You, Sir, have missed the pleasure and satisfaction two people can give one another. Your role as a husband was abysmal and your role as a father is pitiful!"

"You better stop, Daniel. You have said enough!" John Custis's face was chalk gray and he began to cough. "How can you expect me to turn over my estate to you when all you whine about is love. Love, what is this you are speaking about? You should be talking of expanding wealth for your heirs, learning how to understand the exchange of goods, when to change commodities, how to keep books and interpret cash flow, profit and loss. I sent you to England to learn those skills.You came home with nothing except how to womanize some low-life!"

"Low-life?" Daniel's voice and temper raged. "What about Mrs. Moody? Your transgressions are public knowledge. The family treasures you have given her are publicly displayed in her tavern!"[24]

John was coughing between every sentence, spitting into his handkerchief. "Go tell Jack I need him," John ordered. "Get yourself out and close the door when you leave."

MARCH 20, 1749 A horse's hooves hammered the road up the drive to Chestnut Grove. Martha and Anna Maria were practicing a duet on the spinet when the sound of the horse reached Martha's ears. She was certain it was Daniel. Rushing to the doorway, she saw a robust cloud of dust, hiding the rider's identity. "Nancy, I think it might be Daniel. Come here and take a look." Anna Maria joined Martha on the porch but couldn't make out the rider either. "Oh, Nancy you can't see two feet in front of you. Where is one of the boys?"

"Patcy, it is Daniel. I can make out his hat. It is that odd tricorn he loves to wear for riding. Hello, Daniel Custis," Anna Maria hollered, waving her arm briskly, running down the drive to greet him.

"Hello to you, Martha and Anna Maria," Daniel shouted. Martha, following her sister, ran down the drive to meet him, smiling her biggest smile.

"Give me your hand," Daniel demanded of Martha. "I'll pull you up on the horse to ride with me."

Laughing, Martha reached up and locked her tiny hand into Daniel's. He gently drew her up behind him as she threw her leg over the horse's back and settled herself safely behind him. "We probably could not do that again if we tried," laughed Martha.

"My dearest, I have so much to tell you. I just couldn't wait until Church on Sunday," Daniel said. "Will it be all right if we ride together like this for awhile? I don't want your mother and father to be angry with me for taking a risk by riding double with you."

"My parents will never be angry with you for any reason." Martha's arms reached around Daniel's waist and hugged him tightly. *"Besides, one day we will be together forever, I just know it,"* she thought.

"Oh, my darling, you are such a child. That is why I want you to be only mine forever," Daniel teased.

"I am not a child! You promised not to call me such an unflattering word." Martha began to tickle Daniel.

"Stop that. You are going to cause us to spill."

"I will not stop until you promise never to call me a child again. Promise?" Martha begged. Daniel drew in the reins and brought the horse to a standstill. He jumped to the ground first, then offered his hand to help Martha.

"Let's rest and talk for awhile before I take you back to Chestnut Grove."

"What is it, Daniel? Something has happened, and I need to know what it is right now," Martha said.

"I will get right to it, Martha," Daniel said as he stroked her hair. "This is something I want you to hear from me and not Williamsburg hearsay. In opposition to my request to marry you, my outlandish father has begun to take some of the family silver pieces, walnut furniture, and a roan horse and given them to Mrs. Moody. My mother is turning over in her grave, because some of the pieces are inscribed with the Custis-Parke coat of arms. Rumors have been rife for years that my father has enjoyed the company of Mrs. Moody even though there is a Mr. Moody! He may have financed the purchase of the Moody Ordinary for all I know.[25] Supposedly, that woman begged Father to take back the things, but he told her that he would dispose of his property as he pleased, and if she refused he would throw them into the street for anybody to pick up. She must have taken him at his word, because she is displaying the silver in her tavern and bragging where the things came from and why they are there. My dearest, I do not want this to discourage you or bring you embarrassment. The Dandridge name is a proud and strong name. We both knew there would be bumpy times before this was settled."

"Daniel, I am a very strong girl. I can rise above any adversity we may face. It may be time for me to meet your father so he can see that I have only one head instead of two." Daniel took Martha's hand and gently kissed her palm, then turned it over and kissed the back of her hand with his warm lips.

"Yes, my dearest Patcy. We will get permission from your father today so you can go to Williamsburg as soon as possible."

April 2, 1749 Tomorrow I leav for Williamsburg to stae wit Dorthea and Nat. Assemble begins the week next. D will not go. he neds to start planing Papa will plant to. I am nervus to meet Mr Custis. I hav a new dres to ware. Oh dear lord, pleas help me to be a kind unerstaning person. I'm sur I lov D. He maks me lauf. I lik his mustach.it ticles my hand. Yours sencirly. AMEN! Patcy

Martha gazed into the Pamunkey waters on the trip back; they were so still she could see her confused reflection looking back at her. The activity of the two-week visit to Williamsburg had left her struggling to sort through her mixed feelings. Smiling to herself, she thought thankfully of Nate and Dorthea who had lifted her spirits, Nate with his wit and charm and Dorthea with her kindness and sincere friendship. Trying to set a priority on the events of her visit, Martha realized it was not the profusion of parties, fine dining, and visitations every day. It was not the rooms full of gaiety and laughter, yet noiseless. It was not the dining tables set with fine china, and silver candlesticks with lighted candles presiding over engaging conversation, yet empty. The vacuum? The missing piece? It was Daniel!

Dragging her journal from her satchel, Martha decided she would try to catch up with her writing. The waters were calm enough that she could firmly prop the ink well and keep it from spilling. She had written only once since leaving Chestnut Grove, and the entry was written the night before the disastrous meeting with Colonel John Parke Custis. He was late returning his card accepting the invitation to attend Nate and Dorthea's dinner party. The lone entry in Martha's journal abounded with her excitement and anxiety when she learned of his attendance.

April 12, 1749. Im barging on the Pamunky returning to Chestnut Grove. The parties wer gay. I met many people and dancet amost evere danc at the Assemble ball. Salle Cary mae be maried to Georg Fairfax a English grandee. The gossip was they wer alredy maried or about to be. She did not atten the Asemble Ball. I dancet with young men mi brothers age. All sille and clumse. Dorthea and Nate gave a lavis parte. Lots of guests. I was melenchole for most of the time. Whi do I miss Daniel? He is onle one yer youner than mother but all the youner men seem childish and foolish. My mopishness is becas I know Daniel and I will never be tagether. His father is rude and uncivil. I do not want to see him again. Daniel will be disapointet when I tell him about our meeting. Dear Lord please help me to behav like a lade. Give me the words to explan to mama and papa and Daniel what happen. Amen and the Lord have merce. Patcy

John Custis sent his card accepting Dorthea and Nate's invitation to supper at the last minute. The invitation read in "Honour of Martha Jones Dandridge, visitor from Chestnut Grove, New Kent County." Apprehension grew as the day of the party drew closer and no word of acceptance or refusal had arrived from the Six Chimneys house. "It is incomprehensible for John Custis not to respond," remarked Nate.

"Mr. Custis may feel that I am so unworthy that he destroyed the invitation when it arrived to his home," Martha replied. "Daniel has said many times that his father is unreliable and unreasonable. He easily makes his own rules."

Word arrived two days before the party that Mr. Custis would attend. Martha nervously planned her wardrobe and hair style. Her daydreams about the event began to draw her into deep distress. "What if my words are imprecise or inaccurate? I want to be clever and sharp-witted and not sound like a fool. What is the word Mother always says I should be? Is it reserved or preserved?"

By afternoon, Martha was in a frenzy; her hair was unmanageable; the dress was too big, and the shoes hurt her feet. "Patcy, you have lost weight this past week worrying about your meeting with Mr. Custis," Dorthea said. "Don't tighten your waist. No one will know the difference."

Nate, Dorthea, and Martha stood in the passageway greeting the guests as they arrived. Dorthea was a charming hostess. She had planned an elegant party, with candles glowing on the mantel pieces and tables, piano music playing, and a punch bowl decorated with fresh picked magnolia blossoms. The last carriage to arrive belonged to Colonel Custis. He came into the house with Jack on one arm and a cane in the other hand. Martha curtsied deeply upon her introduction to him. "For Godsake, woman, I am not the King's Governor. Get yourself up and stop acting like a ninny!" Martha maintained her composure, straightened her back, and held out her hand for Mr. Custis to shake in greeting.

Looking straight into his eyes, Martha said, "Mr. Custis, it is my pleasure to make your acquaintance. I have heard so much about you and your garden. I need your expert advice on how you have accomplished such grandeur. I, too, am a gardener. I hope you will have time to allow me a stroll in yours sometime soon." Martha dropped her eyes as she leaned toward his ear, and said. "I do hope you will share some of your secrets with me." She flirtatiously lowered her eyelashes and fluttered them several times.

"You were magnificent, Patcy, darling," Nate whispered in her ear as he escorted her to the dining table. Dorthea and Nate had their table set for sixteen. Martha and John Custis, the only single guests, were placed side-by-side. Dorthea's cousin Paul Fairchild was seated on Martha's right and John was on her left. Sarah Wills Howard was seated on John's left. The conversation was lively and jovial. The wine glasses were never empty as many toasts were made, from those to the King and the Governor's Council to the wish that hogsheads never be empty. John chatted mostly with Sarah, about the new Rector at Bruton Parish Church. Paul Fairchild conversed with Jonathan Milton about frontier movement into the Ohio Valley. Elizabeth Milton sat across the table from Martha. Since they shared so many of the same friends, and with Elizabeth living in Williamsburg, she brought Martha up to date on new babies, marriages, and deaths.

The dessert was being served when the Colonel turned to Martha and asked, "Did I catch your name as being a Dandridge? My hearing is limited with my old age and I wasn't sure I heard it right."

"Yes Sir, it is Dandridge. Martha Jones Dandridge," she articulated carefully.

"Used to be a bunch of Dandridge brothers came from England many years ago. Don't know what happened to them. I think one brother lives out on the Pamunkey someplace," said John, leaning over the chocolate layer cake set before him.

"That would be John Dandridge from Chestnut Grove," answered Martha reluctantly. She realized he didn't know who she was. "Maybe it is just as well. I'll plan to earn his respect on my own," she told herself.

"So you want to see my English garden, do you? It is at its best this time of year. The tulips and hyacinths are exquisite. You seem like such a child to be interested in gardening. Tell me, where do you garden—here in Williamsburg?"

"I work the Pamunkey soil. My mother's grandfather was the Rector at Bruton Parish for many years and his garden was the envy of the townsfolks and visitors. That, of course, was before yours became the finest in the colonies. My mother is a genius getting the sickliest plants to grow. I guess one can say it is a hobby passed down from generation to generation."

The conversation between Martha Dandridge and John Custis was going well in spite of John's calling Martha a child. The English teacups had been placed on the dining table, and many of the guests requested more wine be served with the tea. The toasts became more frequent and boisterous. Protocol called for only men to give the toasts, but as the wine flowed a few ladies took turns rising and giving humorous toasts. Martha sipped slowly from only one glassful, but began to get caught up in the frivolous behavior and good fun. She stood, planning to give a toast to John Custis, the world's master horticulturist whose plants bring the purest of human pleasures. As she rose from her chair, a house servant began to pour hot tea from a silver pot into Mr. Custis's cup. Mr. Custis had his full wine glass to his lips just as Martha's arm struck the teapot, spilling hot tea on his lap and dumping red wine down the front of his ruffled white shirt.

"Mr. Custis, I am very sorry," said Martha as she took her napkin and began wiping his shirt.

Nate was out of his seat, concerned the hot tea was soaking into John's clothes. "Patcy, darling, let me help Mr. Custis. You go and sit down in my chair until we have him cleaned up." Nate quickly asked for towels from the serving kitchen to assist in the cleanup. Mr. Custis insisted he was not hurt.

"The tea was barely lukewarm," Custis assured Nate. "Will someone get Jack for me. He will take me home and you may continue this most enjoyable evening. It is time for the old people to be in bed, anyway." Turning to Martha he said, "And, young lady, you are such a child, it is time for you to be in bed also." The color started in Martha's neck and worked its way to her forehead. This was far more than a blush; it was intense embarrassment.

April 28, 1748
My Dear Mr. Custis,

It is with regret and sadness that I send you this letter. Due to my deep embarrassment of the event taking place in the home of my cousin, Nathaniel Dandridge, recently in Williamsburg, I write to ask your forgiveness for the untimely accident taking place at their dining table. My carelessness caused you pain for which I am truly sorry. I suffer pain from deep despair because of my imprudent decision to propose a toast to your beautiful garden and your reputation as the world's finest horticulturist.

Before leaving Williamsburg, my cousin Dorthea Dandridge and I visited The House of Six Chimneys. Your garden is a masterpiece.

Remorsefully,
Martha Jones Dandridge

Frances and Martha strove to give tone and substance to the letter of apology to John Custis. Martha's papa helped with correct spelling and grammar. Distraction and confusion overcame Martha and increased daily because she had been home for two weeks and had not heard from Daniel. Finally, when a message came explaining his delay in calling, Martha collapsed in tears after reading Daniel's letter.

My darling Martha,

I know you have been back for some time. The care and management of Poplar Grove has kept me quite occupied. I am sure you understand the reason I have not called upon you. I will attend church at St. Peter's on Sunday. I await seeing your dark eyes and beautiful face putting smiles upon mine.

Yours anxiously and lovingly,

Daniel

Frances wrapped her arms around Martha's shoulders, trying to bring comfort. "Mother, he has heard of my conduct and misbehavior in Williamsburg. I wanted to tell him, but by now someone will have visited the Custis plantation and brought the latest gossip, of which I will be the subject. Oh, why did I try to be clever? What ruination have I brought upon myself by trying to draw attention by making a toast to John Custis."

"Patcy, dear, do not be so hard on yourself," Frances consoled. "Daniel knows you are a refined young lady with character and judgment. You are kind and thoughtful and do not make hasty decisions. When you see him again, you will tell him exactly what happened, as you are the only person who experienced the misfortune."

"Thank you for your kindness, Mother. I will try to make Daniel understand, my intentions were for the very best." Martha kissed her mother on her warm cheek.

The red oak log was burning itself into embers. The sunrise was slowly creeping through the shadows of the trees, bringing enough light to extinguish the stars hanging overhead. Thomas Milton turned inside his beaver fur robe to find comfort for his throbbing back and cold feet. His companion, Robbie, still enjoying the pleasure of restful sleep, kept steady rhythm with his snoring. Bold Man, the Iroquois scout, had already left his bed to look for game for breakfast. He had failed to shoot a white-tailed deer he had been tracking for several days. "He'll bring back a possum or a squirrel," Thomas told himself as he rolled over, hoping for more sleep.

Bold Man stepped quietly in the wooded underbrush of the forest where he had set a trap the day before. His trap contained not one possum but two, giving him hope of finding the deer he had spotted several days ago. "*Mr. Thomas wants to make it to Fort Duquesne by no later than tomorrow,*" he thought. Bold Man felt Thomas was growing more and more disturbed about the whereabouts of his twin brother David. No word from him in over a year. With Bold Man interpreting, they had asked at many camps, which acknowledged knowing David but said he hadn't been seen in many months.

The encampment was west of the Allegheny Mountains, on the Ohio River. Thomas had just returned from Montreal where his beaver furs were loaded and put aboard a ship headed for France. Trading with the Indians was still a profitable venture for the Milton brothers. Most of the furs were traded from the Algonquins and the Iroquois in exchange for pots, pans, knives, and guns. This enabled the Indians to carry out their own trading among themselves.

The tensions between the British and the French continued to worry Thomas. Thomas's ingenuity, and ability to negotiate with the Indians, had made the three Milton brothers prosperous. Jonathan speculated early upon arrival in Virginia that exporting goods through the St. Lawrence River on French ships would bring monetary gain more quickly than dealing with the King, the English Parliament, and their Navigation Laws and export duties. Trusting his own judgment, Jonathan set out plans to carry out this scheme. Beaver fur was the first priority for export. Otter and fox fur would be secondary. The aristocratic Europeans, with their appetite for embellishment, would provide an immediate market.

Jonathan arrived first in Williamsburg, hanging out his sign which read "Honest and Experienced Attorney." His education had stopped at age twelve, but he continued to self-educate until he became knowledgeable in English law. Thomas, younger than Jonathan, had no education further than learning the alphabet and the letter sounds. Jonathan arranged passage from London for Thomas when John Custis agreed to hire him as an accomplished and skillful gardener to manage his House of Six Chimney's English garden. Thomas and his identical twin brother David arrived in Williamsburg a year later. The twin brothers first travelled west to set up the fur trading business with the Indians and the French. Since David could speak French, he stayed there to manage the business while Thomas returned to Williamsburg to work for John Custis. Thomas had no skills as a gardener, but he convinced himself it was an easy task and a good way to establish credibility. He wanted to move to Albany, New York, with impeccable credentials as the gardener for the best-known horticulturist in the colonies. Albany would also give entrance into the most respected fur trading market in the colonies.

Respectability was the goal of the Milton brothers. Jonathan arrived in Virginia in 1739. Mr. and Mrs. Franklin Carter, well-established Virginia plantation owners, had arrived several years before. Anne Carter was Jonathan's older sister, and sent letters home, to encourage her younger brother to join her. Business opportunities were aplenty:

"My dear brother, you can receive a charter from the King—and begin your own farm growing tobacco. I know Franklin will help you get started. Please come. I am very lonesome for someone of my own kin to visit. Think about staying."

The Milton family had seven children, four girls and three boys, the last of which were twin boys—Thomas, blessed with strong lungs, and David, weak and underweight. The children's mother had a long and difficult labor, leaving her near death before their birth and dying shortly after their arrival. The boys were raised by their grandmother and sisters Anne and Mary. The oldest sister, Elizabeth, had married and left home to have babies of her own.

The invitation to sail to the colonies appealed to Jonathan. His motivation since childhood had been the desire to live luxuriously. Jonathan and Thomas studied the news from the colonies looking for ideas to earn a livelihood, most of which dealt with tobacco. Farming had no appeal to either brother. They did not decide to ship out until they discovered information about the Hudson's Bay Company and its trading rights to the fur industry. The exclusive rights, given by the English government, were being intruded upon by the French. "What would happen if a troop of men, not knowing a Frenchman from an Englishman, moved in and started their own fur trading business?" Jonathan asked Thomas. They had found their reason to leave England.

Jonathan Milton paced nervously back and forth across the floor of his office. Every time he stepped on one strip of oak flooring behind his desk, a squeak sounded beneath his boot. He walked to the water pitcher, pouring a cup he didn't drink, then to his desk where his restless body wouldn't allow him to sit and concentrate on the distressing news he had received the night before.

The Allegheny Company, the name given to the new trading company, had achieved the objective of the development of two hundred thousand acres. The men had a weekly meeting every Thursday. They usually met at four o'clock in the Raleigh Tavern to deliberate their scheme over food and wine. Their rendezvous usually ended with cards and jesting; frequently leaving several men ending the evening sharing a bed with four or five other overserved men.

Jonathan finally placed himself in his chair and quickly opened the drawer searching for stationery. His quill dipped into the inkwell as he scribbled a letter to all the Allegheny troupe. He offered no salutation, as he hastily jotted the missive. He told the men he was calling a meeting of utmost importance in his office that afternoon. "No excuse will be accepted for non-attendance," he said. Then he scratched his name.

Jonathan opened the back door of his office and called Dil, his manservant. "I need you to take a message to all of these men. Thrusting an envelope into Dil's hand, Jonathan said, "Here is the letter you are to deliver, and don't return until you've made sure all the men have seen it! Do you understand?"

"Yes, Sir, Mr. Milton." Dil's horse was saddled and waiting. "I'll be back in no time."

Jonathan watched as Dil rode off, leaving dust hanging in the air. Jonathan rubbed his eyes as the dust drew into his lungs, causing a dry cough to spill from his open mouth.

Settling back into his chair, Jonathan drew his knife from his pocket and began to pick at the dirt under his fingernails. He reflected back on the night before when his brother Thomas paid a surprise visit.

Jonathan sat staring at his fireplace, watching the burning fire melt into embers. All the candles were extinguished, making the fire's shadows project irregularities across his face. Thomas, unrecognizable with his long hair, full beard and mustache, sat quietly sipping a glass of brandy. "Tell me again what you know about the Ohio Company, Thomas," Jonathan asked.

"All I know is that the Privy Council gave Governor Dinwiddie and the Ohio Company a land grant for two hundred thousand, acres with a promise of three hundred thousand more acres if enough people settle on their land," answered Thomas.

"Give me the names of the members again."

"Governor Dinwiddie and George William Fairfax. I am not sure, but maybe the Washington brothers, Lawrence and Augustine, are members," said Thomas. "There are many members, some living in England."[26]

"How did word get out from the twenty members of the Allegheny Company? We took an oath to keep this secret," Jonathan reiterated.

"Jonathan, you know there are no secrets in Virginia. When you asked the General Councillors for the land grant, word was out."

"I didn't ask the General Council," Jonathan retorted. "I have been accumulating frontier land on my own since I became Anne and Franklin's attorney years ago. I have been waiting until the time was right to start developing my own land. This seemed like a way to get the trees down and a road built using someone else's money. There will be enough money for the men to get a handsome return on their investment from the rents—but the land will still be mine, because I have the deeds."

"Good God! How have you maneuvered the deeds for two hundred thousand acres?" Thomas was incredulous. "Are they true deeds or have they been falsified?"

"My dear brother, you leave the accuracy and veracity of the deeds to me," Jonathan answered. "The news of the Ohio Company will be whispered tomorrow, but by the next day it will be spoken everywhere.

"Papa, Papa, are you still working?" Mary Milton asked her father as she started to enter the parlor. "Oh, you do have company, I'm sorry."

Jonathan rose from his chair and intercepted Mary at the doorway. "Yes, pet, I am talking to a client. What is it you need?"

"I knew I heard voices. I could hear your voice and I thought I heard Uncle Thomas."

"No, dear, this is Mr. Wells and he is someone you have not met. Say hello to him. Mr. Wells, this is my oldest daughter, Mary." The man raised his hand in salutation and nodded.

"Happy to meet you, Mr. Wells. I'm sorry for interrupting, Papa. I must have been dreaming." Mary reached her arms around her father's neck and hugged him tightly.

"Yes, I am sure you were dreaming. Goodnight, my dear." Jonathan turned to examine Thomas to make sure Mary had not recognized her uncle. Only his shadow was visible as he sat near the fire with his back to the doorway. "Children have an uncanny sense of distinguishing unusual sounds that do not belong inside their home. I am glad your back was to the door, Thomas."

"I will saddle up and begin my journey back at daylight," Thomas whispered to Jonathan. "Robbie is waiting for me at King's Point with supplies. We'll head west as soon as we can."

"Before you go, tell me about David. Do you think you will find him somewhere living as a Frenchman with the Chippewas, or do you think he has become a white Indian?" Jonathan queried.

"If I can't find him, maybe I can locate someone who has seen or heard of him and the squaw. I'm sure they have wintered someplace north; and now that it's spring they'll show up. I can't answer the white Indian question. There have been a number of English captives taken by the tribes, and stories abound about the captives never wanting to return to a civilized society again.[27] How any Englishman could live the Indian ways and be happy is something I cannot understand."

The mystery of David's disappearance troubled Jonathan even more because of his relentless reliability these recent years. When Thomas and David arrived in Virginia together, Jonathan was overwhelmed. David, the frail and pallid brother, was not included in the plans of Jonathan and Thomas to move into the fur trading business and deal with the French. The generosity of John Custis in purchasing a first-class ticket for Thomas allowed its exchange for two third-class tickets. Thomas explained David's passage as a necessity because Grandmother Milton had died, Mary and Elizabeth were married and living in Bristol, and Ann lived in Virginia.

David was a scholar like Jonathan. His love of literature and books gave him an enlightened worldliness. David had found a benefactor willing to pay for a French tutor who doubled as a music teacher. David was an accomplished flutist, learned the dance, and developed an impeccable fluency in the French language.

After the Milton twins' arrival in Williamsburg, plans were reconstructed to find a function to fit David's expertise. Jonathan's disappointment at his arrival turned into exultation when he learned David could communicate with the French. "This is the missing piece to making our plan flawless," shouted Jonathan. "We will buy from the Algonquins and ship on French ships, nearly duty free," he told his brothers. "David, you will be the negotiator with the French. Thomas, while you establish yourself as a horticulturist in Williamsburg, David will be working the fur business years before our original plan would have gotten off the ground. We'll be stockpiling bank receipts, somewhat deceptively I might add, until Thomas's reputation is in place so he can enter Albany, New York,[28] as a professional gardener and work his way into the elite establishment. As his reputation grows, he will move into the fur trading business as a well-experienced English fur trader, buying from the Iroquois market and shipping to England as an ethical and moral businessman."

David worked diligently to make the plan work. He was adroit at impersonating a French fur trader, once his hair and beard grew to an unseemly length and he had traded his clothes for the animal skins worn by the Indians.

Jonathan sat motionless, staring at his knife and fingernails and reviewing the news brought by Thomas. "I'm grateful he realized the importance of reporting the formation of the Ohio Company. Damn!" said Jonathan as he hit his fist on the desktop. "Where did the Washington brothers get the idea? This was my idea. Who from the Allegheny Company told of my plan?" Jonathan leaned back into his chair reexamining the names of the twenty investors. The name Nathaniel Dandridge surfaced as the most likely to betray the pact. "I did not trust his presence from the beginning. His cynicism and acrimony irritate me. His investment came from his wife's inheritance, which meant he had to advise her of our plans. Yes, it was Nate! It had to be. He told Dorthea about the purpose of the Allegheny Company and she gossiped her way to our oblivion."

The misery Jonathan Milton felt caused his stomach to clench and somersault. "I introduced my plan first. Between the French who want the valley and the new Ohio Company this may deliver me into ruination. I'll tell the men what I know, then we can plan our strategies."

Jonathan, grim-faced, greeted the partners in the Allegheny Company. He offered rum, brandy and sherry. Small talk filled the room with pleasantries, joshing, and banter during the wait for all the members to arrive. Once all were settled, Jonathan cleared the mucus from his throat and announced, "Gentlemen, I called you here to report of activities in the Ohio Valley that concern our Allegheny Company. We have all known of the conflicts between France and England over the Ohio Valley. As Englishmen, we realize the Treaty of Aix-la-Chapelle solved nothing for either country, and it is only a matter of time before another skirmish began.[29] That time, Sirs, may be sooner than anticipated.[33]

Paul Fairchild, a late arrival, limped across the wooden floor, his cane thumping with each step. "We've known about the French moving down the Ohio River, Jonathan, for a long time. Your pallor tells me there is more urgent news and your voice has a sound of desperation."

"I feel another brandy coming on," said George Howard. "Give it to us, Jon."

"There are several situations we need to discuss," Jonathan replied. "It has come to my attention that the Ohio Valley holdings are being raided by the French Canadians."

"What are the French up to now?" asked one of the men. "I heard they've started building a fort somewhere near the Monongahela River."

"Those sonsabitches! Are you sure? That's way south of Erie Lake."

"Listen, that is why I have asked you here," Jonathan said. "My sources tell me the French are pounding lead plates into the ground along the rivers flowing into the Ohio."[30]

"Lead plates! What for?" interrupted William Byron.

"We've already got settlers on some of our land, don't we?" asked George Howard.

"Can't answer that yet. I have a team of surveyors ready to go," answered Jonathan. "It will be several weeks before they'll be on their way. We need to start clearing as soon as the plats are laid out."

"Tell us more 'bout these lead plates. What can they do for the French?"

"There's words engraved on the plates declaring French ownership of the Ohio River and the tributaries flowing into it," Jonathan answered.

"What the hell!" Will Byron scratched his head and asked, "What language they written in, Algonquin?"

"Speaking of the Algonquins, the rest of what I heard is that the Iroquois are moving toward an uprising of some kind. They are put out that the French are supplying the Algonquins with guns and ammunition while the British have never traded for guns with the Iroquois. The French have been negotiating with White Eagle, the Iroquois chief, to side in with them," said Jonathan.[31]

"Does our treaty with the Iroquois allow them to start something?"

"What treaty? We're talking about a truce, not a treaty, anyway. We'll just stand back and wait for the fighting to start again," one of the investors offered.

Jonathan reached into his pocket and dug out his knife. Picking at his dirty nails nervously, he said "Gentlemen, we have to do two things. One is to find a competent surveyor and get our land platted as soon as possible. The second thing—"

"Wait a minute, Jonathan," Paul Fairchild interrupted. "You said you already had a surveyor."

"Yes, yes, I did say that; but I'm not sure of the competency of the man," Jonathan replied.

With furrowed brow, Will asked "What do you mean?"

"Let me finish laying out my plan, then we can discuss the survey." Jonathan intently continued to pick at his nails. "We need to send someone west to gather information for us so we can know what is happening first hand."

"You mean we need to pay two different people to do the job of one man?" asked Will. "Can't the surveyor find out the situation and report back to us?"

"That all depends. The surveyor has little experience."

"Well, tell us, where did you find him and what's his name?" asked Paul impatiently.

"George William Fairfax recommended him. He is going west to do some surveying for his uncle and it seemed prudent to ask him to do ours at the same time," said Jonathan.

"You mean the Washington boy?" George asked incredulously. "He is only sixteen years old."

"Well, there is another complication that we need to discuss." Jon said looking colorless. "The young Mr. Washington is quite accurate and certainly building a reputation as a qualified surveyor. However, there is an informant that gave me very disturbing news. We are not the only men developing a plan to get patents in the Ohio Valley. I have received word that the Privy Council has given two hundred thousand acres to a group calling themselves the Ohio Company. A promise was made to grant three hundred thousand acres more if enough people settle on their land."

"What are you telling us? We've got company going into the Ohio?" asked Will. "Who are these men?"

"This is where the complication begins," answered Jon. "The men are George William Fairfax, Governor Dinwiddie, and the Washington brothers, Lawrence and Augustine. There are English members also."[32]

"How and when did this happen?" And what challenge will this present to us?"

"This, my friends is why I called this emergency meeting this afternoon," Jon answered dolefully.

Martha busied herself with housekeeping duties. Frances was expecting her seventh child, so Martha took over duties that ordinarily would be her mother's. Some days Martha felt overwhelmed. Mim was gone; Oney was nearly two years old, needing attention; Daniel still worked for approval from his father for them to marry. With John Custis back in Arlington, communication was difficult. Disappointment settled in when Martha did not receive a reply from Mr. Custis regarding her letter of apology. "Dearest, do not anguish over my father's indolence," Daniel said, trying to give comfort. "He is a thoughtless man with hate and rancor in his heart."

"Your father does not have hate in his heart, Daniel," said Martha. "He was never taught how to express his feelings. The only way he can put his feelings into words is to sound abrupt and irritable."

"Thank you for the kind words. I wish he could hear them from you," Daniel replied.

May 5, 1749 I'm waiting for Daniel to return from Williamsburg. He will see his father and i no there will be no progres on his aprovel for us to mary. Mother is feeling tired the babe will arrive in about 3 weeks. Ol Joe thanks me for helping wit Oney I do luv her. My hart is breking becaus of John Custis. My feelings are geting strongr for Daniel. He maks my hart sing. Mama told me that her luv for papa was difernt then her luv for me and the other chilren. She promised to hav a talk about "things I shud no" befor Daniel and i mary. my hart is so full that somtim I think it will stop. Please Lord help me be worthy I no you will direct my course. Patcy

Frances Dandridge always managed to give birth when thunder and lightning hovered overhead.[33] She lay peacefully examining her baby daughter's fingers and toes, counting to make sure there were ten of each. Iris was in attendance when Elizabeth Jones Dandridge gave her first cry, with Martha assisting in the tying of the cord. Frances lay in shallow slumber after thanking the Lord for her seventh healthy baby. "Please God, help me explain to John that Your plan is for Dandridge girls instead of Dandridge boys." Young Frances, age five, and Oney, age two, clambered up on the big bed to roll back the small blanket and take a peek at the tiny head with its eyes tightly closed.

"How did God know to give her black hair like Oney's?" Franny asked her mother.

"When you were born, you had lots of black hair just like Elizabeth," mother answered. "Now give her a gentle kiss on the top of her head and tell her goodby. You may come and tell her goodnight before you go to bed."

"Kiss, too?" Oney asked, as she gave Elizabeth an easy smack on the head.

Frances lay her head back on the pillow and began to think about Mim, who had attended the births of her first six children and had given unconditional love to each one. Frances, with her deep faith, never questioned God's will, but a tear dropped onto the pillow as she wished Mim could behold her own child, who had never felt the loving arms of her own mother.

"Frances, darlin', I heard the news about another beautiful Dandridge daughter," John Dandridge called out as he entered the bedroom and sat down on the side of the bed.

Frances reached up and stroked her husband's cheek. "I hope you are not disappointed, John. Isn't she is beautiful? She is so much like Patcy and Nancy. She is sleeping soundly. I wish you could see her eyes. They are as blue as the sky with sunshine. I believe her eyes will always be blue. Won't you be happy to have one blue-eyed child, my love.

"We would love a child born with blind eyes, because it would be a part of you and a part of me. My greatest fear is for you. I always worry about your discomfort and your ability to sustain the pain."

"Each birth becomes easier, John. Elizabeth started letting me know just three hours before she was ready to enter this world." Frances laughed as she said, "If ever there was to be an eighth Dandridge I would probably have little notice."

John Custis sat in the high-backed brocade chair placed next to an open window, reading the *Virginia Gazette* in his bedroom. Footsteps were taking the stairs two at a time, informing John that Daniel was on the way up to his room. "*I do not want to deal with Daniel today*," John said to himself. "*What brings him to Williamsburg, anyway*?"

"Good day, Father," Daniel warmly said, closing the door behind him. "When did you arrive from Arlington, and I hope your trip was a pleasant one. The weather has been Virginia's best."

"I've moved home for good, Daniel." John squirmed in his chair, trying to find comfort. "I have been in Williamsburg for nearly a fortnight. The nights in Arlington are too cold by the water. Jack has tried to convince me to move back for some time."

"I have need to speak with you about several matters. When will be an appropriate time for us to talk?" Daniel asked.

"Are you in Williamsburg for the Assembly or do you have other business?"

"My business is to talk with you, Father. Since you moved to Arlington, it has been difficult to converse with you." Daniel endeavored to keep himself composed. "I will be available tomorrow morning, if that is a good time for you."

"If you want to talk to me about marriage or my will, I won't be available tomorrow or any other day. James Power assaulted me because I asked someone else to attend my will. And who, may I ask, told James about my will? I told him it was none of his business," John rebutted. "Who are you wanting to marry this year?"

"Father, there is only one woman I have ever wanted to marry and you know who that is."

"I know, I know. It's that inferior Dandridge woman! Please do not mention her name in this house again."

Daniel politely asked, "May I sit down, father? I want to tell you what Martha says about you."

"What would she have to say about me? She has never laid eyes, foot nor finger on me," Colonel Custis said.

"Oh, but she has. She sat next to you at the dining table of Nathaniel and Dorthea Dandridge last April. Do you remember having hot tea and red wine spilled on you?" Daniel reminded his father.

"I remember a beautiful, young, sweet-tempered child sitting next to me at the party," John recalled. "I felt she was out of place at a table with adult married folks. I was flabbergasted when she took wine. I thought my waning eyesight was deceiving me when she began sipping the best of Italy's imported malmsey wine—a shame to waste it on one whose palate is undiscerning."

"Father, that is Martha Jones Dandridge, the woman I want for my wife. We care for each other and want to be married."

"Psst . . . she is just a child." John pulled a pillow out from behind his back and squirmed to make himself more comfortable. "You usually consort with such coarse women, Daniel. But I do remember the young lady at the Dandridge party. I would prefer her to any lady in Williamsburg,[34] considering some of the other wretches you have brought before me. But she is just a child, Daniel!"

"No, Father, she is not, and she becomes upset if called a child. She is a mature, kind, and loving human being and I cannot think of living my life without her."

"Oh, Daniel, you are a whining nincompoop."

"Call me what you will . . . My so-called whining is that of a man who deeply loves a woman. One I have searched for and finally found. It is a pity you have not allowed yourself her acquaintance. As a matter of fact, she likes you very much and says she thinks you really, deep down have feelings for your family. She thinks that anyone who cares for and loves the flowers and trees as you do must have passion and be warm-hearted, Father." Daniel's eyes were watching John carefully for signs of relenting on his position with Martha.

"Let's talk of this tomorrow morning, Daniel. As you can see, I am very uncomfortable, and feel a need to imbibe a finger or two of brandy to ease my throbbing hip and back. Find Jack and have him come to see me right away."

LATE SEPTEMBER 1749 Harvest was complete, and the storing of fruits, vegetables and meats in preparation for winter kept the Dandridge family busy. Martha had not seen or heard from Daniel for nearly a month. The Poplar Grove plantation was as hard-working as the Dandridge farm. The fall months meant picking, clearing out the garden remains, and turning the soil to wait for spring.

Since Elizabeth's birth, Martha had assumed many of her mother's duties. She took pleasure in supervising the women on the plantation. Her natural disposition delighted the slaves, as she often worked beside them, knowing the responsibilities of running her own household someday would give her impetus to master the duties she herself would ask others to do for her. Those discussions gave opportunity for her to learn who was ailing, pregnant, or needed comfort because of disagreements, which were frequent. The best part of the day was after the light supper, when Papa always read passages from the Bible, and either Martha or Anna Maria played the piano while the family sang hymns together.

"Why do I have to take a bath?" Franny moaned. "I don't have dirty fingernails, and my elbows are scrubbed." She pushed up her sleeve to show Martha, who was in charge of the Saturday bath. "Patcy, you are so bossy. Mother doesn't make me take a bath if I'm not dirty."

"Mother is not making the decision today. I am, and you can be first in the tub before the boys," said Martha firmly.

"I will pee pee in the tub," replied Franny defiantly.

"Where do you find such talk?"

"Bartholomew told me he always does pee pee if he is first," Franny held her head proudly as she announced this revelation.

"Your brother is teasing you, Franny. He wouldn't do that."

"Yes, he did. I could smell it."

Mother, overhearing this impish conversation, intervened. "You, young lady, will have your mouth washed with soap as well as your whole body," she said leaning down into Franny's face. "I am ashamed that you choose such distasteful words. Pee pee; you are never to utter those words in this house again."

"Will and Bart go outside to pee pe—"

Mother quickly put her hand over Franny's lips stopping her mid-sentence, "Remember, not in this house."

Martha was trying to hold in her laughter at watching Franny try to manage and shock her mother. "I will speak to the boys about befooling her," Martha said to herself. At that moment she thought she heard hooves on the road beyond the drive. "That sounds like Daniel. But it couldn't be; tomorrow is Sunday." Martha hastened to the door to see who was speeding toward the house. Dust and dry leaves flew in every direction making discovery impossible. Martha pulled on her mobcap, pushing her hair inside. "I look plug ugly," she said, pulling off her pinafore and wiping her hands on the apron, now lying in a heap on the porch. "It is Daniel! What news is so important that it can't wait until tomorrow?" She quickly ran down the drive to meet him.

The day at the White House plantation had started as a routine one. Daniel closed his ledger after spending several hours going over receipts. He felt satisfied that the farm had exceeded last year's proceeds. His father's words rang in his head: "I will give you Poplar Grove, but there are two rules you must follow. One is sound agricultural management, and the second is avoidance of debt." Daniel had achieved both. He removed his glasses, rubbed the bridge of his nose and leaned back in his Windsor chair to relax and enjoy the success of the harvest. Daniel closed his eyes, and was on the threshold of slipping into an afternoon snooze when he thought he heard several horses coming up the long drive. Daniel could see it was his close friend James Power, with his house boy. The falling leaves were scattering in every direction as the hooves pounded them into the air. Daniel hurried to the porch to welcome his visitors, "What brings you to Pamunkey?"

"Hey, Daniel. We have ridden hard today because I have some news that could not wait," James said cheerfully, "Assembly time is weeks away but I was sure you'd be angry with me if I didn't bring it to you before then."

The two men entered Daniel's parlor. "May I offer you a glass of sherry?"

"Do you have brandy, or perhaps rum?" James asked.

"Yes, of course. Will Pennsylvania whiskey do?" Daniel was growing impatient as he tried to read James' face. He seemed in high spirits. Did it mean his father had changed his will, given permission for marriage to Martha? Or could he be happy if Father had passed on. No, James was an old family friend. He would not show such pleasure at the death of John Custis.

The two men settled into their chairs, James with a glass of whiskey and Daniel a glass of sherry. "I have word from your father, Daniel. It is about your request to marry Martha Jones Dandridge."

Daniel rose up from his chair. "Good God, man, has he given his permission?" He turned around and faced James.

"Sit down. The letter I have is one I wrote. I was going to send it by messenger but decided to bring it myself. I couldn't miss your reaction, Daniel, my dear friend."

Ripping the letter open, Daniel knew his father had finally acquiesced.

Dear Sir,

I am empowered by your father to let you know that he heartily and willingly consents to your marriage with Miss Dandridge, that he has so good a character of her, that he had rather you should have her than any lady in Virginia. Nay, if possible, he is as much enamoured with her character as you are with her person, and this is owing chiefly to a prudent speech of her own. Hurry down immediately for fear he should change the strong inclination he has to your marrying directly.

Your most obliged and affectionate servant, J. Power.[35]

Daniel spun around in his chair. "How did you do it? I can't believe he finally gave his consent." He held out his hand and the two friends slapped each other's shoulders while shaking hands. "I must go and tell Martha right away. Do you want to ride with me? I'll need you to verify the veracity of the letter. Hmmm?" Daniel was breathless. "We're nearly five miles from the Dandridge farm. Please come with me."

"No, Daniel, we have had a long ride from Williamsburg. I hope we can expect food from your kitchen and maybe a bottle of your finest Bordeaux, which I wish we could share together in celebration. But I will see you tomorrow morning."

"Of course my cook will take care of you and direct you to one of our beds. I may not return until tomorrow morning. There'll be much to discuss and many plans to make. Thank you for serving me so well, my friend." The men embraced, then Daniel was gone.

"Daniel, my dear, I am overpowered by this news," Martha said through her tears as she clung to Daniel's neck. Mother was now on the porch with the younger girls. "Franny, go and find Bart. Tell him to come here quickly." The squeals and crying continued as Mother wiped tears from Martha's eyes as well as her own. "Bart, go to the fields and find Papa, John, and Will, and tell them to come quickly," Frances ordered. "Hurry!"

Bart ran as fast as his young legs could manage and found the three cleaning the hanging shed. "Papa, you'd better get up to the house quick. Somethin's happened. Mother and the girls are all on the porch bawlin' their eyes out."

"What's happened?" asked Papa. "Where is Franny? Has something happened to her?" John Dandridge searched his mind for the cause of this family crisis. "Bart, is it Elizabeth?"

"No, Pa, she's fine. But Daniel Custis is with them. I don't know why," Bart answered.

John Dandridge took quick steps to the house with the boys following behind. The tears had disappeared, and the chattering that met John's ear gave assurance that the crisis was not life or death.

"Papa. Oh Papa," Martha called to her father. She ran down the steps and greeted him with open arms and caressed his neck. "Daniel just brought us the most wonderful news. His father has given permission for us to marry."

Daniel followed Martha and held out his hand to John. "I received the news today. My close friend, James Power, rode all the way from Williamsburg to tell me."

John Dandridge heartily shook Daniel's hand, giving his approval of his acceptance into their family. Daniel's emotions spilled over as his eyes began to fill with tears. He swallowed hard to keep his feelings from overcoming him. He held Martha close and kissed her head, then her hand. "This is probably my happiest day. I am so full of emotion knowing I've waited for the woman who will make all my days joyous, and full of sunshine no matter the skies."

"Daniel, you will make me a proud father-in-law. I now have the same number of boys as I do girls," he said, as his twinkling eye winked at Frances. The family, all gathered around embracing, kissing, congratulating each other, shedding tears, were still a family, drawn together to share a significant moment of warmth, devotion, affection, and love.

November 9, 1749 Daniel want us to mary in December. I can't imagin a weding in winertim. Dorthea and Nate's weding was a purfect day. The trees wer in bloom and the flowers showing there colors. I have a dilema becaus mother thinks December will be a butiful time for a weding. She encourages me to remember the pin wreaths in the windows and on the doors. The pin ropes swaging on the staircas. The baybery candls berning. Daniel says a Christmastide weding will be buteous and memorabl. Mother says are decorated hous will be a resplendent backdrop to the parties befor, after an during the weding. What does Martha say? A reluntant yes. Keep me on course, dear Lord Let me folow your plan Amen Patcy

Jack carefully carried the breakfast tray up the stairs. He had spent a restless night because Mr. Custis had three coughing spells. Each time, he went downstairs, boiled water, and made a hot poultice to put on the old man's chest. The last number Jack remembered the clock chiming was four, but Mr. Custis was awake again at his usual six o'clock, coughing.

Colonel Custis spent most days either in bed or sitting up in his library. He had not left his bedchamber for three weeks, and had not left the House of Six Chimneys for several months. John Custis talked little these days, his voice diminished to a whisper, which didn't prevent him from complaining vociferously about his painful hip.

Jack opened the door and greeted Mr. Custis. "Are you feeling like a little warm tea, and maybe a boiled egg this morning?" Jack sat the tray on the table and worked to prop the pillows. Almost immediately he realized that Mr. Custis was not responding, not even moving. Cautiously, he shook his lean arm, waiting for a nod or a gesture. He carefully shook his arm again, with no reaction, and clearly understood John Parke Custis was dead. Jack sat down in the blue brocade high-back chair by the window. He leaned over and put his head in his hands, hypnotized by the knots in the dark wooden floor. Fully aware of the magnitude of the Custis estate and the rumor of himself as beneficiary to it, Jack had cause to question his future. He looked across the room and saw his reflection in the cheval glass. "*Alice! I need to find my mother and tell her about the Colonel.*" Jack stood up and walked to the mirror. He turned to observe himself front and back, pulling on the bottom of his leather vest, his head held high, tilting back and forth and from side to side. His image resembled a young man preening, full of confidence and hope that the man who had consumed his existence had just given him his freedom.

Jack had lived a solitary life, with few friends, no relatives, only John Custis and Alice. Alice had given birth to two other children, a boy and a girl much older than Jack but they had been sold separately when ten and twelve, leaving a grieving Alice who neither saw nor heard from either one again. "I must get word to Mister Daniel, somehow," Jack said to himself. "I want to go, but I'll need either Billy or Lee to take me, unless there is a barge heading to the Pamunkey." He rose from the chair and slowly walked down the stairs to inform the household, and to prepare for the journey to Poplar Grove.

Jack had never travelled alone. Mr. Custis had always been there to direct the drivers of his carriages or supervise the ferry captains when travelling by water. Jack, sitting inside the carriage all by himself, felt a freedom he had never experienced. He reviewed the instructions he had left for the house servants to carry out while he went to see Daniel. The first was to bring the undertaker to ready Mr. Custis for burial. The second was to clean the bedchamber upstairs and make sure fresh linen was on each bed in the house. Third was to make sure a messenger was sent to inform Jonathan Milton and James Powers about the death. Finally, the cook needed to prepare ample food stuffs for extra guests.

The twenty-five miles to Poplar Grove put Jack's arrival time well into the night. Daniel took the news indifferently. Jack was not comfortable bringing such news, but Daniel's reaction perplexed him. "Please, Jack, take a bed here for the night before you return to Williamsburg. You have spent long hours on the road to bring me this news and I want you to understand how I appreciate it." Daniel sounded somewhat patronizing.

"Mister Daniel, I wouldn't be comfortable sleeping in one of your beds. I'll sleep outside with Billy and Lee."

"I will not hear of you doing that. Dolly will fix something hot for all of you to eat before retiring. Then she can show you where to sleep," Daniel said. "I'll talk to you in the morning before you leave."

Sleep evaded Daniel. He was not surprised to hear of his father's death. His mind was twisting like a spinning top. It seemed inevitable that the marriage would have to be postponed. He climbed out of bed and began pacing from window to door, his thoughts running together. "*The wedding plans are well underway but a postponement would mean Martha will have her wish for a spring wedding, if six months can be considered proper mourning time. But what about the will? I can't believe he would not leave the Pamunkey plantation to me. And Jack? What will happen to him? I will leave for Williamsburg day after tomorrow, after I go to Chestnut Grove to pass on this dreadful news. The first person I must see in Williamsburg is Jonathan Milton!*"

Novemer 15, 1749 Dere God, pleas watch over my lov. He needs your derection and wisdom Giv me instrution and guidance to bring comfort to him. the weding will be postpon until spring Mother is sad She had her hart set on Christmas Decorasons. You hav granted my prayor for a spring weding but I weep that Daniel will hav no Family ther. and the reason for postponin. I will obey your plan knowing your plan is worthy of us all. In Your Name dere Lord, amen November 14, 1749 is the dae John Parke Custis died. God rest his soul. Mae he find his Famly in Heven and find peac and hapines wit the angles.

I wory abot Jack. He is vere upset over the death of Mr Custis. He has no one in his famly enymor My wish is to hav him stay wit us after the mariage. We do not no Mr. Custis will an tesament or what his wishs for Jack ar. giv us the powur an strenth to cary the berdon of the daes ahed. I am yer fathful servant and gloreus folower. Patcy

The winter winds were still, the sun hung low in the cloudless sky. Martha filled her days with spinning, weaving and stitching. She took pains to help care for Elizabeth, who Papa had promptly nicknamed Betty. Frequently she tried to read to Franny and Oney from the Bible, but Franny had difficulty sitting for more than a few minutes. "I think I'll go out and find Papa and John," she announced to Martha. "Oney can come too. Her Papa's working the field and she needs to tell him something."

"Not today, Franny. Papa said you and Oney could not come out today because they are readying the dirt for a rest before spring planting," Martha replied, preparing herself for an argument. "Old Joe is too busy plowing and fertilizing. Papa does not want you girls out in the fields when they fertilize."

"It's just cow poo. I like to watch them with their handkerchiefs tied on their noses. Papa never puts his on, but the rest look funny," Franny laughed.

"Poo, poo," Oney repeated. "Can Oney see poo, too?"

"Frances Dandridge, you are teaching Oney words that she does not understand! Mother will wash your mouth out with soap if I tell her what you said." Martha's exasperation was beginning to become visible. Diplomacy was needed with every task that Franny was asked to do, and preparedness was needed to answer her inevitable "Why do I have to do that?" questions. Martha decided to speak to Mother about Franny being old enough to be given chores. She was always full of questions, observations, and opinions, all articulated in a most mature manner for a child of five years.

SPRING 1750 Martha's days, as full as they were, dragged by slowly. Daniel spent most of his time in Williamsburg after the death of his father. She anxiously awaited word from him each day, and imagined she heard his horse several times each week. She had not seen Daniel since Christmastime. It was now late spring and once again planting season. Martha was sure Daniel would return to the White House to oversee his plantation while the seeds were laid. Many visitors came to Chestnut Grove, bringing news from the Capitol, but none seemed to know when Daniel planned his return to the Pamunkey.

Martha found solace in her journal writing. The journal enabled her to pour out her deepest passion when describing her feelings for Daniel, but distress overshadowed her concern about the marriage plans. Mother busily began plans for a sizable wedding. The family discussed a Williamsburg wedding, but decided the marriage would be held in St. Peter's on the Pamunkey where Frances and John Dandridge had attended services before the children were born. The Dandridges owned a pew in the fifty-year-old church, and the parish Rector had come to the church before Martha's birth.

Wedding arrangements came to a standstill when word came about the death of John Custis. Just when Martha had changed her mind about a December ceremony, the plans abruptly stopped. Mrs. Kidwell, a widowed dressmaker living close by, had moved into the Dandridge home to help plan Martha's wedding dress and new dresses for Frances and each of the girls. Mrs. Kidwell helped pick patterns and choose the brocades and satins for the dresses. After the postponement, she stayed on with the family to complete the sewing of each gown, and then went to work on new shirts for the men. Mrs. Kidwell became a companion to Martha, sharing her own experiences as a new bride who also married a man she truly loved. Martha loved to listen to her stories about their meeting, falling in love, the wedding, and the telling of their first night together. Frances had promised to tell Martha about the wedding night, but the conversation had yet to happen. Several of Martha's friends had already married and told her tales—from pain and agony to bliss and pleasure. She waited to learn from someone with maturity and wisdom.

March 31, 1750 Daniel returned todae. He looked tired but he still gave me the smile showin his sno whit teeth. I am sure his mouth with the scar over his lip is why I fell in lov wit him. I luv to watch his lips move as he talks. (Please God forgive me for talkin so much about my feeling for Daniel) We have much to talk about. Tomorrow we will hav the date. Mrs Kedwill has almos finisht my dres. Nance, Frane and mother has ther dress finished. we think Frane broke her arm tadae. She fall of the porch chasin Oney an hit her lbow. she cryd Hard. I don no bout the wil an tesament yet. daniel to tired to talk. Tomorow Thank you O God of my lif. Thank you for bringin Daniel bac to me. I do lov him. God bles my famly and por litle Frances Thy wil be don o God. AMEN

Patcy

"Martha, darling, let's go for a ride this morning," Daniel begged. "The wildflowers and blossoming trees will inspire us both, especially you, who love them all so much."

"I'll have Iris pack us a lunch so we can ride out to Double Tree Park and eat by the river," Martha said. "We can go by Uncle William's house and say hello to the Dandridge cousins if you want."

The two rode slowly at first, with little conversation. Daniel seemed preoccupied with his own thoughts. "Daniel, a penny for your thoughts. You seem so far away. Please can you tell me what it is, or is it something so painful you don't feel free to discuss it?"

Kicking his horse's ribs, Daniel rode away like a rushing mighty wind. Martha, squeezed both legs against her horse's sides and followed in his wake. Martha's horsemanship had improved as she transformed from child to woman. Because of her small proportions, Martha straddled her mount, giving her more control over the horse's movements. Nate had taught Martha to lean forward in her saddle when galloping her horse. She seldom ran Fatima at a gallop, but today she moved parallel with Daniel, all the while talking to her loyal horse, giving courage and "Atta girl" along the way. "Daniel, let's stop and let the horses cool!"

Daniel pulled himself backward in his saddle, increased the pressure on his reins, and eased his horse to a stop.

Martha, trying to find humor, said, "Oh, Fatima is getting to be an old lady, but she can still keep up with the best of them," her lips forcing a smile.

"Let's find a place to have our lunch," Daniel said as he helped Martha climb down from Fatima. He leaned over and kissed the top of her head and gave her a generous smile. "I am so proud and pleased you have accepted me to be your husband. You honor me and I adore you."

Martha went to tip-toes to reach Daniel's cheek. She kissed him warmly. "My dearest Daniel, you have given me your affection and devotion. What more could I ever expect to complete my being? Every day I thank the Father for bringing you into my life." Martha, her deep, brown eyes beaming, gave him another kiss on his soft cheek.

The two ate their lunch silently, enjoying the peace of the hilltop, soft clouds, and a warm breeze that rustled the buds on the trees. At last, Daniel spoke. "I have suffered with anxiety these past months. My father, I am sorry to say, left his estate in a state of upheaval. I regret my long absence, my dearest, but untangling his last will took patience and forbearance. As you know, James Power has been my father's attorney for many years. Some time ago, I learned that James had not drawn up his will. James has handled all his legal work, but not his last will and testament."

Daniel shifted about restlessly as he spoke. "John Custis filed three different wills, as it turned out, with a lawyer I consider unscrupulous. However, the man says his associate attended the will. The first will was made in affront at my refusal to marry Evelyn Byrd. There seemed to be a change of heart then, because will number two left his full and complete estate to me. I cannot remember a time when he and I had a bond of compatibility. His reasoning is lost with him. Will number three, again, was filed with the rakish Jonathan Milton. This time Jack regained full control."

"Your father's generosity is overwhelming," said Martha, aghast. "Especially, endowing a black house servant."

"Yes, yes. I will explain his reasoning later. Of course, you knew about the will not being in my favor. I told you when we first discussed marriage, and you so graciously agreed to move west away from the only life you have known here on the Pamunkey. I enlisted the help of my dear friend James to intervene on the strength of an enduring friendship to implore my father to give his approval to our marriage."

"Let me interrupt for a moment, please, dear." Martha placed her forefinger over Daniel's lips. "Your father opposed our marriage because he was an accomplished member of the Governor's Council, making your family a part of the colonial aristocracy. He owned thousands of acres of land and several hundred slaves to farm his plantations. He also was a horticulturist with a reputation known here as well as in England. My family own only five hundred acres of farm land and a handful of slaves. My father is a Deputy Clerk for New Kent County and a vestryman at St. Peters, hardly a match for the litany of Custis accomplishments."

"Martha, darling, your family has so much more than mine. There is more to a family than inheritance, good agricultural management, and debt avoidance. Your family is respectable, with love between your mother and father, your brothers and sisters. I know that our marriage, based on love, will bring us children who will pass on our love to their own children, our grandchildren. I have waited a long time to find you. Nothing can keep us apart."

Daniel looked towards the sky, then lowered his eyes as he grappled for words. "I have something I must tell you now. My father changed his will again on fourteen November, 1749. As you know, he died on twenty-two November, just eight days later.[36] It is in our favor; his estate will come to me."

"Oh Daniel, I know how important this is to you, and all the anguish you have endured." Martha beginning to cry, said, "I feel blessed to have spent one day with him, even though it was not my best day."

"There is a contingency to his will, Martha. My father had an illegitimate son. His legacy leaves him property; a house to be built on Custis land, as well as furniture, a riding horse, and a working horse. The irony of these circumstances is that Father also left him five slaves. He is to be under my watch until death."[37]

"Daniel, that is wonderful news! But I have prayed with worry for you, too. All your family, except for cousins, are gone."

"Martha, listen to me very carefully. There is more in his will that we will discuss later. But you must realize that my father's houseboy Jack is my half-brother. My unscrupulous father gave him his mother, Alice. She is one of the five slaves. She has become her own son's slave!"

May 15, 1750 Tomorrow is our weding dae. Daniel and I hav waited long time for this dae. Thank you O Heavenly Father for working out our problems in Your Devine ways. Rev Chichley Gordon Thacker wil mary us bcause Rev Mossom is gon sumwhere.[38] *He was here for Decmber ceremone but bcause of Mr Custis died we pospon. I have been forunat to have my famile for support. My mother herself looks like a bride. My father himself is happier then eny dae I can remember. Nancy, Frany have dresses that make them look happe. Frany will have her broke arm in a sling. She still crys somtimes. My brothers promised to take baths tonite. There shirts are bran new. Mrs. Kedwill sewed them. Our kitchen has been hustle bustle for weeks making food. We will go to the White House after the wedding. Nate says we will dance all night and into the next day in celebration of joining the Dandridges with the Custis' family. Dorthea will have a new baby in August but she will be ther. Dere Father Above please look down upon us tomorrow. Help my weding day be as happe as Nate's and Dorthea's. I will still be happy if all things don't go as planed. Your Plan is my plan. AMEN. Daniel and I will liv in the White House on the Pamunkey. We will be in attendance at the House With Six Chimneys in Williamsburg sometimes. Mostly Assembly times. My stomach is dancing the quadrille tonite. If I had one wish, it would be to have Mim here to fix my hair and powder my face. O Father i envy that she is with you now. If only I could borrow her just for tomorrow. Her little girl is doin good. When i go to bed tomorrow I will have Daniel by my side. He will give me his name and his luv. That is more than I could possibly ever want. When mama and I had our weding talk she quoted Matthew 19:6 "Wherefore they are no more twain, but one flesh. What therefore God hath joined together, let no man put asunder." O Father of us all, I humbly give thanks for all my blessings and No you will watch over Daniel and me. Tonite we are two but tomorrw we will be one. One Forever. Amen Patcy*

GEORGE WASHINGTON

1731-1752

Mary Ball gripped the reins tightly as her dappled gray horse jumped gracefully over the fallen log. Her hair, fluttering in the wake of the moving animal, had fallen loose when her protective hat blew from her head. Her strongly set jaw tightened as she urged the horse to make the second jump, over a four-foot-wide ravine. "Good boy," she said, briskly patting his mane. Mary, at eighteen years, was learned in the skills of reading, writing, sewing, dancing, and embroidery, but riding was her favorite pastime. Her mother and step-father felt she was ready for marriage, but a suitable husband had yet to come calling.

Mary's father had died when she was three years old, and her mother, with miserable luck, married three more times before leaving the world at age thirty-five. Her estate provided Mary a dowry of furniture, livestock, land, a small amount of cash, and a good horse. She preferred the company of horses over spending time feigning female charm for some unsuspecting, eligible man.

Mary was considered a loner by many of her acquaintances. By the time she reached age twenty-five she was considered a strong-willed spinster, when she met a widower named Augustine Washington.

Both Mary and Gus were of English heritage and loyal to the English Crown. Their similarities stopped there, but after a brief courtship they married in the spring of 1731.[1] Gus needed a mother for his children, Lawrence, Augustine, and Jane, so, reluctantly, Mary agreed to begin married life with a ready-made family. She moved into the Washington home on Pope Creek in Virginia, a house that was small and overcrowded even before she moved in her inherited furniture to sit alongside Gus's. She also brought several slaves to the Pope Creek home.[2]

Three months after her marriage to Gus, Mary realized she was receiving messages from her body that signalled a probable pregnancy. That meant curtailing the daily horseback ride. Three months into her pregnancy, her belly protruded such that Gus suggested there possibly could be more than one baby inside. "Absolutely not!" Mary retorted. "This baby will be a strong, sturdy, and fearless son! And I will make sure he rises to some sort of importance." Mary, eyes flashing under her heavy, dark brows, spoke with such conviction there were few who doubted her determination. No one challenged her forthright manner, her straight-from-the-shoulder approach that was brusque and had little tact.

Gus provided reasonably well for his family. His two older sons, Lawrence and Austin, had tutors in their early academic years, then completed their education at the Appleby School in England. Gus was away from home for long periods trying to increase his land holdings and searching for iron ore. He farmed several thousand acres, producing tobacco and eatables.

Mary Washington and Gus's young daughter Jane maintained the Pope Creek home, welcoming frequent guests while Gus was away. One hot Sunday afternoon in the middle of August, 1731, the Fuller family came home with Mary from church to eat dinner. They were sharing stories about family experiences over fried chicken and mashed sweet potatoes, ignoring an unexpected thunderstorm blowing in. The frivolity was high-pitched, laughter permeating the dining room, when a bolt of lightning struck the chimney. "Oh, that one was drawing close," chortled Mary, looking over to her side as Nancy, the Fuller's young daughter, picked up her knife to cut a piece of meat. Instantly, Nancy dropped the knife and fell forward into her plate. Mary screamed and reached for Nancy, grabbing her dangling arm. Mrs. Fuller leaped from her chair and took Nancy's free arm and both women pounded on her back while her head flopped back and forth.

Mrs. Fuller shrieked to her husband, "Henry, do something! I don't think she is breathing. She may have choked on a piece of chicken or has a bone lodged in her throat."

Mr. Fuller joined the women and tried locking his arms around Nancy's torso to stimulate her breathing. Both parents hovered over their daughter, begging for a response.

"Mrs. Fuller, Mr. Fuller. I do believe your child is dead. The lightning has stricken her dead. She is with her Maker," Mary announced.[3] Certain that Nancy's fate had been determined, Mary began to fret about the health of her unborn child. Praying silently, she began to rub her abdomen. "Please don't let anything happen to this strong child I have in my belly. That lightning hit the chimney, and then the knife and killed the girl, and that was that!"

The remaining months of her pregnancy seemed endless. When several more thunderstorms bashed the Washington home in the late summer, Mary placed herself in the passageway, waiting until they passed.

Gus Washington was on a trip to the western frontier when Mary began her labor. Sending one of her service people to fetch a midwife, Mary was alone when her son drew his first breath and broke into a healthy cry. The date was February 22, 1732.[4] After she counted his fingers and toes, Mary lay back smugly smiling to herself. She had her strong, hulking, and Herculean son, and knew this was an accomplishment she alone had achieved!

The first seven years of Mary and Gus's marriage brought four more children into the Washington household: Elizabeth, born sixteen months after George, then three brothers—Samuel, born in 1734, John Augustine, born in 1736, and Charles, born in 1738. Mary and Gus discussed the cramped quarters of the Pope Creek home and decided a larger home was needed for their growing family. Gus acquired a twenty-five hundred–acre farm on Little Hunting Creek that emptied into the Potomac River. The home was inadequate for the Washington family, so Gus made plans to build a new dwelling on a bluff overlooking the Potomac. Construction began on the one and a half story brick farmhouse. Plans called for a long porch on the back side facing the river. Tall trees shielded the house from the river, but offered cool breezes blowing in from the water. A dock was needed to ship tobacco and other goods, but it would wait until after the move was completed.

Epsewasson, the new home on the Potomac, was forty miles down river from Pope Creek. Gus carefully planned the move to be, by water rather than overland. Large rafts were built to ferry the household goods, farming equipment and animals, service people, and the Washington family.[5] However, Mary decided that her young family would not make the trip by water. Early one morning several weeks before the move, Mary announced to Gus, "I have decided the children will not make the trip on the Potomac."

"If the good Lord pleases, when did you make that decision and why?" Gus asked with astonishment.

"I have studied this situation for some time and decided it is for my peace of mind and the health and safety of the children." Mary looked at Gus with her determined eyes and her stubborn and unyielding mouth and chin.

"God forbid . . . I know that I can't change your mulish mind when you give an ultimatum! You and the children will go by land, which, by the way, will take two long days . . . all except George. He will go with me on one of the rafts."

Mary, looking at Gus with contempt, unlocked her lips to utter, "Oh no he won't—"

"Yes, this is my decision and it is final!" Gus interrupted. "George needs to learn the waters, tides, and ways to take fish from the river. He'll be under my supervision. This conversation is over, Madam." Gus pulled his hat from the hook, slapped it on his head, and slammed out the door. Mary was left standing wordless, floored by Gus's proclamation.

Lawrence, George's older half-brother, arrived at Epsewasson from England shortly after the move. He brought with him manners, fashions, idealism, and a system of values, all English. Lawrence soon became George's beau ideal, the archetype exemplifying all the characteristics needed to be an English gentleman. His impressionable young mind began its tutelage in imitating the life of an aristocrat.[6]

Gus, a restless man, worked to increase his land holdings, to enable him to attain his ambition of rising in the social and political institutions of a growing Virginia. Another move by the Washington family took place when Gus purchased a home on the Rappahannock River across from Fredricksburg. The bulk of George's growing-up years were spent in this, his third home. The family lived modestly; Gus never realizing his goal of serving in the House of Burgesses, on the King's Council, or any appointments that came from England. At best, the Washingtons were considered minor Virginia gentry.[7]

"Go tell George to hurry up or else he'll have to swim across to school today," Mary shouted to Betty. "Mr. Williams will be very angry if George misses one more day."

"Mama, when can I go to school with George? The boys always get to do the bestest and most funnest things. I hate being a girl!" Betty sulked.

"I will teach you to read and write when the time comes," Mary answered. "You'll have much to learn before you have a family of your own, but you will do your learning at home. Girls do not go to school!"

The log schoolhouse was located in Fredricksburg, across the Rappahannock. A boat ferried George every morning, leaving promptly at eight o'clock. The schoolmaster rang the bell precisely at eight fifty-five, announcing to the students that they must be in their seats at nine o'clock sharp. Mr. Williams locked the door so any tardy student had the duty to chop wood for the fire until the morning recess began. George did not mind chopping wood if he was late. He only dreaded the work because it was treated as punishment, which brought teasing from the other boys. The weather usually cooperated, but some days the winds caused the ferry to list, cant, or heel over. Wintertime weather was usually unpredictable. Mary decreed whether school was in or out for George. She had a sturdy pole driven into the ground close to the river, to which she tied a cloth, creating a flag. She then watched the wind direction before making her decision. When George began studying reading, writing, and mathematics, Lawrence offered encouragement to him to study hard in preparation for matriculation into Appleby in England.

Gus was spending long periods of time at the frontier surveying lands, some for himself, most for others. George looked forward to the homecomings because his father always included him in his daily chores. The skills taught him by Gus served George throughout his life. His excellence as a horseman began with his father's teaching. He watched his father labor harder than the slaves in the fields. No man worked harder loading and unloading goods or toiling in his grist mill. George watched and listened to his father handle his slaves, always giving precise orders with great clarity. The slaves, always obedient, carried out his directives easily. Gus's presentation as a model for his son had began none too soon because when George was eleven years of age, his father died.

George was visiting his cousins over an Easter holiday when a message arrived from his mother to come home immediately; his father was very sick. Gus took occasional trips to England, and while sailing on a recent return trip, he had become ill before his arrival home.[8]

"Mother, I am here to help with Father," shouted George as he entered the house.

Mary ran to greet her oldest son, giving him a surprising embrace. "We have him in the passageway. Come quickly and tell him you are home."

"Mother, before I go in to see him, tell me how he is. Are Lawrence and Austin here?"

Often inconsistent, she answered, "He is sleeping now, but do be careful not to wake him. And no, they have not arrived." Mary spoke in a halting whisper.

George tiptoed into the passageway where his father lay propped with several pillows, breathing rapidly. George had never seen a dying person before, but he knew the colorless pallor meant he was very sick and probably would not recover.

"Sit down beside your father and hold his hand while I sponge his face." Mary's voice became nearly inaudible as she said, "I don't think he will live through the night."

Crying softly, George wiped his nose on his shirt sleeve, his tears raining on Gus's arm and hand. His sister Betty patted George on his back, trying to offer comfort, his tears causing hers to begin falling again. "Mother seems angry because Father is sick. I am so glad you are home. Maybe Father will wake up when he hears your voice."

"He needs to sleep, Betty," George said trying to offer comfort to his young sister. George tried to envision the Washington family without their father. "I'm eleven now and the oldest son at home. Charles is five, John is seven, Samuel is eight and a half and Betty, you are nearly ten. I wish Lawrence and Austin were here." His tears were out of control, falling on Gus's nightshirt and quilt.

"George, stop that blubbering, now!" Mary spoke harshly. "You'll be the man of the house now, and men do not cry. Do you understand? And stop wiping your nose on your shirt. That is your best one and you'll have to wear it to your father's gravesite."

"Yes, Mother. I'll take Father's place if it is to be." George caressed his father's hand while he tapped his own chest with his other hand, trying to gain control of his emotions. "*Mother is probably right. He will not be with us tomorrow.*" George laid his head on his father's chest and endeavored to curtail his tears. His broken heart seemed to press upon his breastbone, causing his own breathing to become uneven and out of control.[9]

Gus was buried in the family plot, which then held four generations of Washingtons; himself and his father and grandfather alongside Mary and Gus's youngest child Mildred, who had died from the fever at sixteen months. Three weeks after Gus's death, his will was filed for probate. Augustine Washington had owned several thousand acres in seven tracts.

His first born son Lawrence was left Epsewasson on the Potomac where he already resided. Austin received the Pope Creek home, Mary and Gus's first home. George was to receive ownership of his present home, Ferry Farm, on the Rappahannock, when he turned twenty-one years of age. Three city lots in Fredricksburg also were left to George. Mary was left one-fifth of Gus's personal property, which included the harvests of five years and a home to be built on a piece of George's property after he became of age and took control of the Rappahannock home.[10]

Mary took complete charge of running Ferry Farm. She became an intense disciplinarian to the slaves and her children. However, she did not follow through on her directives, which caused the subordinates confusion about the do's and the don'ts. Her indecisiveness was reflected by the condition of the farm. It soon started to fall into decay.

George felt adrift without his father, knowing his future held few possibilities. The desire to go to England to complete his schooling, to become cultured and well-educated like Lawrence and Austin, could not be fulfilled without financial help from his father. The enigma of Mary's domineering manner confused George at first, until he realized that she had always been overbearing and willful. George found relief in riding alone or visiting his half-brother Lawrence, and spending weeks with his cousins. Mary managed to scrimp enough funds to keep a tutor polishing George's mathematical skills, grammar, reading, writing, and history. George found a manual on the art of surveying which had belonged to his grandfather and carefully studied the fine points, thinking he might need them in an uncertain future.

When George reached age fourteen, he and Lawrence developed a plan for George to join the British Royal Navy. "I have spoken to several friends who are willing to use their influence so you can become a midshipman in the British Navy," Lawrence told George. "A career in the Navy will enable you to see parts of the world that otherwise would not be open to you because of Father's death. An Appleby education will not be possible either. I'm sure you'll be assured of rising in rank at a rapid pace if you choose to follow the military discipline."[11]

George remembered Lawrence dressed in his dazzling, brightly colored Royal Navy uniform with his shiny silver sword over his shoulder. George was eight years old when Lawrence was given a commission as a captain, leaving an unforgettable image in George's mind. Then Lawrence was sent on a expedition to roust the Spanish settlements in Cartagena. His commanding officer was Admiral Edward Vernon, a war hero in earlier sea battles in the Caribbean. Lawrence was away for two years, battling in a war that the British could not win. The obstacles included starvation, dysentery, yellow fever, malaria and disagreements between the British sailors and the American recruits. Lawrence came home a hero, with a written document from Admiral Vernon to commend his bravery. He still wore the dashing uniform on his return, but he also brought home a body that never fully recovered its health and vitality.[12]

George listened carefully to Lawrence's idea about joining the Royal Navy. "As her oldest son, Mother will refuse to allow me to leave. She thinks I should stay home and take care of her," George told Lawrence. "She'll want to send a letter to her brother in London to ask his opinion, and that will take at least six months."

"Your mother won't be pleased if she thinks I've manipulated you into signing on."

"Yes, you are correct. She questions me every time I come to visit you. She knows how much I like to be here with you. Besides, she has become overly domineering and obstinate since Father's death."

Mary Ball Washington did not give her approval or her disapproval to her son. She sent a letter to her brother, just as George had predicted. As a British ship lay waiting in the harbor for George to come aboard, Mary insisted on delaying her decision until she had a response from her brother.[13]

With few prospects, George at age fourteen, pondered his future. With only a small inheritance, his mother failing to give him permission to be part of the British Royal Navy, and no way to go to Appleby School in England, he turned to his half-brothers Lawrence and Austin for solace and consultation. Lawrence arranged for George to spend more time at Mount Vernon. A tutor was enlisted to continue George's studies and it soon became apparent he had remarkable skills as a mathematician.[14]

Lawrence had married Anne Fairfax, the daughter of one of the most prominent and wealthiest families in Virginia, who had brought into the marriage a four thousand acre dowry which Lawrence controlled.

Anne planned and oversaw the rebuilding and refurnishing of Epsewasson, now renamed Mount Vernon after Lawrence's commanding officer in the British Royal Navy. The story and a half brick house became a symmetrical two-story home, a fashionable Georgian building that had style and grandeur. Young George was overwhelmed with the luxurious home and visited frequently. The addition to the house allowed for separate rooms where parlor games and music and dancing could go on simultaneously. Anne's connections also drew Lawrence into circles of the socially conscious Virginia aristocrats. He soon was elected to the House of Burgesses and was appointed Adjutant General of the Virginia Militia by the Virginia governor.[15]

The relationship between George and his mother deteriorated rapidly after her refusal to let him join the navy. He spent more and more time with Anne and Lawrence, drawing himself into their highly social lifestyle. George soon felt the pleasure of lively conversation, games, and dancing, mostly as a silent observer, but a conscientious student of aristocratic behaviors.

Mary Ball Washington gave George permission to take music lessons so he could become an accomplished dancer. There was, of course, a stipulation—the money for the lessons was to be only a loan. George's athleticism had seen him through lessons in fencing and wrestling, and now gave him the ability to master the dance. At fourteen years his growth had reached its maximum, drawing his long and lank body to nearly six feet four inches—a presence which dominated any minuet or quadrille with rhythm and grace. He scrambled to find dance partners willing to let him practice his new-found activity, and with his youth and vigor he quickly wore out most of his somewhat older partners.

Upon returning to Ferry Farm from a week-long stay at Mount Vernon, George was greeted by his mother with her usual hateful vituperation, "Why don't you move into Lawrence's house! You never think of anyone but yourself and your own pleasure! I labor day and night with your brothers and sister. Betty is sick with a fever right now and it looks like we are in for a storm, with thunder and lightning. You know how I fear lightning!"

"Hello, Mother." George fixed his eyes on his mother's scowl. "I always look forward to my return to Ferry Farm. Especially after enjoying several days with Anne and Lawrence. I'm sorry that Betty is ill, and yes, Mother, I'd like to help you with the children and the farm. Every time I ask you what chore you have for me, you never answer. I can guide our farm workers and oversee their duties, but every time I give an order, you rescind it, making me feel quite inadequate. Father helped me learn the farming business. I have studied manuals of agrarian practices, and I feel quite confident I can manage Ferry Farm."

"Your father has nothing to do with this farm now. It is my responsibility," Mary retorted.

George continued to study Mary's face. He was sure their conversation would end the same as most of their exchanges, so he quietly placed his hat on his head, went outside, mounted his horse, and rode into the trees where he could smell the sap in the pine trees. The smell of fresh soil overturned by the hooves of his horse accompanied him as he sadly gathered his thoughts about his future. "*What fate does my future hold? Is Ferry Farm my destiny? Mother, as long as she lives, will not allow me autonomy. Lawrence will be my salvation. I need his advice and counsel. His encouragement always gives me hope.*" The horse and rider began the twenty-mile trip back to Mount Vernon.

"George, Anne, and I want you to come and live with us here at Mount Vernon.[16] We have extra room, besides, this will allow you to continue your studies. Do you think your mother will give her approval, or will she need your uncle to make the decision again?" Lawrence asked.

Swallowing hard and wiping his hair back with his large hand,

George was stunned. "I am speechless. I don't know what to say. Are you sure it is what you wish?"

"Of course, it's what we want. Your mother's disapproval would be the only deterrent to this proposal."

"My mother be damned!" George replied vociferously. "My future is so uncertain, and as I see it, with few possibilities. I spend most of my time riding while I pray for some clue to my destiny."

"Is your answer a yes, without your mother's approval?"

"How soon will you be prepared for this to become my permanent residence?" George asked.

"My boy, you can consider this your home as soon as we put aside this conversation. I will send someone to ride to Ferry Farm tomorrow, to inform your mother and to pick up your things."

Lawrence Washington made a brilliant choice when he chose Anne Fairfax as his wife. Her distinguished ancestral line carried back hundreds of years and her uncle, an older brother of her father, held the inherited rank of baron. Known as Lord William Fairfax, his family had been granted five million, two hundred thousand acres in northern Virginia and West Virginia through a royal charter from King Charles II in 1660. The land grant took nearly ninety years to be confirmed in Fairfax ownership, since the king was exiled in France at the time he made the grant. Virginia colonists vehemently protested the size of the grant, but in 1746 the issue was settled and the Fairfax family readied the area for mapping and development. After confirmation was won, another unforeseen problem developed with the Indians who inhabited the Fairfax territory. A treaty had to be negotiated that allowed the colonists entry into the newly acquired land so surveying and mapping could lay the groundwork for development.[17]

The Fairfax home, called Belvoir, was located two miles from Mount Vernon. The Lawrence Washingtons spent long days and numerous nights at Belvoir while Mount Vernon was being rebuilt. George frequently visited the Fairfax home with Anne and Lawrence. This was his introduction to the resplendent life style of the very rich. His impressions of the opulence, of brilliant color and millwork, plethora of furnishings and paintings, lavish silver flatware and service pieces, overwhelmed him. The home had drawing rooms, a dining room, a music room, and a library filled with volumes of history and the sciences. All family members and guests were required to wear shoes inside this lively home, which George supposed was because of recurrent dancing.[18]

In contrast, the Ferry Farm house on the Rappahannock was a plain, dreary, dark and common place, slowly collapsing into disrepair. The move to Mount Vernon inspired George to see a small opening in his future. Anne and Lawrence entertained guests several times a week. Their dining table was overflowing with the finest wines, meats, fish and fowl, tarts and cakes—and conversation. George seldom entered the lively discussions, for fear he would reveal his inability to use the King's English appropriately and would sound illiterate and dim-witted. He attentively listened to the dinnertime talk planning the survey of the great territory that belonged to the Fairfax family. A fixed boundary line was needed between their western properties and the colony of Virginia before plans could begin to build settlements, and sell parcels.[19]

"Anne, dear, do you suppose George could borrow some of your father's library books?" Lawrence asked. "He is wont to learn about English politics and wit. The dear boy continues to fret about his poor intellectual abilities."

"Poor intellectual abilities?—Ha!—He continues to take my coins when we play cards. I taught him to play, pulling back so he could win a hand or two. Now, I struggle to win on my own," Anne replied. "Of course, he can borrow any book he chooses. Has George thought of William and Mary as a possible educational resource?"

Lawrence, with a mirror in his hand as he picked at his mustache, replied, "Yes, as a matter of fact he has approached Mary about funds, but she has refused. George is practicing with our father's surveying tools and may want to help your uncle on the frontier. He is quite brilliant with the chains. I allowed him to practice on my herb garden, and his measurements were precise to the number. He has been running lines at Ferry Farm and Mount Vernon for some time. He has studied our grandfather's surveyor's guide and seems to comprehend the principles.[20] George is a very tenacious young man. He may develop into a most reliable man. . . . God knows, his size—and those muscular arms and powerful hands—give him an edge. And his skill at handling a horse is exceptional. Lord Fairfax may be wise to mentor him and make ready for his help with surveying on the frontier."

Mary Ball Washington had predicted her first-born would be tall: he was indeed; well-built, with enormous hands and feet, well-coordinated and athletic. His equestrian skills were touted as the best in the county. He became a wrestler, hunter, and fisherman, with strength and endurance.

The biggest dilemma facing George at age sixteen was still his mother. After moving to Mount Vernon, he promised himself he would make frequent visits to see her and visit with his brothers and sister. However, his mother, with her cantankerous ways, filled George with guilt because he had left her with all the Ferry Farm responsibilities. After one such unpleasant afternoon spent with his family, he measured his feelings of self-worth in his life at Mount Vernon against the antagonism of his mother at Ferry Farm. As he cantered his horse homeword, he thought, "*My mother struggles to keep me at her side, but I feel so satisfied with my life at Mount Vernon and Belvoir. I am beginning to feel I may have a place in the world of the titled and high-born. Now, at least, I feel somewhat proficient with my ability to contribute at the dinnertime palaver.*" Chuckling, he gathered the reins and galloped Neddle, his thoroughbred, until the wind from the run chilled him. The twenty-mile trip between Ferry Farm and Mount Vernon passed quickly. Neddle seemed full of vitality and spirit, so George cantered then galloped; galloped and cantered back to Mount Vernon, thanking the Lord for Lawrence and Anne, who had delivered him from Mary Ball Washington.

Sam, Lawrence's house boy, greeted George as he made his way up the long drive. "Mister Washington, you are to go straight to Belvoir. Miz Anne's brother just arrive from Englan'."

"Thank you, Sam. I need to change horses." George stroked Neddle's head, "This horse ran almost the whole way home and he needs a rest. Cool him down for me, please."

The front door of the Fairfax home was ajar, so George stepped into the large passageway, announcing his arrival. "George, George, I am so glad you are here." Anne was jubilant as she entered the hallway from the east parlor. "Come in quickly and meet George William. He is very tired, but anxious to meet you. I have told him all about you and what a naughty boy you are." George had never seen Anne so gay and light-hearted.

"I'm sure you told him I can take all your money when we play lanterloo," rebutted George happily.

George William Fairfax, Anne's brother, was a rather immature twenty-three-year-old man, seven years older than George. George William, born in the Bahamas, had moved to England for his higher education. George and George William became close friends, playing cards, hunting foxes and game, and visiting back and forth between Mount Vernon and Belvoir. Like Lawrence, George William became another mentor to George, bringing to life the expectations of conduct and appropriate fashions of the English aristocracy. He also encouraged George to continue borrowing books from his uncle's library and offered to elucidate information that George questioned. George continued to study and practice the profession of surveying, hoping the Fairfaxes would soon invite him to the Shenandoah.

In March 1748, George William invited George to accompany him on a surveying trip to the frontier. A commissioned surveyor was recruited to head the survey, so George knew this good fortune would afford him the chance to observe an expert. His mother's permission was needed because of his age. When hearing George was to receive payment, she gave her approval.

The month-long trip introduced George to the life of the raw outdoors, with no shelter and only grass or leaves for sleeping. Each man in the party was responsible for catching his own food. George William turned back when the weather became blustery and bitter cold, but

George and his leader forged onward, completing their mission.[21]

The trip to the Shenandoah was a watershed in George's life. For the first time he had earned money on his own, making him less dependent on his mother's meager allowance. By the time he turned eighteen, he was earning one hundred and twenty-five pounds yearly as a licensed surveyor. He spent wisely on land investments and carelessly on frivolities, such as the latest English fashions, and fencing lessons to provide another outlet for his need to embellish his athletic expertise. George was often borrowing when his cash flow evaporated.

George was developing the skills and endurance needed to subsist in the wilderness, facing hazards such as overflowing rivers, and pioneering trails while hunting for food. He learned to make expeditious decisions using his compass and chains, while advancing his reputation as a trustworthy surveyor. This fortunate experience would serve him advantageously in a future that George was beginning to mold for himself.

"Anne, I am greatly concerned about Lawrence's deteriorating health," George said with a deep sigh. "His continual cough keeps him from getting much-needed rest."

"He has not felt completely well since his return from Cartagena a decade ago. He often speaks of the poor living conditions and rampant spread of disease there. What he really needs is a rest in the balmy West Indies. With winter upon us, warm sunshine may be the best treatment."

"My dear brother so hoped he would improve from the herbal treatments of Doctor Walters. Do you think he'll be well enough to attend the spring Assembly in Williamsburg?"

"Hardly! I fear he is suffering from melancholy, as well," Anne said. "Would you entertain the thought of accompanying Lawrence to Barbados? The winter weather will soon be upon us, and maybe a trip to a warmer climate will help restore his health."

"Have you spoken with Lawrence about such a trip?" George studied Anne's face, waiting for her answer. "Are you sure it is wise for Lawrence to leave you so soon after Sarah's birth? You have recovered so quickly, but I'm sure you must also worry about her health."

"George, you're very thoughtful to think of my condition, but it's Lawrence I'm concerned about. The consumption is overtaking his body. Any new treatment must be administered without delay and I understand there's a doctor in Bridgetown who has been successful in treating lung disorders."

George continued to gaze into Anne's eyes, which betrayed her anguish. Her new baby daughter seemed healthy, yet after losing three children shortly after birth, and now with the strain of Lawrence's declining physical condition, George could see that Anne was distraught with heartbreak.

"I'll go with Lawrence anywhere in this world if it will cure him and bring vitality back into his flesh and bones," George said as he arose from his chair, walked to Anne and gently patted her outstretched arm. "Let's speak with Lawrence at suppertime and let him decide if he is up to a sail. He may feel he can't be away from you and Sarah."

In late September 1751, the brothers embarked on the six-week sailing trip to Barbados. The trip nearly brought George and Lawrence to their knees. Inclement weather, a diminishing food supply, and the poor navigation skills of the eight-man crew kept both men in their bunks a good deal of the time.

The doctor treating Lawrence in Bridgetown was, at first, optimistic about his recovery. However, neither the treatments nor the warm climate brought about improvement, for Lawrence continued to cough and spew. Unexpectedly, George developed a raging fever leaving him incoherent and motionless. When he broke out with red itching pustules, the startling diagnosis was the smallpox! Nearly four weeks passed before George felt strong enough to pull himself out of bed. While George continued to recover, Lawrence realized the Barbados journey was a failure. "*I am wasting away*," Lawrence told himself. "*George has been exposed to the most abysmal of ailments, and I feel responsible for his great sacrifice. It's time we consider going home.*"

Lawrence and George talked about a return to Virginia. George's ambivalence to the idea surprised Lawrence. “I know it is time I go home, but this is such a paradise. It will be difficult to leave this lush, green landscape and the delicious pineapples and avocados. Let’s stay awhile longer. Perhaps we both can advance our health a bit more in this agreeable weather.”

“I am homesick. I want to go home and see Anne and baby Sarah before I die,” announced Lawrence two months after their arrival in Barbados.

“But Lawrence, it is still wintertime in Virginia. It is not advisable for you to thrust yourself into the chill after the warmth of Bridgetown. Besides, I’ve never heard you talk about death. You can’t give up on your illness. Your choice of words upsets me.”

“I know, and I don’t disagree, but it is nearly Christmas and my place is to be with my family. My dear brother, it is time we face head-on the probability of my demise. This will likely be my last Christmas season.” Lawrence seemed resigned to this possibility.

“I don’t feel comfortable with such talk,” George argued. “You must consider finishing the winter in warm weather. I’ll go on home, but you need to consider moving to another island—just for variety. Perhaps you are bored with Bridgetown.”

“I have given thought that a change in venue might raise my spirits and my well-being,” replied Lawrence. “As a matter of fact, I have charted a plan for both of us. You book passage back to Virginia and I will sail on to Bermuda. When spring arrives, I’ll come home. Does that sound like a satisfactory plan, George?”[22]

“Your comfort is my first concern. The harsh Virginia winters are not suited for delicate lungs so Bermuda sounds like a good choice for completing your recovery.” George refused to believe his beloved brother was facing death.

“You can prepare Anne for my homecoming,” Lawrence said. Then whispered to himself, “By that time, I hope I’ll still be ambulatory.”

The journal kept by George while in Barbados was full of observations about the economy, the military, and the social mores of the islanders. This would be his only trip outside the American colonies. His written account of the trip would later be interpreted by scholars who would note his growing abilities for observation and analysis. This was one of three results of the voyage which had great effect on George Washington's preparedness for his destiny. Arriving home, his twentieth birthday only days away, George realized his mother's refusal to allow him to become a part of the British Royal Navy had kept him from a career he could never have endured because of his propensity for seasickness. And having had smallpox, the scourge of the eighteenth century, gave George immunization to a disease feared by the most fearless.

George rode slowly and half-heartedly toward Mount Vernon. Dreading the reunion with Anne, he lowered his head and appealed for courage and cogency in explaining Lawrence's health. Resigning himself to the fate of his brother and best friend, George's spirits fell into a dolorous pit. The prosperous future he had hoped for would not be within his grasp with Lawrence gone. His fear of the end of the happy days spent at Mount Vernon and Belvoir put him into a bottomless chasm. "My surveying and meager land investments will not carry me far," George thought. "I'll go back to Ferry Farm and try to convince Mother that I'm capable of handling the planting and harvesting."

"Oh, my dear George, I am so glad to have you home. I've had no one to challenge me in the game of loo since you went away!" Anne was ecstatic to see her young half-brother-in-law. "Sit down and tell me about the trip. I want to hear everything, the sail back and forth, the extraordinary people who entertained the two of you, the unusual foodstuffs and all about Lawrence's treatments. Is he well, and when will he be coming home to Sarah and me?" Clasping her hands together, she said, "Wait until you see her. She is so beautiful. Her eyes twinkle just like her father's and she has his high spirits. First tell me about Lawrence. His letters said little about his progress."

"I know he wrote to tell you about sailing to Bermuda and spending the rest of the winter there. He worried about coming back to Mount Vernon this time of year. He wanted desperately for you and Sarah to join him, but an ocean voyage is treacherous with seasickness and the worries of poor food and disease."[23] George felt heat rising in his neck and throat as he continued trying to render his explanation of the lung disease consuming her husband's body. "The outlook is not an optimistic one. His coughing is causing such a gasping for breath that he is unable to sleep except for short periods of time. I regret having to bring such bad news, but the outlook is not good. I sense Lawrence is giving up."

Anne, reached for her handkerchief, gently pulling it out of her bodice, and began to wipe her eyes. "George, I have tried to prepare myself for this inevitable outcome. What a wretched sickness this tuberculosis is." Anne fell over onto the chaise, sobbing.

"He plans to come home sometime in early June," George consoled. Then he added, "I have yet to see my mother. I am going to ride over and bid her hello. She is anxious to know my whereabouts. I'll come back in three or four days, Anne." George tenderly kissed her on the back of her head as she lay doubled over on the cushions.

Ferry Farm was a long ride for George. Exhaustion sliced through his body, bones weighing heavily in his usually straight back "*I'll ride to Belvoir to see my dear friend George William and his captivating wife Sally after I visit Mother for a few days.*" George was immersed in nostalgic memories of Belvoir and Mount Vernon—the brilliant conversation, the lively parlor games, the music and dancing. "*Where will I find myself after Lawrence is gone? What will happen to Mount Vernon? And Sally and George William? Will our deep friendship come to an end?*" George guided his horse across a shallow river that was ready to overflow its narrow banks. Melting snow pushed the currents over the rocks that sparkled in the brilliant sun. His pensive mood threw his thoughts back to the day he met Sally Cary Fairfax.

In the spring of 1748, Lawrence invited George to Williamsburg for the Publick Times Assembly. The parties, balls, card games, and drinking were pervasive. Lawrence, a member of the House of Burgesses, carefully interpreted the business agenda for George, but as someone who had just turned sixteen a few months earlier, his interest was strictly social. The Governor's Ball was well-attended by the Burgesses and their wives, but George was overwhelmed by the young, fashionably dressed debutantes. With his size and stature George was not overlooked by the girls, especially after he garnered enough courage to ask them to dance. George Washington's six-foot-four-inch height gave him prominence in any room. Standing against the wall, at first, he looked for a familiar face. There was an unusually tall girl who seemed to be the choice partner for many of the single men. He did not know her name, but became instantly smitten with her poise and grace on the dance floor. She surrounded herself with male admirers who seemed to clamor for her attention. George moved to the punch bowl and plotted his introduction to this belle. He carefully poured the pink refreshment into a cup and walked across the room to offer it. At that moment, Lawrence called from the hallway to announce they were leaving because he was not feeling well. Shortly after Lawrence gave summons, George learned they were not only leaving the ball, they were leaving Williamsburg. Lawrence was sick and wanted to return to Mount Vernon.

George William Fairfax, also a Burgess, returned several days later from Williamsburg and announced his engagement to Sarah Cary. "My father is delighted with my choice," George William told George. "She is exquisitely beautiful, has had an impeccable education, and she speaks French fluently. Her grandfather was a Rector of William and Mary College, where her father studied before going to Cambridge.[24]

"Will I manage an introduction before you bring her home to Belvoir?" asked George. "She sounds like a perfect match for you, old friend."

"Indeed, you will meet her at dinner this afternoon," George William said in anticipation. "She will be arriving for a stay to meet the family. You are adjudged as part of our family, so please join us for this most happy occasion."

Sarah Cary, or Sally, as she was called, arrived surrounded in grandeur. Her carriage was drawn by four perfectly groomed white horses. Her entourage included three black slaves, two drivers, and a footman. As she entered the large passageway of Belvoir, George was overcome with awe as she gracefully pulled her white scarf away from her face to reveal raven-colored hair with eyes to match, and milk-white skin with a touch of pink on her cheeks. Sally held out her hand to George after the introduction and said, "I believe you were in Williamsburg during the Assembly. Am I correct? I somehow remember watching your polished minuet, or am I being too bold to ask such a question?"

Gripping Sally's hand and intently studying her eyes, George realized she was the tall and lithesome girl at the Governor's Ball. Grasping for appropriate words, he incoherently said, "No...no...It couldn't have been . . . I mean yes . . . It was me . . . I was there for a very short time." Clearing his throat, he bowed his head in embarrassment and looked at the floor.

So full of confidence, Sally pulled her hand away and giggled, "I remember you because after I saw you dance, I wished for you to invite me to the floor. I consider myself taller than most women, and thought what a handsome couple we would make because of your exceptional height." Sally smiled broadly, then turned away to greet the remaining Fairfax family.

Since the marriage of Sally and George William, George had spent many days in their company, playing cards and dancing. Even though Sally was two years older, with far greater maturity, George became enamoured with her charm, humor, ability to speak French and her extraordinary self-confidence. He observed and scrutinized her every move and was attentive to every word, using her as the model for the expected behavior of all the Virginian aristocratic women. He often fantasized that she was more paramour than mentor or friend.

Lawrence's ordeal ended at Mount Vernon in July 1752. His will named George and Austin Washington, George William Fairfax, and several friends as co-executors. Lawrence had been a poor manager. His investments were not giving good returns, especially the investment in the Ohio Company. An auction was necessary to pay his creditors, leaving Mount Vernon boarded up and abandoned. He left most of his estate to Sarah, his young daughter. A small interest in Mount Vernon and half of their slaves went to his wife. Anne would receive Sarah's legacy if she did not live to legal age. If Sarah did not survive to inherit Mount Vernon by her twenty-first birthday, the farm was to go to George.[25]

Continual melancholia swept over George as he reviewed his future. Rebuilding Ferry Farm seemed to be his only positive option, but was his last choice. Going back into the Shenandoah to survey had moderate appeal. Lawrence had held several appointments, so George conceived of a plan to apply to the Governor of Virginia to replace Lawrence as Adjuntant General of the Virginia Militia. Four generations of Washington men had spent time in the military, compelling George to feel he should carry on the tradition. He knew full well that his lack of experience might disqualify him for Lawrence's position. After looking over George's qualifications, Governor Robert Dinwiddie, a British loyalist, appointed by the King, must have agreed with George, so he appointed him a Major of the British Royal Army to oversee training of the men in the southernmost part of Virginia; another job in which George had no training.[26]

Unbeknownst to him, this appointment placed George on the threshold of building his infinite reputation as soldier and officer. Dinwiddie could not possibly have imagined that the inexperienced twenty-one-year-old Major would eventually be the commanding general of the Continental Army fighting *against* the British Royal Army to gain freedom for the American colonies.

Mrs. Daniel Parke Custis by John Wollaston
Courtesy of Washington-Custis-Lee Collection, Washington and Lee University, Lexington, Virginia

Daniel Parke Custis by John Wollaston
Courtesy of Washington-Custis-Lee Collection, Washington and Lee University, Lexington, Virginia

John Parke Custis and Martha (Patcy) *Custis* by John Wollaston
Courtesy of Washington-Custis-Lee Collection, Washington and Lee University, Lexington, Virginia

The Courtship of Washington by John McRae
Courtesy of The Virginia Historical Society

Daniel Parke
Courtesy of The Virginia Historical Society

Sally Fairfax
Courtesy of The Virginia Historical Society

Martha Washington
Courtesy of The Virginia Historical Society

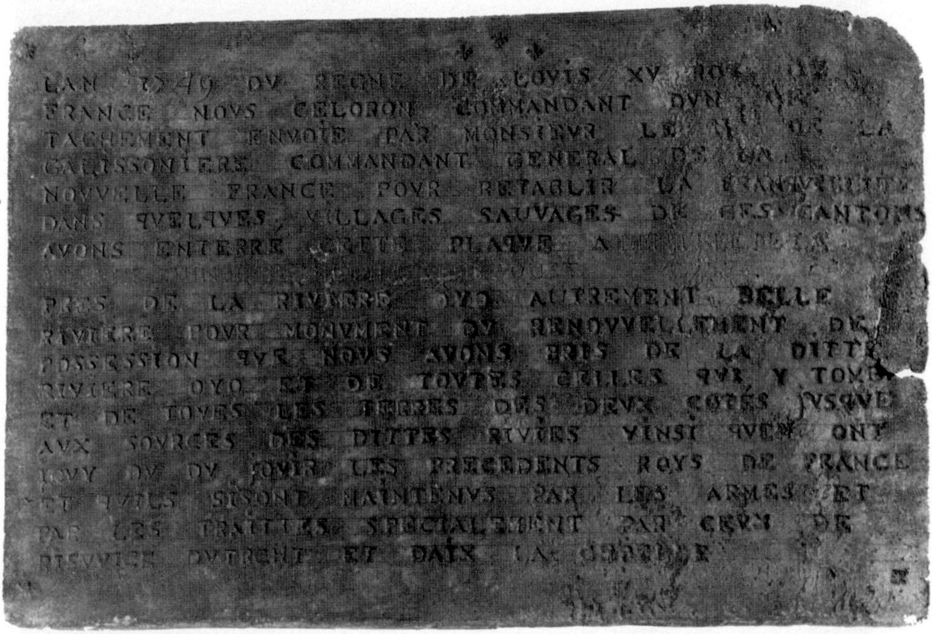

Celeron Plate
Courtesy of The Virginia Historical Society

MARTHA, DANIEL & GEORGE

1753-1758

The Custis's White House on the Pamunkey River teemed with activity and energy. Mr. and Mrs. Daniel Parke Custis were, with John Parke Custis's final will, one of the wealthiest families in Virginia and one of the most sought-after couples for dinner parties and galas. With their wealth came responsibility and expectations. Martha was accountable for overseeing the running of the house in a proper and aristocratic manner. Since the White House had not seen a woman's touch for some time, Martha needed to retrain the servants to her satisfaction in cooking, washing clothes, soap-making, weaving, and dressmaking. Her mother had taught her well in most general household duties, but the duties of choosing menus and training the servants to serve house guests ceremoniously were skills she needed to master herself. Numerous family members and friends called daily, many staying for weeks at a time. The Frances and John Dandridge home had been meticulous in making sure the linens were snow-white and ironed without obvious wrinkles. Martha spent long hours supervising her staff to make sure their performance of their duties met the strict Dandridge standard that she wanted transferred into the Custis home.

The first three years of the Dandridge-Custis union transformed Martha from a giddy adolescent into a mature and respected woman. With maturity came tears of joy with the birth of a son, followed by a daughter. Tears of sorrow flowed when John, Martha's brother, died unexpectedly. Sickness and death were always around the corner, and Martha, with tremendous resilience, resorted to her Scriptures and prayer when tragedy struck.

Martha and Daniel, devoted to one another, took every opportunity to proudly show off their two young children—Daniel Parke Custis II and Frances Parke Custis. They were the center of the Custis household. Daniel, delighted in parenthood, showered his children with toys, clothing, and love. He made sure the catastrophic family relationships in his own family would not be repeated with young Daniel and Fanny or any future children. Daniel also gave generously to Martha. Their clothes came either from London or were fashioned by the best seamstresses and tailors in Williamsburg. Daniel indulged Martha with jewelry and watches exquisitely made by the most well-known artisans in London.

The House of Six Chimneys, the John Custis home in Williamsburg, also belonged to Martha and Daniel. At first, Martha was overwhelmed with the care of both homes. She worked diligently to reorganize and retrain the help in the capital home on their visits during Publick Times. Daniel chose not to ask for an appointment to the General Council or to run as a Burgess. He chose, instead, to follow his father's advice and use sound judgment in agricultural management and avoid debt. He tenaciously kept the Custis plantations producing quality tobacco and made sure there was no need for credit.

Managing two large homes, well-staffed with house servants, was a challenge for Martha. Both homes contained furniture, paintings, and silver pieces that were mostly family heirlooms. She planned carefully the redecoration of each home. The White House, as the primary residence, was her first target for paint and paper. The new colors and brightly printed wall coverings in the White House begged for pictures to fill the empty spaces. The House of Six Chimneys had many family portraits hanging, most of people Martha could not identify. Martha made a trip into Williamsburg to study the pictures hanging there and bring back those that were best suited for the White House redecoration project. Daniel had specifically asked for his grandfather Parke's portrait.

Martha looked forward to her trips to Williamsburg. The maintenance of John Custis's garden was a responsibility Martha appointed herself to manage. Her plan was to keep it trimmed, fertilized, and preserved as her father-in-law had left it. Martha's orders were for daily care consisting of pinching back, transplanting, and separating overgrown bushes and flowers, though the garden had never looked the same since that horrible man took over the care years ago. "*What was his name?*" Martha could not get the name out. "*His name is on the tip of my tongue... Milton, I think... yes, that is it. He was Jonathan Milton's brother.*"

Martha had risen early so she could spend the day in the garden. As she surveyed the shrubs, trees, and plantings, she heard a single horse cantering up the drive. Jack entered the courtyard riding a black stallion with a coat like lustrous satin. "Jack, I'm surprised to see you!" Martha watched as Jack climbed down from his horse. "What brings you to the House of Six Chimneys?"

"I received word you were coming to Williamsburg and I want to send a message back to Mister Daniel," Jack smiled sheepishly.

"Of course, I will dispatch information back to Daniel," Martha replied reluctantly. "I hope it's not bad news. Is the building of your new home at Queen's Creek Plantation going well?"

"No, no, it's not bad news. I want to ask Daniel if he remembers a portrait of his father that has been in storage for some time. If he has no plans to hang the picture, I wish to ask permission to hang it in my new house. I will consider it a loan, of course. Daniel's children may wish to claim ownership at some time in the future. That would be understood." Jack's eyes betrayed his discomfort in asking the question. "If you recall the distribution of Mr. Custis's will? Well, he gave Mr. and Mrs. Moody the portrait Mr. Custis had painted of me.[1] You do know about that, I'm sure. I would like to have that too."

Studying Jack's uneasiness, Martha realized that Jack was asking for a portrait of a father he and Daniel shared. "I will discuss this with Daniel as soon as I return to the Pamunkey. I will send a message back to you when I have an answer. If he gives his affirmative, you may pick up the picture before we return to Williamsburg. I suggest you see the Moodys about your portrait. I know nothing of its whereabouts."

"You asked about the progress of my new house. It is nearly ready for furniture now. I'm waiting for the next ship from London. The chairs and chaise should be arriving. Tell Mister Daniel how grateful I am . . . about . . . you know . . . the . . . the will."

"Yes, I will tell him." Martha watched as Jack mounted his horse and slowly rode down the sandy drive and through the open gate. She crossed her arms and gave a deep sigh. "*I'm having some strange feelings about this conversation with Jack. I can't decide if he is maudlin and lonely or if he has become impertinent and unmannerly. Goodness knows, the will of John Custis left him emancipated with a handsome yearly stipend, a new home fully furnished, and with farm animals also.*" Martha began to stab at the soil with her small shovel. "*I do believe I am somewhat angry with John Custis at this moment. I need to stop working and go pump myself a fresh ladle of water while I put some logic in this conversation with Jack.*"

The carriage entered the extended drive to the White House, lined with the poplar trees that had leafed out in Martha's absence. She was anxious to see her precious children. Two weeks was a long time to be away. "They both have probably grown," sighed Martha. Danny, at two and a half had become a chatter box, while Fanny, at eight months, had begun to sit up, sprout teeth and jabber. The conversations between brother and sister were unintelligible to others as they chattered and jabbered back and forth, then laughed to keep each other company.

"Where are my two babies?" shouted Martha, as she entered the front door. "I brought you candies from Williamsburg!"

"Mis Custis, so glad you'rn home." Dicey met Martha in the passageway, rubbing her nervous hands down the side of her apron. "We's been awaitin' ya."

"Is something wrong, Dicey? Where are the children and Mr. Custis?"

"Mister Custis . . . well, he be out in the field but the chil'ren . . . they be upstairs. Master Daniel, he gots one of his spells again. Just coughin' and coughin." Dicey, reluctant to look at Martha said, "He's better taday, 'cause I tol' him you be home by dinnertime." Dicey, swaying her body, looked proudly at Martha, as if this revelation had made his cough disappear.

Martha was nearly up the stairs before Dicey finished her sentence. Daniel's room was dark and malodorous. She stumbled as she entered, trying to find her son. "Mama's here, my little darling." Martha reached up and pulled the heavy damask curtains apart. Daniel stirred from his sleep and wearily said, "Mama, Mama." Reaching up his arms, he begged, "Up, up."

"Of course, dear one." Martha brushed aside his curly dark hair, picked him up, and tested his forehead for fever. "Are you feeling better now that mama is home?" She rocked him gently back and forth as he laid his head on her breast. "If you were a kitten, you'd be purring," she said to give a little bit of assurance to Daniel's comfort. His frequent bouts with croup seemed to be increasing, giving Martha cause to worry about this susceptibility. "*Thank heavens it is spring and the warm weather is upon us*," Martha told herself.

Daniel pranced around the front parlor and picked up his wife and swung her around like a rag doll. "Do you know how happy I am to have you home, Madame? I am going to give you at least a thousand kisses before you go to sleep tonight."

Martha still had difficulty responding to Daniel's deep and demonstrative affection. He still made her heart sing with the sound of his voice, but she was reluctant to return his open and physical affection, which seemed out of place for daytime display. Drawing away from Daniel's playfulness, she quickly changed the subject. "Daniel, I saw Jack while I was gone. He asked me to give you a message, actually more of a request."

"Really. I must say, I am surprised that he would send me a message. He is seldom in Williamsburg now that his house is nearly finished. Where did you see him?"

"He came to the House of Six Chimneys. I was working in your father's garden when he rode up the drive. I tried to hide my surprise. He looks well. I asked about his mother and he said she is well." Martha saw that Daniel was growing impatient to hear the message. "He wants to know if he can hang your father's portrait in his new house so he . . ."

Daniel broke in and interrupted before Martha finished her sentence. "Most certainly not! He is well taken care of through my father's will. How dare he make such a request!"

"Let me finish before you make a harsh judgment. He suggested that it be only a loan. He knows the picture has been in storage for some time. Jack said that if our children want the portrait at any time, it would be theirs. He would like his own portrait too. The one your father commissioned."

"What, pray tell, does he want with John Custis's picture? His own portrait is one thing, but to request my father's is absurd!" Daniel was pacing around the table with his hands tightly clasped.

Martha had somewhat prepared herself for Daniel's reaction. "*But he has such balanced temperament and never engages in confrontation*," she told herself. Then she said, "You and Jack share the same father. That is the only reason I can think of."

"He just wants to show off to his black cohorts where his roots are."

"Daniel, sit down and listen." Martha's voice quivered.

"No, I want you to listen to me. We have suffered the embarrassment of the whole of New Kent County and the people of Williamsburg knowing about the recipients named in John Custis's will. I will not allow just a slave, really, an enormous albatross, to haunt me by the transgression of my father, flaunting a picture over Jack's fireplace in a house that Custis money built. The next news we'll hear is of Jack calling me his half-brother and our children his niece and nephew! I do not want my children to be drawn into this sordid affair by having them recognize they have a black uncle, who by the way, will marry and have black babies that will be our children's cousins. They will not share a picture of their grandfather! I don't give a damn about the black-faced portrait. If he can get it away from Anne Moody, let him hang himself."

Daniel fell on his knees in front of Martha's chair. He clasped her hand in his, and looked deep into her eyes. "My Dearest Patcy, I prayed I would never disclose my profound feelings concerning this matter. Let us promise each other that we will never discuss Jack or the portrait again." Daniel rubbed his fingers down her cheeks and smiled his everything-will-be-all-right smile.

"My dear, please forgive my shallowness. I have presented myself as frivolous and thoughtless. I did not think the situation through. He receives such a handsome amount of money each year from the Custis estate.[2] Perhaps he will want to find a painter who will copy John Custis's picture."

"Please, let's not mention that as a possibility." Daniel seated himself on the brocade settee. He patted the cushion and said, "Come join me. Now, tell me what items are being shipped to the White House. Did you pack my grandfather's portrait? With the robin's egg blue color in our east parlor, his picture will be well-suited over the fireplace. I am going to commission a portrait painter to come here and paint each of us. The children need to be a bit older, however. Sitting for long periods will be quite impossible for them. I must have a few names submitted to us the next time we are in Williamsburg. I want the best artist in the colonies to paint your magnificent face, my darling."

April 18, 1753 Im hapy to be back wit my famly. The long trip home gav me time to cont my blesings. A husband who luvs me an too butiful chilren. Thank you, LORD for blesing me wit so much luv. Daniel surprisd me. My misgivings were correct He was so angry wit Jack abot the picture. But I did not no how wrong I was to think the picture shud be okay to hang in his new home. I have deep concern for Jack and his resons for wanting to hang it in his house. John Custis was his father! Jack had nothing to do wit his own creation. I will study abot having a artist mak anothr picture from the orginul to giv to him. Daniel wil not lik the idea I no. Im vere woried abot

Danys coff. He neds warm sunshin to dri it up.Plac yer hands on his brest Lord to mak him wel. I no you ar in his hart and he wil gladle acept your hands. AMEN

Mother used to say, "Time and tide wait for no man." What about women? Martha rolled the idea around inside her head. "*It is nearly harvest time and before I can blink my eyes, Christmas will be here. Danny is nearly three and Fanny will be close to a year old. This will be a joyous holiday for our family. I think I will insist that Mother and Papa bring themselves and the children here this year. The renovation of the house is nearly completed and the redecorating will lend itself to the pine swags and boxwood with apples and oranges made into wreaths for the windows. We must start the candle making at once.*"

On Christmas Day the sun hung low on the horizon. The afternoon sun was unusually warm, allowing the younger Dandridge children and the Custis children to play outside. Fanny tried to run and jump with the older children. She spent most of the time on her bottom because her unsteady legs could not hold her upright. Her happy disposition allowed her to laugh and coo at herself and the others as she worked to get on her feet again. Daniel joined the outside games and organized new ones, keeping a vigilant eye on his young children. After consuming a plump Christmas goose cooked to perfection, the family gathered around the spinet while Martha played hymns and carols and the family sang along. When the children were tucked into bed, the adults sat before the fire and shared stories, gossip, and laughter. "Martha, your home looks beautiful," Frances Dandridge told her daughter. "I am so proud of your choice of colors for the walls and tapestries. The portrait of Daniel's grandfather hanging over the fireplace puts the finishing touch on the whole room. The colors of his clothing match the walls perfectly."

"Your grandfather Parke was quite the warrior, wasn't he, Daniel?" asked John Dandridge. "I have heard numerous accounts of his war years and then Governorship in the Leeward Islands. I suppose most of the stories are myths."

"I don't know what you may have heard, but his biography would make exciting reading," Daniel answered. "He was very ambitious but was born too soon and in the wrong place. His first mistake, which was not his doing, was being born in York County, Virginia, instead of England. His mother took him to England as a baby, while his father remained in Virginia accumulating royal charters. After his English education, Grandfather came back to Virginia and became an accomplished businessman. He grew tobacco, developed brickyards, shipyards, docks, and warehouses. Of course, the politics of Virginia became attractive to one with all his holdings and he became an officer in the Militia, a Justice of the County Court and a member of the House of Burgesses. His credentials in the colonies included vestryman at Bruton Parish. He was a heavy contributor to William and Mary College. His bricks built the main building."[3]

John Dandridge sat down and lighted his pipe. "Daniel, I haven't heard about his Virginia contributions. Most of the stories I've heard concern his war years and his rather untimely death."

"Now, Papa, you need to listen to the true story of Colonel Parke. Your stories filled me with beans and applebutter when I was younger." Martha began to laugh. "Daniel, have I told you the tales Papa told me about your grandfather? He told me he chased women, had an illegitimate son that he asked his wife, your grandmother, to raise, and was killed by irate husbands whose wives were debauched by him."

"Martha, I am shocked that you would speak of my proud and stately grandfather like that." Daniel turned toward the portrait and began to laugh. "Look at him! Does he look like a scoundrel . . . umm?" Daniel turned away from the picture grinning. "Every word your father said is absolutely true."

Frances Dandridge had been silent during this profound conversation. "Well, Daniel, dear, are you going to finish the tales of Parke? I, too, thought John exaggerated all this time."

"Grandfather Parke won the favor of Queen Anne after Marlborough won a crucial battle in Blenheim. He had the privilege of taking the message of this success to the Queen and she rewarded him with the miniature of herself you see in the picture. She also lavished gold and diamond trinkets and money on him. My grandfather was rather puffed about the recognition given by the Queen, so he asked her to appoint him Governor of Virginia. She refused because he had the impropriety to not be born in England, so she appointed him Governor of the Leeward Islands in the Caribbean instead. At the time of his arrival, skirmishes with the French had left the military nearly depleted—a situation which Grandfather tried to remedy. Political unrest was rampant, so he tried to replicate reforms he had witnessed in Virginia—unsuccessfully, I might add. His opposition carried out an assassination attempt that left him with a useless arm. Grandfather was accused of being an autocratic militant, illegal trader, and rake. Yes, he did have a propensity toward women, with lascivious intentions. He brought "Cousin Brown," as he called his mistress, and her illegitimate son, sired by him, to live in Virginia. My grandmother raised the boy along with her two daughters—Frances, my mother, and Aunt Lucy. Cousin Brown became a servant in the Parke household. And yes, Grandfather was a womanizer in Antigua. And yes, he supposedly had numerous affairs with other men's wives. The attack on and ultimate death of my grandfather was planned and carried out by his political enemies. Rumor persists that the assassins were also irate husbands."[4]

John Dandridge leaned into the soft cushions of the high-back chair, drawing on the stem of his pipe. "Well, tell me, didn't he die a rather pathetic death? Seems the stories always ended with him lying naked on the steps of the Governor's Mansion and left to die. Of course, I believe the embellishment of the story of his death is just that—embellishment!"

"Actually, that story is credible. My father told about his death quite often to anyone willing to listen. The Custis family did benefit from his holdings. A group of the Antigua militia assaulted my grandfather and his bodyguard. Two against many does not bring negotiation. The story goes that Grandfather Parke had his back broken with the butt of a musket and then was dragged down the steps of the mansion and abandoned. He cried out for water but no one offered solace. Supposedly, he lay there several days. It was there he met his Maker."[5]

"Daniel, we will all have nightmares tonight," Martha said. "That is a most gruesome story. I have never heard you mention how he died."

"Daniel, do you know when and where your grandfather sat for this handsome picture?" asked Frances.

"I only know the name of the London portraitist, John Closterman," Daniel replied politely.[6] "I plan to have the Custis family sit for pictures as soon as the children are a bit older. I hope we can find an artist of the quality of Mr. Closterman."

Martha sensed her family was ready to retire. "Mother . . . Papa . . . do you have a story about the Dandridge family that matches Colonel Daniel Parke II?"

"Yes and no," answered Papa. "Yes, I have a story but no, it does not match the Colonel's."

Frances began to shift herself in her lounge. "John, dear, the fire has burned into embers. We need to go to bed. Maybe the story can wait until tomorrow." Frances yawned into her handerkerchief.

"What story would that be, Papa?" Martha asked curiously.

"It's a story about a young girl whose temper was rising so high she rode her horse up her uncle's staircase—inside his house."[7]

"Papa, you wouldn't tell that story!"

"John, not tonight," Frances echoed.

Feb 17, 1754 Lif is to good to me. Ar plantations ar giving us the best tobako Daniels fishere is doing well. He leased ar swampland. He is askd to be vestry man at church. Im vere proud of his acomplismet. Mother askd me let Oney com liv wit us. she is six an old enuf to help wit Dany an Frany. Our mane slave chilren plae wit our chilren but I wil bee hapy to hav her wit us. Now that Old Joe is gon mother tinks she wud be hapy wit our mane helpers. Dany wil be hapy to hav his own companion. The cold wether is wit us now and I so worre about the coff and fever seson. Daniel luvs to tak Dany wit him on his morning ride. He is so proud of his son. he is a good father. Fany has her first coff spell. I gues my chilren were born to coff. John D, Nance and Betty ar coffers too. God Bless John D and keep him wit you always LORD. I miss him so! Pleas keep my chilren well this winter. An my brothers an sisters too. Im yur wiling servant Almighty God. Amen. Patcy

The ambivalent weather of the winter of 1754 was perplexing. One day would be warm and sunny and the next cold and rainy. Daniel worried about soil plowing and preparation for planting. Martha worried about her children's health, especially Danny's for he wanted to be outside with his father no matter how inclement the weather. Fanny was content to be in or out as long as Oney was at her side. Oney had turned out to be a blessing to the Custis family. She had her mother's wit and her father's instinct. Fanny called her O because her small throat muscles had not developed enough to pronounce the O-ney together as one word. All day long, her jabber was calling O-O, which sounded like Oh-Oh.

"Please, Dicey, keep your eye on the girls. I am going out to the kitchen to check on the raspberry tarts. If they aren't made yet, I will roll out the dough and put them together. My brother and sisters will be here in time for dinner today." Nancy, Franny, and Betty were coming for a week's visit, and Will was driving them to the White House. Wonderfully, when the carriage arrived, Frances had come along with the Dandridge children as a surprise for Martha and her two grandchildren. Oney was in the middle of all the hugs and kisses between the Custis and Dandridge children.

"Oney, dear. I've missed you!" Frances knelt down and kissed and held her tightly. Fanny worked her way to Frances for an extra hug. "Grandmother has kisses for both of her girls."

"O-O, no! Me kiss." Fanny gave Oney a push.

Martha intervened quickly, taking Fanny's hand. "Oney wants to hug Grandmother, too. You must never push aside another person. Tell Oney you are sorry." Martha held to her firm stance with Fanny, who began to cry, then sob. Her wails began to move her little body up and down as she continued sobbing. The inhaling and exhaling developed into a deep rattle emanating from her chest. "Oh, dear Mother of God, her croup is back! Dicey, please prepare a cup of tea with honey and a drop of lemon for Fanny. We'll be upstairs waiting for you." Martha struggled to keep herself calm as she made her apologies and then whisked her young daughter up the stairs.

Following a long afternoon nap, Fanny awoke with a smile. The cough had disappeared. A much-relieved Martha played the gracious hostess during the dinner hour as the roast baron of beef, spanked potatoes, and green beans smothered in bacon were served by two well-trained servants. Fanny's recovery seemed to raise the mood of the family. They watched her play with the other children, hang on her father's neck and boss O-O before going to bed for the night. After a leisurely dinner, Martha, Daniel, and Frances Dandridge were comfortably seated around the fire sipping one last cup of strong coffee before retiring. The children were all tucked in and sleeping after an evening song fest and parlor games. "Mother, it is so good of you to come and spend time with us. We hope you can visit us often. You can see how happy your grandchildren are to see you, but I must say it is peaceful having them all in bed."

The words had just fallen from Martha's lips when her younger sister, Nancy shouted, "Patcy, come here," as she hung over the staircase railing.

Martha sprang from her chair, calling, "I'll be right there. Is it Fanny?" She paused and turned to Daniel, "She seemed fine before going to bed."

"No, it is Danny that's calling for you," replied Nancy.

Daniel, Martha, and Frances Dandridge stood guard over Danny. His fever and cough had stricken him suddenly. Dicey wrang out cold rags and wrapped them around his chest, shoulders, and arms, trying to lower his temperature. Martha sat on the side of the bed stroking his forehead and twirling his dark, damp hair around her finger and humming to him. "Where did that nasty cough come from, my sweet son? You usually start with a sneeze or two." Danny was not responding to Martha's words. His mumbling into his mother's ear became inaudible and soon lethargy set in. The lack of response was new to his frequent illnesses, as was the high fever, which was a great concern. "Mother, please go on to bed. Daniel, you need rest, too. I will come to bed as soon as I know Danny is sleeping soundly."

"My dearest, do you think I can possibly sleep? I will awaken every time he coughs. Do you think the cool cloths are what he needs or should we try a poultice instead?" The only children with whom Daniel had spent time were his own. His son was his treasure trove overflowing with gold coins and gems made of silver and pearls; his love, unequivocally.

"Do you think we should send for Doctor Perkins? Mother, what do you think? You have nursed all of us so many times."

"Martha, dear, I am never sure what to do in time of sickness. I always pray to our Lord for strength and calm. Do you remember when our Franny was so sick?" Frances asked. "Remember the day of Nate and Dorthea's wedding? Why don't we try and make Danny comfortable tonight. Croup is always worse at night. We can decide in the morning if we need to send for Doctor Perkins. I suggest we keep him in cool cloths and try to drip water from a rag into his mouth like Doctor Walters said. Daniel, I will show you how to do this so you and I can take the next couple of hours of duty. Patcy, you look like you need a bed."

Morning came. Young Daniel seemed to be sinking into a deeper sleep with a higher temperature. A rider was sent to get Doctor Perkins, who lived over five miles away. Martha began to cling to hope of an outcome like her sister Franny's. She and Daniel prayed and walked the floor together. Frances helped manage the other children while Daniel kept a watchful eye on the mantel clock. "What is taking the doctor so long to get here?" Daniel said with torment.

"Mother, come quickly!" shouted Martha from the second floor. "Please hurry!"

Frances pulled up her petticoat and dashed up the stairs. "What is it, dear?" Frances could read her daughter and son-in-law's faces. She bent over her grandson, pressing her ear to his chest. She stood up and looked into the horror-stricken faces of Martha and Daniel and softly said, "He is gone."[8]

The late winter rains poured incessantly, turning the fields and roads into muck and mire. Mim always said the wet mud was like looking at gumbo, all brown and squishy but without the okra. Martha, giving out a deep sigh, put a half smile on her face. "Just thinking about Mim lifts my spirits some." She watched Fanny and Oney playing with a rag doll, each trying to decide who was the mama and who was the papa. "Children love being the grownups. If only they understood the heartaches of parenthood." Martha was certain she had a new life growing inside her belly. Fatigue and the need for extra sleep were symptoms of her first pregnancy. "Maybe I will have another boy," she sighed. "A son may help Daniel edge out of his grief and despair," Martha said to herself. "His sorrow is imbedded so deeply in his heart that sometimes I worry he will have no room left for the love of another child."

John Parke Custis was born in early 1755. His father was euphoric, and very possessive of his newborn son. Jacky, as the family called him, was a healthy boy with a strong cry and a demanding disposition. Daniel delayed his early morning call to the fields nearly every day so he could watch Jacky eat his breakfast. He sometimes helped with his bathing and would be the first to pick him up for a nighttime feeding. As soon as he was able to sit up Jacky rode on a horse with Daniel, placed behind him on the saddle. The two were inseparable.

A year later, a sister arrived—Martha Parke Custis, also strong-voiced and demanding. Martha's fourth child came into the world with an older sister, an older brother, Oney, and a new Aunt Mary born to Frances Dandridge—her eighth child—several weeks before little Martha. The new baby was called Patcy, like her mother. Babies spread over two generations kept the Custis and Dandridge homes humming with feedings, diapers and colic. Both young Patcy and Mary suffered from upset tummies, always inconveniently in the early morning hours. Daniel delighted in helping with the late night interruptions. Patcy's crying usually caused Jacky to awaken, so Daniel would bring him into his bed to offer comfort. Young Patcy, when well into her sixth month, still suffered with her nocturnal tummy aches. Early one morning, as Daniel readied himself for his morning ride, he complained to Martha that the midnight intrusions were causing him daytime fatigue. "Do you think our children will soon outgrow this need to awaken us each night? We have not experienced an entire night's rest since Jacky was born. Mind you, I'm not complaining, but perhaps Dicey could take over the night-time care."

"Of course she can. We both worry so about our children. Perhaps we have been overly cautious because of Danny. I will make arrangements today. Fanny has not had the croup for some time, which is a great relief."

Daniel insisted that he and Martha go into Williamsburg for the Publick Times. They both needed new clothes, shoes, and household goods. "We have been so devoted to our children and their needs. Let's have a holiday and attend the festivities and the Governor's Ball," Daniel suggested. He did not tell Martha that he had employed a portraitist to paint both of them. Martha needed to feel young and gay again. The stress of losing her beloved son, birthing two babies very close together and giving loving care mixed with perpetual concern about the children's health, had given her worry lines and dark circles around her eyes. She needed companionship with friends and family.

Thomas and David Milton sat around the open fire drinking watered-down rum traded from a lone Indian looking for gunpowder. David wanted to head north, because an early winter had settled into the valley, bringing rain, wet snow, and chilling winds. "Dammit, David! You cannot get yourself all het up about the Choctaw squaw. We've got work to do. I need to start back to Williamsburg to talk to Jonathan, and I need you to stay here and help talk to the French soldiers. They are behind every bush and tree."

"We've got plenty of furs and we need to get them ship-bound before the real winter weather starts. The season has been a good one, but it is only mid-October and I predict a long and unbearable winter. Why don't you head for Albany and I'll head north for Quebec?" said David. " I want to get myself started."

"David, you've got your head stuck in the wrong place. What's this influence the squaw has over you? Let your sense prevail and get off that Injun! I need to talk to Jonathan. I'm sure the King is about to start something out here, and we need to know how soon and where,"

Thomas said. "Jonathan will tell us what to do. He's got indentured men, volunteers, and farmers out here working his plats, I mean, our plats. We've invested a lot of our time, mostly miserable time, out here."

The two brothers were rolling out their fur robes to wrap up for the night when they heard the sound of horses approaching the campsite. "Hello," a deep voice bellowed. "May we join you for the night? We saw your fire, and have been following your light for some time."

Thomas used his gloved hand to shade his eyes from the fire light. He made out two horses, one ridden by a small, lean man and the other by a large, imposing man, both dressed in buckskin. There were two packhorses fettered to each saddle. "Where you headed?"

The burly man replied, "We are going to Logstown and then Fort Le Boeuf.[9] Have you been out in that direction, or are you headed east?"

Thomas quickly sat up, his attention focused by their destination. "Fort Le Boeuf? Why are you going there this time of year, with winter setting in?"

"I am an emissary sent by the Virginia governor to meet with French officers there. We have had a long day and would like to camp here, with your permission."

"Yes, of course. We have only rum to offer you, but it may warm your innards," Thomas offered.

"We have our own store, thank you. We'll roll out robes and get some rest. Tomorrow is another long day."

The winds coming from the north kept Thomas open-eyed while David slept soundly. Sometimes the dead of night caused nightmarish images, with sounds exaggerated by the silence of the wilderness. The significance of what the stranger said about their mission caused Thomas to puzzle out a plan to learn more about the meeting of an English emissary with French military officers. His judgment told him it must be over French infringement into the Ohio Valley. Thomas decided that somehow he and David must be a part of this English entourage. He needed to know if there was going to be negotiation, or an ultimatum to get out of the Ohio Valley.

Virginia Governor Robert Dinwiddie received word of a French buildup of eight hundred men on the forks of the Ohio, Allegheny, and Monongahela Rivers. The British King ordered Dinwiddie to send warning to the French to peacefully depart. "A refusal to do so may force the British to bring a call to arms," said the statement.

George Washington learned, while in Williamsburg, of an assignment for someone to go into the western frontier. He offered his services as a volunteer to carry the message. George convinced the Governor he was experienced in the wilderness due to his years as a surveyor. He insisted that the winter weather that was coming would not be a deterrent to his strength and persistence, because he had already endured the harshness and hardship of Ohio Valley winters.

Dawn brought more cold and chill, with Arctic winds coming from the north. The two strangers were packing up and ready to mount their horses when Thomas awoke. When he sat up, a drip of ice fell from his nose. "You're up early, I see. Looks like another bitter winter day."

"We want to get an early start, because the dark sets in so early these days," the large man said. "Where are you two headed?"

"I'm headed north," David answered. "Going all the way to Quebec, God willing."

Thomas broke into the conversation, "I'm going north, too. By the way, I'm Thomas Milton and this is my brother, David." David reached out to shake the hands of the strangers. He turned towards Thomas, and raised his left eyebrow and furrowed his brow in astonishment.

"My name is Major George Washington, and this is my guide, Christopher Gist.[10] Pleased to meet you both. If you want to ride with us today, please join us."

"Most obliged to do that, Sir. Me and my brother know these parts pretty well. Maybe we can show Mr. Gist some shortcuts to your destinations," Thomas said, as he hurriedly swallowed his coffee and chewed on a bite of hard bread.

"Our destination today is Logtown, where we'll meet a group of Iroquois who will accompany us to Fort Le Boeuf. Your company is welcome."

The Milton brothers were standing back to back saddling up their horses. "I thought you had a mind to get to Williamsburg. What changed your mind?" asked David.

"If these men are who they say they are, we better stick with them. They can help us find out if another war with the French is headed our way. Jonathan will be pleased if I can give him first-hand information about an imminent war and where it might be fought. You'll be needed to translate, probably. I don't want you to say a word about speaking French. We'll maybe get more news for Jonathan if we just tell them we're guides, too."

Christopher Gist was an experienced guide assigned to accompany George to the Ohio Valley and to help communicate with the Indians. Thomas and David were equally as experienced but did not chose to take the lead. Excessive rain fell the first day the Washington party and the Milton brothers headed northwest. Thomas tried to ride side by side with George but conversation was impossible because of heavy winds.

Day two started out dry and windless. The conversation was lively at first but Thomas worked to direct George into talking about his mission. "I'm curious, Major. Your trip to visit the French must be of utmost importance to make such a journey as the winter sets in." Thomas waited for George to reply.

"Yes, Governor Dinwiddie received a letter from the Board of Trade in London requesting a meeting with French Canada. The words are very clear. They are to vacate immediately or else we will bring the British Army into the Ohio Valley. I have volunteered to bring this message." George turned to Thomas. "What, pray tell, brings you into this mountainous country?"

"My brother and I are fur traders."

"Really, do you supply the Hudson's Bay Company? They are successful with the beavers furs and also have good relations with the Indians, I might add. At least that is what I have been told."

Thomas reflected on the Major's question. "Yes, we do business with the Hudson's Bay. But tell me, what are the French up to now? I know about the lead plates they have put into the ground stating their possession of the Ohio River."

"Yes, it's true. Our government is sure the French are intending a full takeover of all the territory between Canada and Louisiana. They want an unobstructed passage to reach the mouth of the Mississippi and New Orleans. As you know, there are many Englishmen moving into the frontier. It's the Crown's wish to protect this westward movement. The Ohio Company already has a large investment in the Valley, and I understand smaller companies have invested large sums to clear land and build roads to the Cheasapeake as well. The Indians are upset because the French are claiming land that the English have already agreed, by treaty, to give to them. The agreement says that the colonists will not infringe on Indian land, but the French have ignored this treaty. I'll be meeting with Half-King, the Iroquois chief, and he'll go with me to see the French Canadians."

Thomas looked into the ominous sky. Clouds had begun covering the blue sky as the breeze blew in prelude to the winds that were about to return. "Will we have another war with the French?" Thomas asked.

"I will be able to answer that better after we reach our destination. The letter from London seemed quite resolute."

Major Washington and Mr. Gist met with a Frenchman named Legardeur de St. Pierre on Presque Isle on the Lake Erie shore.[11] Thomas and David travelled with the group, which by now included a French interpreter, Half-King, and several other men. The Milton brothers were disappointed with the interpreter but disingenuously carried out their plan not to divulge David's ability to speak French. "We'll work on a way to put you inside when Washington presents the letter from Dinwiddie," Thomas told David. "It'll be imperative to know exactly what the letter says and how St. Pierre responds. We'll continue as unconcerned guides until we see what happens when the French meet the English."

Major Washington changed into his red and blue army uniform while his interpreter waited inside for St. Pierre and his interpreter to arrive. The meeting place was a one- room shack, barely standing, but it brought shelter as a blazing fire warmed the men for the first time in many weeks. The Major began pacing as he waited for the adversaries to arrive. "What can be keeping St. Pierre?" he asked his interpreter. "Go and see what the delay is."

Thomas and David observed the impasse in the meeting. Men, mostly French soldiers, were moving in and out of the small cabin. As the two brothers tried to eavesdrop, the French chatter was lost in the wind. "Move closer to the window, David!" Thomas ordered. "Try to look inconspicuous so's ya can pick up the babble. Somethin's going on."

Meandering to the door, David squatted down on one knee pretending to tie his buckskin boot. The French soldiers stood beside an open campfire to keep warm, so David took a place beside one of the soldiers and leaned in to warm his hands. The British interpreter came rushing by and pushed his way through the door. David heard him announce to Major Washington that the French interpreter was ill. "Why can't you interpret for both sides?" George asked impatiently. David could hear the conversation clearly.

"They seem to fear I won't be honorable and translate impartially," was the reply from the English interpreter. David rushed to tell Thomas another interpreter would be needed because of this turn in events. "Now is your chance—go over and ask what is wrong, using your best French. Get into a conversation with the soldiers. Just act like an unconcerned fur trader and let them make the first move," Thomas instructed. The plan worked. The rendezvous convened and David was inside, using his most valuable skill as a neutral translating for the Frenchman, St. Pierre.

George Washington gave Governor Dinwiddie's message. The response from St. Pierre was adamant. "There will be no withdrawal of French troops from the Ohio Valley.[12] You have come on this long journey for naught. This has been a complete waste of my time and, certainly, yours, Major!"

George took immediate action, asking for volunteers to make haste to give St. Pierre's response to the Governor. The Milton brothers, with no forethought, quickly answered in unison. Thomas raised his hand to gain Washington's eye. "Sir, I can leave immediately. To expedite the trip, I feel with plenty of supplies and several men I can reach Williamsburg in several weeks. I am the best man for the job because of my unlimited knowledge of the terrain."

By dawn's early light, Thomas Milton, two detail men, and a pack horse were underway. Thomas was euphoric, in disbelief of the good fortune that lay ahead. Jonathan Milton would be the first to learn of the probability of another war between England and France.

The grandees of Virginia embraced the Publick Times in Williamsburg. The renaissance of spring after the drab 1753–1754 winter season blazed with color from the flowers and trees. Adding to the brightness were the English fashions worn by both women and men. Martha and Daniel were inundated with invitations to dinner parties and balls. In return, they invited numerous friends and family to sit at their table. The dinnertime conversations centered on the young Major who had returned from giving the French military the ultimatum to get out of the Ohio Valley. The seven thousand–word report which he had turned over to Govenor Dinwiddie was reprinted not only in the Virginia newspapers, but in newspapers in other colonies and even several in England.[13] "Do you think the Governor will raise troops and start training for retaliation?" was the question that usually started an exchange.

"The Algonquins will be a French ally. They have murdered and scalped over fifty Virginians already."

"No, no! Not fifty, the number is under ten," an exasperated Virginian said.[14] "But just the same, they are killing our people."

"Even Colonel Washington said the Indians fired at him. He said he had holes in his hat and coat. The French will be sorry they gave them guns. We'll probably end up giving the Iroquois guns before this is over."

"My worry is that the Indians will get into Williamsburg."

"We're going to need to build a fort or two to store supplies and house men. The French have already built several forts. Oh, and by the way, unless Governor Dinwiddie has commissioned Washington, he is not a Colonel. He is still a Major."

"I hear this young upstart is a member of the Ohio Company. He is just trying to protect the five hundred thousand acres. Since his brother died, he has been overzealous in trying to replace him. Well, I even heard he was trying to take over as Adjutant General of the Virginia Militia, his brother's position."

"The Ohio Company has been the exemplar for many companies. Benjamin Franklin and Thomas Jefferson's father each have developed a company. I hear tell that Jonathan Milton has organized twenty or so men into the Allegheny Company and they may have a charter for two hundred thousand acres."

"Who is this brash young man? Has anyone actually seen him? I hear tell he is a Goliath, nearly seven feet tall."

"One thing is for sure, Major or Colonel, whatever his rank, Washington will have trouble finding men to join the Militia. Protecting Virginia borders will not be a simple task if there is all-out war"

A deep melancholy hung over George as he returned to Williamsburg. The failure to negotiate the French out of the Ohio Valley overwhelmed him. When he learned of his reprinted journal in the Virginia Gazette, his spirits began to rise. His observations on the clear and present danger of the French intrusion became the subject of discussion of many Virginians. The name *George Washington, the Courageous,* lay on the lips of the populace.

Governor Dinwiddie asked George to find recruits and lead an assault into the frontier. With little military experience himself, poorly-trained men, a shortage of horses, wagons in disrepair, and a limited food supply, Lt. Colonel Washington (his new rank) headed west to rout the French. The campaign was a disappointment from start to finish. Washington had pledged to dislodge the French or face the consequences of losing the fertile Ohio Valley. The first set-back was the rest of a preemptive round fired by Washington's men, killing numerous French and their commander. This infuriated the opposition, who declared they had been under a flag of truce.

The final trampling resulted in the Virginia soldiers having to show a flag of truce. Given an opportunity to regroup, the French attacked Fort Necessity, where the Virginia Militia was encamped. Surrounded by French Canadians, with supplies diminishing and casualties building, Washington sent up a flag of truce, professing defeat.

After nearly a year in the Ohio Valley, Washington returned home with stomach pain and dysentery, a huge loss of men, and an embarrassing defeat. He had fallen from favor with Governor Dinwiddie as well. Discouraged and disgraced, George resigned from the Virginia Militia, rented Mount Vernon from his brother's widow, and went home to become a planter.[15]

Bartholomew Dandridge took out his handkerchief, lifted his straw hat and wiped the sweat dripping from his brow like rain into a rain barrel. The August day had temperatures into the nineties with humidity nearly the same. "A swim in the Pamunkey would keep me drier than this heat," he said. "My weathervane nose tells me we'll have a storm brewing sometime soon. I need to get the farmhands to tie down the hanging sheds so the tobacco will not get soaked." Bart trudged into the house, shouting, "Mother, where are you?"

"Upstairs with baby Mary," he was told.

A flash of dry lightning illuminated the staircase as Bart started up towards the baby's room. Thunder sounded only seconds later, startling him as he entered the nursery. Baby Mary, who was nursing, began to cry inconsolably.

"I have been so busy today, I didn't realize a summer storm was on the way," Frances said as she cuddled her baby. "There, there. Mama's here." She began humming into Mary's tiny ear.

"Mis'er Dan'ridge, Mis'er Dan'ridge," called Lee as he thundered up the stairs. "Come quick, there's a fire in the hanging shed. " S'cuse me, Mis Dan'ridge. Iris say it okay fer me to come an' tell Mis'er Dan'ridge The wind is blowin' in from the north and we can't control it."

"That's fine, Lee. I'm sorry Mr. Dandridge is away, but I know

Bartholomew and you can handle this emergency. Sounds like the rain will be here any minute," Frances said as she gently patted Mary's back. Another clap of thunder sounded, and either a tree branch or an outside shutter began to slap against the window.

"Mother, I want you to take the girls and go into the storm cellar. The sky is asparagus green—could mean a cyclone is coming. I know if Pa were here, he would insist you take the girls and go. Storms that blow up this fast mean we're in for lots of wind and rain."

Frances studied her son with deep concern. "I won't go unless you go with us!"

"I will join you as soon as I'm sure we have the fire under control and all our people are safe. If things look bad, I'll send the women and children down to be with you. Now, take the children and go!"

Frances walked slowly to the window and observed the clouds moving swiftly across the sky, their colors changing into an ominous dark blue-green that overlay the lighter viridescent clouds. Their rapid movement pushed the colors back and forth. "We'll wait for you in the cellar, but please don't delay until the last minute to join us, Bart."

The raging wind that followed the lightning and thunder continued for several hours while Frances prayed for composure. She tried to hide her fear by playing word games and I-spy with her children in the damp cellar. "Where's Papa?" Betty kept asking her mother, as she pulled on her sleeve.

John Dandridge had left Chestnut Grove a week earlier to visit his niece, Mary Spotswood, who lived in Fredricksburg.[16] The crops were about to be harvested and the tobacco was mostly picked and hanging, so the time seemed appropriate to leave for a family visit. John, at age fifty-six, no longer had to spend as much time with the farming. Bartholomew, young, strong, and capable, seemed a likely replacement to relieve his father from some of the heavier responsibilities of their farm.

"Sshh," said Franny. "He's gone to visit cousin Mary and he won't be home until tomorrow. Now be quiet." Both Nancy and Betty sat listening to the wind and waiting for the gusts to subside. "Mother, I don't like the smell down here. The muddy walls are leaking and I feel like I'm sitting in water,"

Franny said. At that moment, the two wooden doors opened and Bart carefully descended the four mudpacked stairs. "Mother, this nor'easter isn't due to leave us too soon," he said. "We'll just have to wait it out."

The mantel clock chimed half past twelve as the Dandridge family wearily climbed the staircase to find their beds. Too exhausted to even talk about the wind, rain, and fire, the family removed their shoes and fell into bed. As dawn approached, a knock-knocking sound aroused Frances from her deep sleep. "What was that," she said, sitting upright. Usually she did not have restful nights if John was not lying next to her, and baby Mary had chosen to have one of her restless nights, waking Frances several times. When the baby finally settled down in her mother's arms, Frances slipped into a golden slumber. The intrusive noise began again, and Frances realized someone was knocking on the front door. Iris, already on her feet, padded down the stairs and was soon joined by Frances. "Who's at the Dan'ridge door?" Iris called. She was sure it was not one of the slaves, because they used the back door.

A deep raspy voice replied, "I's from Mis Spotswoods in Fred'icksbur' "

Frances, standing behind Iris, felt her heart race while her legs began to shake and her body chilled—in the middle of August early on a summer morning. "Open the door, Iris. Ask him in," she said quietly.

Frances knew before the words spilled from the black man's mouth; something had happened to her dearest husband. "Mis Dan'ridge, I's awful sorry to bring such news, but I's need to tell ya that Mis'er Dan'ridge . . . well . . . he's already in the groun . . . it bein' so hot an all. Mis Spotswood wouldn't allow as how we bring 'im home. Mis Spotswood as' me to stay an' help bring you an' the family to Fredricksburg for a service."

Frances numbly gave directions. "Iris, send someone to Poplar Grove immediately to give Martha the news. I will oversee telling Bartholomew and the girls. We must try and be on our way by noon."

After a sweltering day of travel over dry dusty roads, the Dandridge family arrived in Fredricksburg. Frances insisted on complete details of John's passing and was told he had died of apoplexy. His stroke was immediately fatal, she was told, with assurances that he suffered no pain.[17] John had been interred in St. George's churchyard, where a service was now performed by the Reverend Mossom. Frances sat silently on the hard pew, deeply hypnotized while repeating her prayers. Bartholomew sat beside her. Anna Maria held baby Mary. Franny and Elizabeth sat next to Martha.

Martha hardly attended to the words spoken by the minister. Like her mother, she was numbed by her father's death. Her precious Daniel wrapped his hand over hers and gave a reassuring and loving nod. Anguished, Martha offered her own prayer as Reverend Mossom gave the benediction. "*Oh my Heavenly Father, it hurts me to see my mother suffer such enormous pain. My empathy brings thoughts inside my head of the torment and agony to me and the children if I ever lost my dear husband. Please spare Mother the burden of deep despair and help her to take solace in her devoted family . . . My dearest Father, I have loved you so much. You have given us all so much, especially, the gift of yourself.*" Her tears sprinkled onto Daniel's hand as she looked to him for comfort and peace.

March 28, 1755 Spring is wit us again. As i set riting in mi jornel I feel rested and joyous for the first tim in meny months. Mother has ben buse wit Mary and plans for Nances weding wich helps her lonely dais witout papa. Mi sisters and Mother hav staid wit us at white hous so Mrs kidwel maks us ar dreses here. Nances dres is so beutiful. White brocad and lace. Her shoes hav not arrived yet from england. Ar chilren r well. thank you dear Lord. Fany is almos for years old. Jacky is 2 an Patcy is 1. they ar beutiful chilren. Daniel is a astounding father. He stil gits up at nite to tend the chilren if they need somthing. They luv him so. How can i thank you for mi blesings my DEAR LORD my GOD. Giv me strength to fac any adversitys that mae com my way. Amen and Peace forever. Patcy

An earthquake can strike without warning; movement deep below the earth bringing enormous consequences to the life above. Life's daily events can also strike a blow, delivering permanent life-changing events. Seventeen hundred and fifty-five would be the watershed year in Martha Jones Dandridge Custis's life changes. While she was still mourning the loss of her father, her oldest daughter Frances suddenly died. The onset of her illness was sudden, as had been the fatal illness of her brother Daniel.[18]

"*Another piece of my heart has been taken away,*" Martha lamented. Watching Daniel fall into an abyss of grief, Martha feared he would never return. His health began to deteriorate, causing Martha to agonize over his every sneeze and cough. A strange lethargy had overtaken the bereaved father.

"My dearest, you seem so tired after your morning survey of the plantation," Martha said with concern. "Maybe a trip into Williamsburg would be good for both of us."

"If we take the children, I will agree. I am anxious to see our portraits. Mr. Wollaston should have completed the finishing touches by now. Do you think Jacky and Patcy can sit still for him to begin their portraits?[19] Let us make plans to leave right away. I need to see James Power about some business dealings anyway."

"In answer to your first question, dear, I'm sure Patcy will have no problem sitting for John Wollaston. Jacky? He will be as wiggly as a June bug. It will be good for you to see James again; he is such a good friend. Why do you need to see him?" Martha asked.

"Don't worry about my reasons to see James. I need to talk over some issues left behind by my father."

The trip into Williamsburg was restorative for both Martha and Daniel. Arriving in the off-season without Assembly, their social calendar was still flooded with invitations. Martha had become an esteemed hostess, as well. Her unease about bringing the limited Dandridge heritage into the aristocratic realm of the Custis family had diminished. An invitation to the House of Six Chimneys was considered a prize attached to the importance of the guests. The two-week visit extended into four weeks. The portraitist, Mr. Wollaston, patiently painted the Custis children. As Martha had forecast, Patcy could sit for an hour, even though she had acquired a large bump in the middle of her forehead which had turned black and blue. Jacky's ability to sit was limited to a bare fifteen minutes.

Daniel had two very important appointments in Williamsburg, one to see a physician and the other to see his lawyer about his will, which had yet to be written. Daniel was sure his physical disorder was temporary, at best. "My loss of two dear children has put me into a deep melancholy, I know," Daniel confided to Dr. James Carter. "But I also sometimes suffer from shortness of breath and fatigue."

"You may need to curtail some of your activities," the doctor suggested. "Why don't you relinquish some of your plantation duties to others, then go home and enjoy your wife and children."

"What are you trying to tell me? Are you saying I won't recover from this state I find myself in?" Daniel leaned back in his chair, aghast at this news.

"Mr. Custis, your heart is slowing down. You need to do the same. Weariness and irregular breathing can be expected as one becomes older."

"But I do not feel old—just worn out. My father lived to be seventy-one, and my grandfather died a rather untimely death, so no telling how long he might have lived, if he had not been gluttonous, especially for the comfort of other men's wives."[20]

"Daniel, go back to the White House and spend more time on your porch."

James Power was not in his office, so Daniel rode on to his home. He knocked several times before a large, bent-over, black man answered the door. "Mis'er Power not here. Don' know when he'll be back. I can tell him a message for ya." His dark bloodshot eyes looked weary.

"No, no—I'll reach him later." Daniel climbed into his carriage, puzzling over Dr. Carter's directive and James Power's absence. "Maybe Dr. Carter is correct, I do need to take advantage of more leisure time so I can work out the details of my will. Jack is such an anomaly that I need advice with that situation. Martha will not be burdened with his care!" Daniel told himself. "Sam, drive to Jonathan Milton's office, quickly." Daniel's abrupt decision to see Jonathan was a painful one. But with James out of reach and his return to the White House in a few days, he needed immediate legal advice.

Deliberating his situation, Daniel sat back and prepared himself for the distasteful Mr. Milton, but found his office empty.

The Custis family returned to the Pamunkey without Daniel settling his will. He chose not to tell Martha about his visit to see the doctor, and explained that his legal business was postponed because James Power was out of town. Life on the Pamunkey had become sedate and peaceful for the Custis family. Both Martha and Daniel curtailed many of their social obligations. Daniel, especially, drew pleasure from home and hearth. His days were filled with early morning rides inspecting the plantation, diligent work on the receipts of all the Custis properties, then, after the three o'clock dinner, evenings spent with Martha, Jacky, young Patcy, and Scriptures and song.

The summer heat settled over Virginia like a pile of blankets in winter. May and June blistered the crops and dried up several water sources. Summer frequently brought with it all kinds of sicknesses. Mosquitos were carriers of yellow fever and malaria, while typhoid fever spread by unsafe water.

Jacky was the first to fall victim of malaise and fever.[21] Martha, always apprehensive, was sure it was typhoid fever and wasn't sure which well to blame, the old one or the new one. She sent Sam into Williamsburg to bring Dr. Carter to the White House so he could begin treatment of her precious son. Instead the doctor sent several remedies, giving explicit instructions for administering them. He also sent assurance that Jacky did not have typhoid fever.

Several days later Daniel was taken ill. Martha rotated between one patient and the other. Jacky appeared to begin recovery first, so she transferred Dr. Carter's elixirs to Daniel. "My dear, it is time for more barley water," Martha said as she entered their bedroom on a humid July day. Daniel was resting against propped-up pillows in a high-back chair sitting next to the window.

"I'm feeling a bit better this afternoon. The cool breeze is accommodating to my sticky body." Daniel weakly smiled at his wife.

"Daniel Parke Custis, you get back into your bed immediately!" Martha's petite hand reached for Daniel's elbow. "You'll catch your death if you don't move away from the window. I'll have Iris bring up some more cool cloths. They will have to do for making you more comfortable."

"I know you are right, dearest. Please let me be for awhile longer. I love looking over our meadows and poplar trees moving in the breeze. I can hear the sounds of the out-of-doors . . . the children so carefree, playing and laughing. Listen, can you hear them? The slaves are making their callings to each other in the fields. I even hear the spinning wheels spin. The sounds are like a symphony, all synchronized on the same song. Forgive me for sounding so maudlin. The sounds of the open air give me such peace."

"You are very poetic today. Of course, I hear the sounds of Poplar Grove. We are so accustomed to the everyday goings on, we don't hear it. Sometimes at night when the plantation sleeps, I lie back and listen to the sounds of silence. Now, you get back into bed!"

This was the last day that Daniel was able to communicate with the people he loved. His temperature rose and his lucidity diminished. Martha was overwrought with worry as she scribbled out a note for Dr. Carter. "You ride as fast as the wind, Sam," Martha ordered. "Tell him he must ride back here quickly. I am desperately pleading for him to come. You tell him that!" After Sam explained Daniel's symptoms to Dr. Carter, he packed his bag with different medicines, saddled up, and headed west to travel the twenty-five miles to the White House.[22]

Martha nursed, fed, and bathed Daniel, hardly leaving his bedside. She watched his strength ebb further away each day. His concave eyes, submerging deeper into his head, altered his facial features. His complexion turned ashen.

Three days passed with Dr. Carter and Martha attending. Jacky continued to improve and wanted to leave his bed. Iris kept a twenty-four-hour vigil with him to make sure he did not leave his room.

Each night, Martha found solace writing in her journal to spill out her concern at Daniel's failure to show any vestiges of recovery. She quoted the Scriptures that seemed to fulfill her needs, then blew out the candle and placed herself next to Daniel, praying for sleep for them both.

By mid-July Daniel was dead.[23] Twenty-six-year-old Martha was left with two children, substantial cash reserves, eighteen thousand acres of widely separated farmland, nearly two hundred slaves, bills to be paid, money to be collected, communication with Daniels's English agents and supervision of the plantation's overseers to be carried out, an unresolved lawsuit that began back with Daniel's grandfather Parke, and a heart that was fragmented into a million pieces. The staggering blow of Daniel's death was, at first, a crushing shock, which turned into anguish, followed by an unrelenting anger. Daniel was laid to rest at Queens Creek Plantation, a plantation brought into the Custis family by his mother. He lay beside his two children, Daniel II and Frances.[24]

Several weeks after Daniel's death, Martha learned he did not leave a will. Intestate law declares that an estate without a will is to be divided equally among the heirs; in this case, Martha, Jacky and Patcy.[25] Martha was inundated with advice from several different factions—her brother-in-law, close friends, and her mother—who offered warnings about the numerous men who would be calling upon her seeking marriage.[26] "You, my darling, have become a most attractive and very wealthy candidate for suitors to come calling," Frances cautioned.

Martha was told she needed management help to care for the plantations and other holdings. English factors needed to be replaced. Attorneys bid her favor to settle the estate, especially trusts for her children. Concentration on her children and herself was Martha's primary concern as she began to untangle the intricacies of Daniel's estate.

20, August 1757, Each day I ask the LORD to help mak me hole agin. My dear husban is in heven wit my 2 chilren and I feel helples an hopeles wit my 2 chilren here on erth. I will work to keep ar plantasions prosperous an good return on our tobako. Ar soil is dying says Daniel's manager, mr valentine. ar tobako is poor quality. i'm crying evry nite to tell myself that we wil not ned credit and continu wit good management. John Custis mad Daniel promis he wud not go into debt I wil keep the promis. Wit yur help an guidanc I wil keep the Custis estate for my chilren. But what abot Jack? I hav not seen or herd from him in along tim. I hav not herd from him since Daniel's death. i ned advice becaus he wil come to see me soon. PLEAS give y ur plan o lord. Som daes i am overwhelmed wit worre, uncertanity, sleeplesnes an torment. Mother is mi bigest comfort. She alwaes has the write words for mi soul an hart. Todae Jacky askt if he cud go wit me to Daniel's grave. He has ben a good boy thru his loss to. Daniel sed he is lik John Custis, irasional and demanding he sed for me to be unyielding. He sed "Jacky wil want to tell me what to do an to never go back on mi word. he will be manipulating" Can he be rite? I will obey you an trust you to help me mak mi daes grow shorter not longer, lighten my heart and take away mi dolefulness. AMEN

Martha leaned her head back on the leather seat of her carriage. The blinds were pulled to the top of the windows because the late summer humidity was pressing against her body, the dark color of her mourning gown holding in the heat. A slight breeze flowed through the moving carriage, bringing limited relief. Perspiration dripped down the sides of her face and under her arms, trickling down over her ribs. Pulling her handkerchief from her bosom, she patted her forehead, catching the moisture before it rolled onto the white lace collar attached to the bodice of her dress. Patcy's head lay in Martha's lap while her little body lurched to and fro in rhythm with the movements of the carriage. Martha stroked Patcy's cheek with her damp fingers, "How lucky you are, my little angel, to sleep so soundly on this blistering day." Jacky and Dicey sat across from Martha. Dicey pretended to sleep. Jacky, always restless, played with a wooden top that one of the field hands had carved for him. Martha put her forefinger to her lips, cautioning him to be careful and not disturb Dicey.

Dreading the trip into Williamsburg, Martha had tried to lay out the plans for meeting Daniel's attorney. Six weeks had gone by since Daniel's death and this was her first visit away from the White House. Martha had begged off on the trip but her mother encouraged her to find some solace at the House of Six Chimneys. "How can I find solace in that house?" She asked herself. "The house has so many ghosts. The children and I will sleep outside on the porch tonight! I must start an inventory of the household goods. There will be several things I will take back with me, especially the silver pieces. No one is going to get their hands on them except my children! Least of all Anne Moody, or Jack, for that matter. Oh, dear Lord, don't let Jack show up while I'm here. I just can't face him right now." Martha's uneasiness surprised her. Her shattered heart was beginning to mend, with hostility nudging out the pain. "It's only because I have such anxiety over keeping our receipts in order. And Jack, I have no idea what demands he may make of me because of Daniel's being intestate. He may demand a fourth of the Custis estate. Oh, Daniel, why didn't you have a will? Do you know the torment this has caused me?"

The House of Six Chimneys needed curtains to be opened, along with windows and doors, to let fresh breezes blow in from the Chesapeake. There needed to be people inhabiting the house, to purge the dust, motionless air, and dank, musty, and clammy odor. "I need to make a decision about what to do with this house. I can't possibly manage two large homes and five plantations by myself," Martha told herself. She had not sent a messenger ahead to inform the servants of her arrival.

"Dicey, please open the drapes and then the windows down here; then go upstairs. Fetch fresh water when you are through opening up the house," Martha ordered. "I will go and find the cook and tell her we are here and need something to eat." Jacky and Patcy both still slept inside the carriage, for which Martha was grateful.

"Sam, bring in the valises, but try not to disturb the children. Make sure the horses have fresh water and feed. I am sure there will be help in the barn." Martha tiptoed through the house, as though she had forgotton her children were sleeping outside in the carriage.

"Mrs. Custis, I didn' know you were a comin'," Sally said, running in from the passageway. "We's still cryin' over Mr. Custis, God bless his soul, an worrin' 'bout you and the chil'ren. Can we help git you settled?"

"Yes, Sally. We have had a very long day, but the roads were clear so we made good time. Please find the cook and tell her we want our dinner within the hour. We will be retiring early. I have business to settle in Williamsburg tomorrow. I would like to be rested. Send someone to give

Mr. Power the message that I am here and will call upon him tomorrow."

With a pink puff full of powder, Martha tried to cover the dark circles under her eyes. She looked down on her jet black dress and tried to wipe away the excess powder which had fallen from the puff. She studied herself in the mirror. "Those circles around my eyes match my dress. Maybe I can bring a new fashion to the ladies of Williamsburg."

The Custis carriage lumbering down Gloucester Street drew the attention of the Williamsburg townfolks. Men removed their hats, and women, nodding their heads, stopped and waved greetings. Martha responded with a wave of her handkerchief. James Power was not in his office, but a young, handsome assistant offered his services, promising familiarity with the Custis family legal file. "When will Mr. Powers return?" Martha asked.

"Not until a fortnight. He is in Baltimore on business."

"I plan to return home soon. Waiting for Mr. Powers will be quite impossible. I need advice, so I will appeal to your legal expertise to answer a few questions for me," replied Martha. She settled herself on a wodden surfaced chair and took out her handkerchief to pat her brow and lips. "I am sure you understand that my dear husband, Daniel Parke Custis, left no will. This tells me he was not ready to depart his family. His unexpected death took us all by surprise." Nervously wringing her handkerchief, Martha uttered, "Daniel was one who tended to details. His father instilled in him principles, conscientiousness, and honesty."

"Yes, he was a man of immense morality and ethics." The young man sat behind the large oak desk looking intently at Martha.

Martha knew that women usually did not handle their own affairs. She strove to dominate the dialogue, knowing she was displacing an emissary that could be taking care of her estate for her. She felt an urgency to hear for herself, from a legal professional, what intestate meant. "Mrs. Custis, Mr. Custis's estate will be divided equally among his heirs. As I understand it, you have two children. Is that correct?"

"Yes, yes. That is correct." Martha began to feel the oppressive heat.

"Each of your children will need a trust drawn up, to be turned over to them when they become of age. You will need to name a trustee to manage the trust. You, of course, will be able to draw upon the trust for their care and education or any needs they may have. Now, if you should marry again, under Virginia law all of your third, including furnishings, animals, household items, and slaves, will be turned over to your new husband. Your children's two-thirds will pass into the guardianship of your new husband after a formal petition is approved by the General Court here in Williamsburg. Have you any questions about the law?"

Martha studied the attorney's face. "*He can't be much older than my brothers William and Bartholomew. Was Mother right about young men seeking my fortune? Could this young man try to court me? I feel much older than he, maybe not in years but in experience.*" Feeling vulnerable and insecure, Martha took a deep breath and said, "I have a question that has been troubling me since learning of the law of intestate. John Custis fathered an illegitimate son with one of his slaves. Jack was Mr. Custis's loyal servant until his death and he received a large legacy from his will. Mr. Custis carefully outlined in his will each item Jack was to receive, including a house and furnishings." Martha bowed her head, blew air from her lungs and softly declared, "Daniel has been prudent in carrying out his father's wishes." Gathering her courage, she raised her head and leaned towards the attorney, "Since Daniel left no will, does Jack have a right to be declared an heir of his estate?" Martha nervously let out all the air from her lungs, straightened her back and sat forward in her chair. Staring directly into the attorney's eyes, she waited for the answer.

"I have not seen John Custis's will. I will need to be given a copy as soon as you can get one before I can answer your question."

Martha looked into the attorney's eyes, sensing deception. Most everyone in Williamsburg knew about the contents of John Custis's will! Dining table discussions and tea-time chatter for weeks centered on the outrageous inheritance left to Jack, a black slave-boy![27] "It is my assumption that Jack is now a free black man, so we will need to review Mr. Custis's legacy to him. Does Jack know of Daniel's death?"

"I have had no word from him, which does surprise me. As a matter of fact, neither Daniel nor I have heard from him in a long time. He may make an effort to contact me while I am here in Williamsburg," Martha replied. "I will get a copy of John Custis's will as quickly as possible." She stood up and offered her hand. "Good day."

"Sally, my dear friend, how can I possibly make recompense for all the kindness you have given me these past weeks?" George Washington was recovering from a prolonged illness due to his military campaign against the French. He lay cradled in feathery pillows to ease the pain.

"Are you sure you are warm enough?" Sally pulled up the quilt that was lying half on the floor and half on the bed. "You look like you need a good game of cards."

"Madame, gaze upon me carefully. My reclamation of fitness is well along. I feel like Lazarus arising from the dead."

His recovery seemed certain after returning to Mount Vernon. George William Fairfax was in England to settle the estate of his father. He had left his wife, Sally behind to keep watch over Belvoir. Sally contributed to George's recovery with her daily visits to his bedside, bringing jellies, hyson tea, and mountain sweet wine from the Canary Islands.[28]

"You are such a poor card player that I find delight in taking your specie." Sally's titillating eyes danced with pleasure as she tipped her head in response.

"When this bloody flux is replaced with my good health, we'll see who carries the heaviest purse. As a matter of fact, I feel so well, I think I will indulge myself with one of life's greatest pleasures." Sally met George's eye with a look of anticipation as to what that pleasure might be. "Why don't you pour me a glass of the wine." George returned a flirtatious grin. "Not the wine with the sap from the acacia tree, but the sweet wine from Malaga."[29]

"George, your doctor said only two glasses a day and only mixed with water of gum arabic.[30] You may be blessed with sinew and brawn, which still need time to recover, but your rationality needs examination."

"Madame, just your presence is the most likely tonic to help me recoup my vitality." George lay back on his pillows with a peal of laughter. "Now bring us the cards. Today, I will take the gold."

George had nearly died on the battlefield, not from the volleys of bullets and the swords, but from rancid meat, poor water, and living in a cold stockade with a smoky fireplace that provided little heat. His susceptibility to intestinal ailments became more prolonged with each bout. Moreover, a new ailment had presented itself, causing George grave concern. A cough with chest pain reminded him of the suffering of his beloved brother Lawrence. George had witnessed Lawrence's slow and painful death from tuberculosis. The combination of dysentery, severe stomach cramps, and now the persistent cough and fever, had compelled George to leave his duty and return to Williamsburg for expert medical advice. Relief overcame George when he was told his chest discomfort was pleurisy and that a long rest at home would overcome the bloody flux.[31]

Home . . . his beloved Mount Vernon! Anne Fairfax Washington, now Lee, due to her remarriage, agreed to rent the house on the Potomac to George. Lawrence's young daughter Sarah was to have inherited Mount Vernon when she became of age. Anne had remarried shortly after the death of Lawrence and moved away, leaving the Potomac home deserted. Unexpectedly, Sarah died, giving Anne total ownership. With her own home and a new husband, she had sold the furniture and closed Mount Vernon. The manor house, outbuildings, grist mill, and several slaves were now abandoned, leaving the house boarded up. Weak, weary, haggard, discouraged, and sick, George went to Mount Vernon for the restoration of his health, reopening of the rented Mount Vernon that he loved.[32]

Five years in the field fighting the lingering war over property rights in the Ohio Valley resulted in frustration and severe illness. His failure to be commissioned by the British as an officer in the Royal Army disappointed George. His loyalty to the Crown began to diminish as the condescending British officers treated him disrespectfully. He suffered frights from having his horses shot from beneath him, finding gunshot holes in his hats and coats, and watching officers lose their lives on the battlefield. One such officer was General Edward Braddock, his British superior. George felt dishonor and shame at being ignored when he suggested battle strategies for the wilderness against an enemy who had learned from the Algonquins how to hide, jump, and attack, in terrain he had surveyed and mapped. Humiliation swept over him when he was thwarted from helping with negotiations with the Iroquois and Algonquins whose customs, mores, and language were well-known to him. The disappointing battles couldn't be won by an ill-trained, poorly equipped, and arrogant British army. General Braddock's resistance to using Indian tactics cost him his life. Overriding the disappointments was the depression brought on by more debilitating dysentery.

As he rode toward home, retreating from the Ohio Valley, George cudgelled his brain to make decisions about his future. "I'm sure I will restore Mount Vernon and bring back the Lawrence Washington standard of a viable country manor with friends, parties, dancing, sumptuous food, and laughter. I think I'll leave my military career behind and become a planter!"

Several months passed by, with Sally visiting daily to tend to George's health. "I see you have more color in your pallid cheeks today," Sally would report as she fluffed the pillows behind George's head. Envisioning her visits each day, he knew it was her company that helped his physical and mental health improve.

"This day, Madame, I will mark on my calendar. I am feeling so well, with or without color in my cheeks," he chided Sally, "I am thinking of returning to the battlefield."

"Your return would be premature and self-indulgent, I must say!" Sally retorted. "Does the general forget your doctor told you three months was the least time needed for rest? You have hardly been out of bed. It will take more time for your strength to return." Looking coquettish, Sally demurely added, "I thought you were never going back to the war; besides, I will be very lonely if you leave."

Sally, the humorous, unpretentious, sociable, and self-confident woman that George had always coveted, was admitting her passion for him? George's thoughts were spinning from this revelation. Was he misinterpreting her statement? His infatuation with Sally Cary Fairfax began the first time his eyes beheld her at the Assembly Ball in Williamsburg. However, his adoration for her had never been reciprocated. This was something he needed to put away in his heart, and wait for more validation.

George's health continued to improve and so did his confusion about his future. After several weeks his recuperation seemed sufficient to decide him to see his doctor, for confirmation of his return to health, and to speak with the Virginia Governor about perhaps returning to the war if a British commission could be arranged. George wanted to train an army that could win.

"Bishop, my loyal friend, we are going to Williamsburg. The three-day trip will be a struggle but I know I'm feeling up to it." George patted his servant's arm. "Do you think if we pile several pillows on my saddle, it will make the ride easier? My buttocks and back are still tender, and maybe the padding of the pillows will allow me some comfort."

"Mr. Washington, are you sure you are ready for such a long journey?" Bishop's black eyes scanned George's face. "Your color is more of a white man's now but it's been so long since you've ridden, your horse still won't recognize ya."

George and Bishop left for Williamsburg with George sitting on pillows placed on his saddle to ease his pain while he rode. The two men did not achieve a full day's ride before they turned back. George's abdominal pain and fever returned, sending him flying back to Mount Vernon for more recuperation, and a return to Sally.[33]

Preparations for harvest were taking place when Martha returned to the White House from Williamsburg. Oney came running down the drive to greet the Custis children, whose heads popped out of the windows of the carriage, waving and shouting hello. "Patcy, darling, let Dicey hold you on her lap until we are up to the house," cautioned Martha. Patcy had several months to go before her second birthday and still seemed unsteady on her feet. Oney, at age ten, was her caretaker, and the two girls were inseparable.

Patcy ran into Oney's arms, hugging and kissing her. Jacky, needing to stretch his legs after the long ride, ran to the stable to check upon his favorite pony, Shepherd. Martha wearily entered her empty house, with a heavy heart. "I think I will send a message to Mother. I need to share with her the events of my trip." Then, to Martha's surprise, Frances opened the door from the passageway and hastened to greet her daughter. "Mother! I am delighted to see you. I was going to send Sam with a message asking you to come." The two women embraced affectionately. "Are Betty and Mary with you?"

"Yes, and Franny, too. I insisted she join us this time. All she wants to do is ride horses instead of helping in the house. Your father was certainly right about her being a rough and tumble. My dear, you look exhausted." Frances caressed her troubled child, gently stroking her head as it lay upon her breast. "I have a fresh pot of tea. Come and sit down and tell me about your trip."

"My lonely heart has overcome my logic, Mother. The advice I so hoped to seek has been withheld. James Power was in Baltimore so my parlance was with his assistant, a young and capable man, at least I thought so at first. He seemed sympathetic and a wise advocate for my situation. He asked to see John Custis's will, which I promptly made arrangements to have delivered to him." Martha struggled to remove her black hat. The ribbons once tied in a bow beneath her chin were now in a knot.

"Here, dear, let me help you." Frances manipulated the ties and untangled the bow. "Have a sip of tea. It will offer some comfort for you."

"The day is much too warm for hot tea. The return to the White House was unbearable. The carriage was stifling; the children were restless, even Patcy, and my clothes are saturated with my own perspiration. Dark clothing does not bring comfort in the summertime, Mother. Do you find that true?"

"I haven't noticed, my dear. Let the tea cool a bit, then continue to tell me what happened."

"Somehow, I misunderstood the young attorney's name, not that it should matter. But when he looked over the will he told me he would need to study precedent. I was astounded! I had no idea what he meant.

He explained the unusualness of intestate and Virginia law. John Custis clearly itemized the goods that Jack was to receive as a result of his legacy. The part of the will that is open to question is the statement relating to Daniel's guardianship of Jack until his death. It is not clear as to whose death, Jack's or Daniel's? I have no definite answer. I must wait until Mr. Power returns to clarify the intent of the will. I assume he will have to consult with Jonathan Milton. He is such a rogue. He will interpret the John Custis will in favor of Jack to embarrass my children by making them aware their father has a half-brother that is black!"

"I am so sorry you have come home feeling so despondent, Martha. Your desire to settle this matter quickly and efficiently will have to wait. Remember, patience is a virtue, and everything comes to those who wait, my dear."

"Of course, Mother. You always seem to find the words that soothe my soul. But I felt fine about his judgment until I apologized and asked him his name again. . . . His name is Luke Carter. There are so many Carters living in Virginia, and I get a chill every time I hear the name."

George Washington's recuperation was continuing to rally his spirits and his disposition. Sally Fairfax's contribution to his recovery was her affable personality—she offered companionship and constant encouragement to return to good health. George awoke every morning feeling rested, and waited for her daily visits. He began to plan a lavish dinner party with Sally's help, as thoughts of returning to the war diminished. Each day's improvement brought George to the realization that he had truly loved Sally from the time he had watched her polished minuet as she smoothly crossed the floor in her elegant snow-white dress at the Governor's Ball so many years ago, with every eye in the room upon her.

Correspondence began to flow into Mount Vernon from military friends and colleagues. A new British General had arrived in Virginia to replace the late General Braddock. There were requests for George to return to active duty, but he declined, answering that his health did not permit his return at this time. In truth, he was not going to leave Sally or Mount Vernon. Making plans for a gala dinner party with Sally as his hostess occupied much of his time.[34]

Each day he made notes on guest lists, china, silver, and menus, waiting to consult Sally about his plans. Then several days passed and Sally did not make her daily visit. George became agitated and sent Bishop to Belvoir to make sure Sally was not ill herself. Bishop returned with the news that George William Fairfax had unexpectedly arrived home from England.[35]

George had always assumed his close friend and Sally's husband suspected his feelings. George was only sixteen years old and vulnerable when they met. Over the years, Sally's sister had spoken to George about his obvious behavior when Sally was in his company. "You must be more discreet about your feelings for Sally. It is time you find a suitable woman that does not already have a husband. Sally will never leave George William." George was devastated.

George was in the process of planning to rebuild Mount Vernon. He meticulously studied the Georgian architecture in Williamsburg and other metropolitan areas that he had visited during the French and Indian campaign. Even though he did not have outright ownership of Mount Vernon, he planned the remodel and chose the wallcoverings, fabrics, and colors for each room. The second floor was to be extended, and windowpanes were to be either added or replaced. He had ordered the furnishings, dishes, silver, and interior changes before and during his recuperation. Sally's intermittent visits now always included either George William or several of her women friends.[36]

George's health continued to improve, and he made plans to once again try and ride into Williamsburg to see his doctor and meet the new Virginian Governor. Four months had passed since George had left the Army and returned home. Now the time had come to make decisions about his future. The one hundred thirty–mile trip into Williamsburg from Mount Vernon usually took three days. George planned two rest stops on the way. One stop would be his duty visit to his mother for several days, and the second stop would be a daytime visit to see Major Richard Chamberlayne, a comrade in arms.[37] George and Bishop rode their horses easily, allowing George no risk of aggravating his sensitive body.

Mary Ball Washington hardly acknowledged her son when he arrived at Ferry Farm. "You look like a bean pole without any beans! Have you been sick?" Her smile was as usual, upside down. Dark curtains hung over the windows making the rooms dark and drab. The only light was one small candle burning on the tea table. Piles of newspapers covered the tabletop, and old letters, yellow with age, covered the mahogany desktop.

"Yes, Mother. I have written you several letters. Didn't you know, I have been at Mount Vernon for some time, recuperating from dysentery and pleurisy? I have been on leave from the Army for nearly four months."

"What brings you here?" Mary stood with her hands on her hips. "Do you want me to fix your supper or something?"

"No, Mother, I came to spend several days with you. Haven't you read any of my letters?"

"No time for letters. I'm too busy trying to keep this farm going. My children don't care about me. Nobody ever comes."

George walked over and sat down in front of the disorganized desk. He picked up some of the letters and found most not been opened. There were three letters from his sister Betty. "Mother, why haven't you read these letters?"

"My eyes don't allow reading anymore. Besides, she never comes to see me. I'm not interested in what she has to say."

George's impatience became visible. "Mother, I am not here to bring you displeasure. I'm here because I have been very ill and I have written you numerous times to let you know. I am much better, and if the doctor says I'm fit, I'll return to the field."

"I need you here! Ferry Farm is too much for me to manage. Can't you see how disabled I am?"

"Father's will made provision for you to move to Fredricksburg at my coming of age . . . and that was five years ago." George tried to control his peevishness. "There is money for me to build you a house. Why won't you leave the farm?"

"Ferry Farm is my home, that's why." Mary crossed her arms over her chest and stuck out her chin. "I will die here."

"Ferry Farm is not your home; it is my home." George struggled for composure. "Father left it to me."

"*Why do I always walk into a battle with her. The Militia needs her on the front; she would scare Half-King into surrendering to the French. Three days will become too long for a visit,*" George thought. At the end of the first day George told Bishop they would be leaving early in the morning, and to plan on arriving at the Chamberlaynes two days early.

11, December 1757, I hav mised sevrl weeks writing. I seem to fall into bed evere nite ready for sleep after a long dae of overseeing the plantation, receipts, conferring wit the overseer and tending mi chilren an the house servants. making sur the pantry is ful of stapls prepare for the coming winter. PLEAS GoD help me to get throo the wintr wit energy an purpos. Im dreading the Christmas holidaes. I need ur guiding principle to show me the rite direction. Im stil waiting for word from James Powers about Jack. No word from Jack yet demanding his shar of Daniel's estate. Befor that hapens, I hope the legal side will be setled. I hav mane suitors calling, it sems. Charles Carter came calling He had the udacity to ask for mi hand.[38] *The old rascel! He jus wants mi plantasions. I wont merri again someone so old. Mi daes r so full wit duties. I hav no time for this nonsens. Mi chilren ned a father one that will luv them kindly an good harted. I can knot see miself or mi chilren in the same house wit selfish an greedy way. i must be able to talk an lauf take walks in mi garden an enjoy a new husband in that way. I PRAY everedae someone is there for me an Jacky an Patcy. LEAD me to the rite one. Im begining to tak pleasur in visiting my friends an family now and again. Patcy*

"Dicey, Molly, and Oney, please come into the west parlor. I have something to discuss with you." The girls were upstairs tending Jacky, Patcy, and their cousin, Mary Dandridge. Frances Dandridge and her baby daughter had arrived two weeks earlier for a visit. Martha and Frances, growing closer each day, brought companionship and comfort to each other. Both women shared widowhood and the responsibility of raising small children. Martha frequently had to remind herself that Mary was her sister and not her own child.

A messenger had arrived two days earlier, bringing an invitation to dinner at the home of Major and Mrs. Richard Chamberlayne. The Chamberlaynes were Martha's closest neighbors. The invitation included Jacky and Patcy, which pleased Martha because she knew she would be staying for several days, and she was not ready for separation from her children.

The three house servants entered the parlor, standing and waiting for Martha's directions. "Please sit down on the chaise," Martha instructed. "Jacky, Patcy, and I will be going to the Chamberlayne plantation the day after tomorrow for several days.[39] Molly, you will return to Chestnut Grove with Mary and my mother tomorrow. Dicey, you and Oney will accompany us to the Chamberlaynes. Tomorrow, I want you to bathe the children and make sure their hair is clean. Make sure their travelling clothes are cleaned and ironed, probably best to see to that today. All necessaries are to be packed in their valises. I will pack for myself, but please air my best chambray and make sure my black bonnet has no powder on the lace. Wash out my black gloves and my white collar, too."

Martha's second day at the Chamberlaynes had been therapeutic. "I almost feel somewhat whole again," Martha told herself, as she gazed at her reflection in the vanity. "My dark circles are fading, I have a little color back in my cheeks, and my spirits are rising." The walk in the early spring morning chatting with Mrs. Chamberlayne had given Martha a sense of renewal and hope. Her worries, about the Custis estate, overseeing the plantation and service people, caring for her children, keeping company with her bereaved mother and helping care for her year-old sister, seemed remote for the moment. Martha heard Jacky's laughter and pleasure outside while he was led around by a groom as he sat upon a pony, shouting, "Giddy-up." Patcy and Oney played London Bridge, Ring the Rosy and other outdoor games, with Dicey supervising.

Martha gave herself one last look in the cheval glass before she descended the stairway into the dining room for the three o'clock dinner. The table was elegantly set, with an array of silver candelabra burning brightly, china plates bordered in gold leaf with cups and saucers to match, silverware polished to mirror-like perfection, and stemware waiting to be filled with the finest claret from Bordeaux, France. Martha, the first to view the sumptuousness, counted the place settings. "*I wonder if a guest has arrived unexpectedly . . . there are eight settings.*" Martha's whimsical thoughts pictured a dashing prince dressed in brocade and feathers coming to dine with a sleeping princess.

"Martha, darling, I'm so glad I found you. We are all in the east parlor. We have a guest making a stopover on his way to Williamsburg. Come, I want you to meet him. He is a Militia comrade of mine," Major Chamberlayne said, as he took Martha's elbow and led her into the parlor.

The men were standing around the spinet drinking sherry, while the women were situated on chairs in front of the hearth chit-chatting. Richard Chamberlayne directed Martha to the group of men where the tall, lanky, unanticipated guest was deeply engaged in conversation, with his backside leaning against the spinet. "George, I would like you meet Martha Custis." Richard Chamberlayne, still holding Martha's elbow, guided her hand to reach out to the guest. "Martha, this is Colonel George Washington, the Adjutant General of the Virginia Militia. He is a very old and dear friend." Martha knew the Colonel was in high favor with the citizens of Williamsburg and the colonists of Virginia. She recalled seeing him at Assembly Balls, in Bruton Parish Church, and on Gloucester Street. The Virginia Gazette frequently reprinted his journal writings and letters about the distasteful war with the French Canadians. "I am very happy to make your acquaintance, Colonel Washington."

"The pleasure is mine, madame . . . . " The blue-gray eyes of this towering man intently scrutinized Martha's sable-colored hair and matching eyes. "When the time comes, please allow me to accompany you into the dining room. It is my pleasure to be invited to participate in this festive dinner. The Chamberlaynes did not expect me until the day after tomorrow, but my schedule brought me here early . . . . And I must say, it may be Providence that brought me here prematurely."

"*His nose is broad and his jaw is set. His mouth is fixed and rigid . . . . His uniform hangs loosely on his enormous frame. He is gaunt and his face is colorless . . . . Has he been ill? But his eyes are full of life and ambition.*" Martha's assessment of this imposing man gave her spine a fleeting chill. "It will be my pleasure to accompany you into the dining room," she answered.[40]

"Bishop, let's make our horses' best speed all the way to Williamsburg today." George sat upright in his saddle, breathing tidewater air already fresh from the springtime which was only weeks away. "I can almost smell the Chesapeake in the cool spring breezes."

Bishop had become a constant companion to George since the Braddock debacle in the Ohio Valley. The manservant of General Edward Braddock, Bishop moved to provide the same service to George after Braddock was killed in battle.[41] A man of immense size, measuring almost the same height as George, Bishop's ebony skin often had a tone of deep purple, especially when he wore his vermilion turban. George confided in Bishop, a quiet man, on a daily basis. If he had been able to read and write he could have recorded the intimate thoughts and feelings of George Washington for posterity. However, they were all buried inside his head, locked for safekeeping.

"I regret waiting so long to inform you about my desire to spend the night at the Chamberlaynes. Your loyalty is greatly appreciated, as is your patience in keeping the horses ready for our departure. My intention was to move on to Williamsburg after dinner yesterday."[42] George, sitting erect in his saddle, looked the quintessential military leader in his dark blue uniform with the cardinal-red, silk lapels. The once-polished silver buttons were lusterless, but were overshadowed by the man occupying the dusty suit, his tricorn hat placed atop his head, looking like the British Army General he yearned to be.

"My restoration is taking place, Bishop. Yesterday morning I was dispirited and weary, feeling rather hollow. Today I feel a greater rejuvenation than I've felt for some time. The doctor will agree, I'm sure."

"Colonel Washington, I haven't seen you look so well for a long time." Bishop rode parallel to George. "If you need to rest, I will guide your horse for you."

While his thoughts were beginning to center on the war again, George needed reassurance about his health. "*Mount Vernon is my home and the plans for restoring the structure and redecorating are nearly complete. If I go back to the Ohio, I will not be available to supervise the restoration.*" George's dilemma was further compounded by his introduction to Martha Custis. "*She must be a very wealthly woman,*" he mused to himself. "*Her name and face seem to be at the surface of my argument. I hardly slept for thinking about her uniqueness. Do I compare every woman I meet to Sally Fairfax? Sally is tall and slender, flirtatous, witty, and lightens every room she enters. Martha, the antithesis of Sally, is diminutive and rather plump, unflirtatious, kindhearted, and a good listener. She can best be described as cozy.*"

George began to lower his head so he could doze. "Bishop, take my reins for awhile. I may try to snooze for a bit." The activity inside his head prevented sleep. The cadence of the horse's hooves beat inside his head. "*Sal-ly Fair-fax—Mar-tha Cus-tis—Sal-ly Fair-fax—Mar-tha Custis. I will never have Sally Fairfax for my own, and Martha will never have Daniel again.*" Drowsiness overcame George as the rhythm continued.... "*Sal-ly Fair-fax—Mar-tha Cus-tis.*"

18, March 1758, Mi hart sometines tries to overide mi judgment. I did not look forward to mi visit wit the Chamberlanes but an iner voice kept nagging at me. Was it divin inervention LORD? Was it yur voice telling me to go? Mi prayers mae be touched by yur hand. Now I no iam capable of filing mi life agen wit the companionship an friendship of another. Col Wasington brot mi hed, hart and sole back to life. Maebe ar fate was to meet so unsuspectingly, both so impoverished. He tring to return from near death both on the battlefield an from an al most certain deathe from disentary an decae. He spent the nite wit the Chamberlanes which was not the intent. Im certain he staed becaws we cud not end ar conversation which ended near daelite. The servants brot us supper in the parlor by candle lite. He let me nurse him some. I suggested red wine insted of the milk his doc sed wud help. Im sur he is a harassed man witout a woman to tern to He suffers from lack of cossetting. We ate brefast together an the Col met Jacky and Patcy. They crawled over his uniform an he bounced them on his knee. he seems to lik chilren. At noon he was gon to Wiliamsberg to see a doc. an the new govnor. He sed he wud stop here on his wae back to Mt vernun. mi chilren askt him to com. I await his visit but promis not to be disapoint if his unabl. the war mae tak presedence. GOD bles us all an Col Wasington. AMEN Patcy

When George arrived in Williamsburg, he was caught in a social whirl. Requests for his presence as a dinner guest out-numbered the days of his planned visit. His first-hand reporting on the war brought his name to the lips of many Virginians as a heroic, valiant warrior.

The ambivalent George still considered his option to return to Mount Vernon. "Bishop. I'm still thinking of the hearth and home I love. My head and heart want to return so I can employ my skills as a planter."

"Colonel Washington, Sir. You have difficult days ahead. Decisions will be looking you in the eye. Why don' ya just listen and wait; the discussions might help ya."

George sat and looked straight ahead, barely listening to Bishop's words. "I guess I can wait to hear what the new English General has to proffer. My poor impoverished men are better trained than the British. Most of them are prisoners from the English jails or indentured. Their officers are ill-equipped to make decisions . . . and I have to take orders from these misfits. I know I can't be treated as an inferior subordinate any longer."

"When the time is right, you'll make the right choice."

George lifted his tricorn and scratched his head. "You know, Bishop, my choices are to go home or go back to the Ohio. I'm still overburdened with grief over the humiliating defeat at Fort Necessity. The death of General Braddock torments my every waking hour. I want to regain my self-respect and honor helping to protect the Virginia frontier. We must be allowed to make sure we never carry arms over Virginia borders," he said. "If the orders give me automony to command my own men without British interference, my decision will be obvious. I will go tomorrow and do as you say, Bishop. I'll listen to the proposition and wait to make my decision."

John Forbes, the latest general to arrive from London to command the British and American forces, brought word from the British Ministry of War for an all-out campaign to oust the French. The strikes were to be three-fold, to take command of Fort Duquesne on the Ohio River, Fort Ticonderoga on Lake Champlain, and Cape Breton in Nova Scotia. The plan called for large numbers of American troops. General Forbes was assigned to seize Fort Duquesne, with part of his force to be using a division of Virginia troops under the sole command of George Washington.[43]

Prepared to negotiate with General Forbes about his assignment, George patiently gave heed to the outline of the battle plan. His new role gave him independence to train the Militia and use the maneuvers of hide, surprise, and attack. The British strategy of forming up in columns in open fields, then firing, was left to General Forbes.

George and Bishop prepared for their return trip to Mount Vernon. The two men rode side by side; both absorbed by what might lie ahead. Bishop broke the silence first. "Colonel Washington, I will go with you to the front. I want to go with you. It will be an honor to go with you."

"My loyal friend, you have already witnessed the worst of war. The death of General Braddock brought us both into the abyss of sorrow." George observed his servant carefully. "I value your allegiance to the depths of my soul. But I can't ask you to return to this alien struggle."

"Who will you take?" Bishop questioned. "There is no one with my experience. I want to be with you when you become a General. I've waited a mighty long time to sew them stripes on your uniform . . . " Bishop paused, "Sir."

"Bishop, let me study this a bit. I have many ends to tie together before I leave for the Ohio again." George cleared his throat, "I have decided we will stop at the White House and see Mrs. Custis before returning to Mount Vernon."

The visit from Colonel George Washington to Martha Custis's White House on the Pamunkey River took place nine days after their meeting at Chamberlayne's plantation.[44] Eight months had passed since Martha's desolating loss of Daniel. Martha and Daniel had shared a love of spring fragrances, serenading birds, and azure skies. Shortly after the birth of Daniel II, Martha had waked to find a Scripture written out by Daniel lying on her pillow. She immediately recognized the words from one of her mother's favorites, one which Frances insisted Martha memorize by age eight.

> *My beloved spake, and said unto me, Rise up, my love, my fair one, and come away. For, lo the winter is past, the rain is over and gone; the flowers appear on the earth; the time of the singing of birds is come, and the voice of the turtle is heard in our land.*

Martha smiled now as she repeated to herself the Song of Solomon. "My heart is overburdened with emotions today. My beloved, taken away too soon." Martha's left hand swiped across her forehead as she adjusted her mobcap. She shook her head, saying, "I must find myself and terminate this reverie."

After Daniel's sudden passing, Martha had set aside one hour each morning after breakfast to retire to her bedroom for meditation and Scripture reading.[45] Her instructions to Dicey called for no interruptions unless there was imminent danger to life or limb of the children. Gazing out the open window to watch the springtime activity, Martha thought she could see dust rising on the horizon. She studied the cloud before she heard the hooves of a horse . . . no, there were two horses. No wonder there is so much powdery dust. Who would be racing their horses at this time of day? Martha continued to watch until the bedroom door burst open and Jacky ran in, shouting, "It's Colonel Washington and Bishop, Mama."

"Are you sure? I can't make out the riders."

"I know it is them. I can tell by the sounds of the horses and how the riders pace them." Jacky clamored to the window to verify his announcement as the riders drew closer. "Yes, yes! I can see the red of Colonel Washington's jacket. See, I told you I could tell the horse and rider by the sounds before I can see 'em."

George sandwiched Martha's small hand between his two large hands. "I am sorry I did not send a message of my coming visit. There was no time for such." George looked down upon her beaming face and smiled. "I have a letter for you from James Power. I met him at the King's Arms, and coincidentally sat for a rum with him. I mentioned a possible stop to see you, and he seemed genuinely pleased when I agreed to bring the letter."

"It is so good of you to bring it to me. I hope it concerns a matter which I have waited to settle for some time." Martha was anxious to look at the letter, but laid it aside as she invited George to take a cup of tea and some tarts in the east parlor. "I do hope you'll join us for dinner—Jacky is very anxious to see you. He watched you ride in—and Patcy is upstairs with Oney—they both will be pleased with your visit." Martha, in her excitement, seemed to be spilling her words one after another. George removed his tricorn as he entered the passageway. Martha led him into the parlor so he could settle in for a visit, and she hoped, a briefing on the state of his health and his plans for the future.

"Your manor house is lovely, Madame. The picture over the hearth? Maybe you will tell me about the subject and all his decorations." Martha felt awkward talking about Colonel John Parke, Daniel's grandfather. She brushed aside his comments.

"The tea will be served in a few minutes. Maybe you will feel more comfortable washing up after the dusty ride? There is fresh water and towels in the front bedroom. Please help yourself while I see about the tea."

Both Martha and George loved conversation—George, witty and lively, and Martha, more passive and attentive. However, she frequently controlled the conversation with thoughtful questions. After dinner George asked to see Martha's garden. The two strolled up and down the paths past spring bulbs ready to pop and colorful primroses in full bloom. The dogwood trees had begun to show their delicate white blossoms. The vegetable garden overflowed with spring seedlings. The bean-poles, already in place, looked like tipi frames. They were surrounded with miniature boxwood. The conversation never dragged and the two began to feel a bond as they discovered the commonalities between them. Martha loved gardening, as did George. The material items in her home impressed George, always intent on copying Belvoir, the Fairfax manor. Her choices in decor of the White House interior left George convinced she was a woman of taste.

The two sat down on a wooden bench under a redbud tree about to bloom. "Martha, the pleasure of your garden, manor house, and splendid meal have given me contentment and pleasure today. Your children are well-mannered and delightful. I have debated several issues concerning my future these past few days and made decisions that perhaps will change my life forever. If I may, I would like to share my decisions and hope that some of them you won't find burdensome." Martha nodded her head giving approval.

"I have agreed to command the Virginia troops in an all-out effort to oust the French for good. I don't have to serve as an officer under British command. I'll lead all American men and we will use the battle strategies of the Iroquois, not those of the British which have cost too many lives. Our uniforms will be suited for forest warfare, instead of the finery of the redcoats.[46]

"Before I leave for the front, I have made provision for my home, Mount Vernon, to begin its renovation. My close friend, George William Fairfax, will oversee the work. I do regret my being elsewhere. I have been convinced by many constituents to run again for the House of Burgesses.[47] One dilemma there was my inability to campaign, so again, George William agreed to manage for me." Martha sat patiently while George explained his plans.

"I'm sure the difficulties of your conclusions have been thoroughly measured," Martha reached out to touch George's hand.

"Yes, I have weighed very carefully my resolutions. But my health is still not of the best, even though I continue to improve. The doctor says my restoration is imminent." George turned towards Martha and took her lace-gloved hand in his, "Which brings me to an unresolved issue that I would like to settle before I return to the front."

Their eyes met. Martha, for the first time, fluttered her lashes in a flirtatious manner. "Does this concern me in any way?" Her powerful intuition that he wanted her for his wife overwhelmed her.

"Yes, Martha, it does. You see, I have no idea of how long this war will last. Nor do I know the outcome. Before I leave for the Ohio Valley I would like a promise from you that you will consider becoming my wife after my return."[48] George squeezed her hand tightly and lifted it to his lips, never removing his eyes from hers.

Martha tried feigning surprise by widening her eyes. "Yes, I agree that would be most suitable. We have much to learn about each other, but there will be time for that when you return, and I'll wait until that happens."

George continued to hold Martha's hand as he asked another question, which did surprise her. " Do you mind if I call you Patcy, as your family does? Sometimes fathers give their daughters pet names to show their deep affection. Did yours?"

"He did, and my family usually still use it. However, there has been confusion with two Patcys in the same household," Martha said, laughing.

"Um . . . Patcy—Then I will fondly call you Patcy from this day forward. My dearest Patcy."

MARTHA & GEORGE

1758-1759

Is it a truism that brides and grooms are consumed with consternation—whether misgiving, fear, or panic—before the matrimonial vows? For Martha's necessities to be met and because of Virginia common law, she needed a trusted guardian for the estates of her children and a person to manage her plantations, dwellings, and slaves. If she remarried, all her chattel became the property of her new husband. Martha, at twenty-seven no longer the giddy teenager, widowed, with two children living and two in the grave, was now a mature and somewhat sedate woman. "My passion and love for Daniel may be never replicated again. My children deserve a caring father and I await an affectionate companion," Martha told herself. "Is this towering military man the one man who can fulfill those needs?"

George, also twenty-seven, and with Sally Fairfax unattainable, set out to find a wife personifying aristocratic conduct—able to converse sensibly and lucidly, insightful and attentive, astute in social behavior and ceremony, while remaining heedful of the administration of a planter's estate. Wealth was an issue he hardly ignored! Did Martha Dandridge Custis exemplify his vision of a polished and well-mannered partner?

Both stem and branch of the ancestry of Martha Dandridge Custis and George Washington came from the same root. While neither was born into the aristocracy of Virginian society, they both quickly learned the distinction between owning five hundred acres of land with ten slaves and owning thousands of acres with hundreds of slaves. A youthful Martha earned her way into the Virginia elite through a relationship whose foundation was constructed on love and admiration, not wealth and social position. George had yet to earn his way, but his mentors had taught him well. The archetype shown him by Lawrence Washington exemplified the achievement of happiness and wealth through marriage, and gave George a panoramic observation point overlooking the rich and famous. This introduction laid the first stone leading him to Sally and George William Fairfax, Belvoir and the craving for their grand lifestyle.

It was sometime in March of 1758 that Martha and George agreed to marry. It was early June before George visited the White House again, his last visit before proceeding back to the Ohio Valley.[1]

Martha had finished her morning hour of meditation and seclusion. She opened the window to allow in the concert of the merry warblers of the morn. With the demanding work of soil preparation in January and February finished, the March weather now permitted planting. In the distance, the sounds of shovels and iron shoes digging into the earth told Martha all was well on the Custis plantation. Laying the seeds was once again on schedule.

Martha carefully scrutinized her pale face in the lacquered mirror hanging over her knee-hole dressing table. "I wonder if Mr. Washington will stop for a visit on his way to Williamsburg?" She reviewed George's plans, as he knew them, and had a strong premonition he would be paying the White House a visit; if not while going into Williamsburg, then he'd stop on his way back to Mount Vernon. Martha was blessed with clear white skin needing neither cornstarch nor orrisroot powders. She added rouge to highlight her cheeks and added a touch of red to her lips as she hummed a whimsical tune. "Where is my straw hat?" Martha reached into an alcove where it usually hung, but all she found was an empty hook. Her garden needed attention, so her plan for the day to hoe and plant. "Dicey, may I borrow your straw hat? Mine is not where I thought I left it."

"Lil' Patcy had it on the las' time I saw it, Mis Dandridge. She do love your hat."

The noon sun bore down on Martha's head through her hat. Beads of perspiration dripped from her forehead onto the ground as she bent over her plantings. "May I interest you in a tall glass of cold tea, Madame?" a deep, resonant voice asked.

Martha turned and looked up into the piercing blue-gray eyes of the tall, imposing man. "Oh, Mother of Heaven! Where did you come from?" Martha jumped up and began brushing her pinafore. "Let's find some shade and sit down. I'll call Dicey to bring us something to drink. I'm so . . . so . . . happy . . . to see you," Martha stammered, trying to hide the rising color in her cheeks. "I've been . . . thinking . . . "

"Yes, I'm sure I can finish your sentence—we need to plan a wedding!" George took Martha's elbow and led her to a wooden bench under the umbrella of a shade tree. "That is . . . when I return from the war."

Martha's crimson face betrayed her fluster. "Then, you are returning to the battlefield. When?"

"Yes, soon. There is no way to settle upon a date, for fear I cannot journey back to the Pamunkey," George delicately said. "I have no idea how long the war will continue, so it is difficult to make plans."

"Yes, I understand. We both need time to make ready," Martha replied quickly. "I am so glad you have agreed the White House will be a worthy and adequate place for our nuptials." Martha patted George's hand as she gazed fondly into his eyes, her lower lip quivering with disappointment. "I do hope you will give your approval for Reverend Mossum to preside when our date is set. He has administered to our family since before I was born. He baptized all the Dandridge and Custis children." Not certain she should mention her marriage to Daniel, she reluctantly said, "Reverend Mossum planned to marry Daniel and me, but because of the death of John Custis, we were married by Reverend Chichley Gorden Thacker. Do you know of Reverend Thacker?"

"Yes, but I have heard Reverend Mossum officiate several times. His ceremonial brings me comfort and peace." George sipped the cool, black tea and devoured the apple tart Dicey had prepared for him. His mood lifted and his deep and powerful voice bubbled over with laughter. "Where are the children? My arms are waiting for their hugs and kisses and it's nearly an hour since my arrival! I want to wrestle with the little rascals."

"I wasn't sure how long your stay would be and I worried that we'd need private time to go over some things. I'm anxious to hear about your departure to the Ohio and you haven't told me yet about your health. Did Dr. Amson give you good news?" Martha, for the first time in his company, began to feel uncomfortable. "I didn't want the children to pester you and be nuisances."

George's laughter wafted across the gardens. "Jacky and Patcy would never bring me anything but pleasure. Nuisances? Never! Let us go inside so I can bid them hello and then a very hasty good-by."

A look of disappointment fell on Martha's round face. "Oh, must you go so soon? We have hardly had time to visit."

"Yes, my dear. I must ride to Williamsburg before nightfall." He took Martha's tiny gloved hand in his and touched his lips to the back of her hand, then turned it over to kiss her palm. "You'll need to lead the way. I haven't been upstairs to the children's nursery before."

George's brief visit and sudden departure left Martha in a confused state. "I wish either Mother or Anna Maria would pay me a visit. Maybe I should make plans to go to Chestnut Grove soon so I can relieve myself of this burden I'm carrying. Mother always seems to know my worries before I express them." Martha sat down on the heavy damask highback chair next to the mantel and looked at the painting of Daniel's grandfather. "You were such a rogue! Maybe I'll just ask you a few questions . . . . Why is this feeling of uncertainty hanging over me? George seemed far away today. He seemed to avoid our need to talk out our marriage plans. Is he fearful he won't return, anticipating bloodshed and carnage? He spoke to me about the untrustworthy Cherokees. They never seem to know which allies are which . . . or has he changed his mind about taking me as his wife? He loves my children and they adore him. Jacky will be on look-out until his return, and Patcy loves the piggy-back rides." Martha's eyes penetrated Daniel Parke's deep-set eyes. She stared for several seconds and imagined his lips moving and whispering, "Don't be hard on yourself. He will be back."

The assault on Fort Duquesne, the French stronghold, was beginning. Many of the volunteer Virginia Militia enlistments ended in December, freeing the men to return home. General Forbes decreed the campaign should be completed by December 1, to avoid sending an inexperienced replacement army into battle. Conflict and disagreement between Forbes and several officers, including George, began early in the western movement. The weather became unbearable as they travelled over muddy and rutted roads. Forbes compounded the differences of opinions with a serious case of dysentery. He was unable to ride and gave his daily orders from a travois swinging from the back of his horse. Forbes insisted on building roads and bridges to reach Fort Duquesne instead of using the routes of General Braddock. This delayed their reaching their destination, along with the hazards of consistent wind and rainfall and poor food sources.[2]

Accustomed to daily letter writing, George rose each morning before sun-up to take up his quill pen, ink and paper. He enjoyed the solitary act of communicating with his friends, family, and political cronies, and even adversaries. The Fairfaxes returned lively letters full of Tidewater events. Sally occasionally wrote to George separately, but his frequent letters to her always begged for prompt answers, especially if he knew George William was in Williamsburg attending the Assembly. Martha was not an accomplished letter writer. George became impatient with her inability to spell and her use of grammar. He promised himself when he got home, he would have her dictate letters to him so she could copy them over correctly.[3] Even between two people who had shared few experiences, he found the content of her letters dull and emotionless.

Since George had shared the news about his betrothal to Martha with his closest friends, Sally began to write George on a regular basis after his return to the front. His letters to her were expressions of his open feelings to the woman he could never possess, hardly appropriate from someone betrothed to another.

September 1, 1758,
My dear Sally,

I am so happy you have renewed correspondence with me. . . . In silence I now express my joy, silence which, in some cases—I wish the present—speaks more intelligibly than the sweetest eloquence.[4]

Sally, always the tease, chided George about the betrothal to one so colorless. Perhaps she realized her manipulation of him would continue, because he wrote a letter to her shortly before returning home to marry Martha.

Twelve, September 1758
My Dear Sally,

You have drawn me, my dear Madame, or rather I have drawn myself, into an honest confession of a simple fact, Misconstrue not my meaning—'tis obvious—doubt it not nor expose it. The world has no business to know the object of my love, declared in this manner to you when I want to conceal it. One thing above all things in his world I wish to know and only one person of your acquaintance can solve me that or guess my meaning. But adieu to this, 'til happier times, if ever I shall see them. [5]

Martha sat at Daniel's very old high-back mahogany secretary. The brilliant morning sunlight shafted through the window across the paperwork that she diligently studied. "I love this time of day," Martha said, as she gazed out across the undulating green grass. "*And God said, let there be light, and there was light. And God saw the light, that it was good, and God divided the light from the darkness,"* she repeated. "*One of my favorite scriptures. Daniel, I do think of you each time I use your desk as the sun shines upon it. The warmth heats the varnish and brings out the essence of the wood. I still relish the memories of our sitting in early morning sipping hot tea together."* She bowed her head and offered a prayer which was really a message to Daniel. "*Please understand my reasons for choosing to give myself to another man. Our young children need the nurturing and love of a father, especially Jacky. No one can possibly replace you.... You, who loved your children so deeply. I have prayed for a substitute who can give them the love and security I thought was taken away from them forever. I feel your presence this morning and pray for your approval of my choice."*

Martha pulled on a wooden knob and withdrew an elongated drawer which held the letter explaining the distribution of Daniel's estate. Martha had read the letter over several times to make sure she understood the contents. Burwell Bassett, her brother-in-law, had carefully surveyed the letter, as well as Richard Chamberlayne. Both men agreed the reliability of the subject matter closed once and for all Martha's concern about Jack taking one fourth of the Custis estate. Martha read aloud the letter reassuring herself the matter was closed.

October 1, 1757
Dear Mrs. Custis,

Please accept my deepest regret at the untimely death of your husband, Daniel Parke Custis. He was a man of distinction and high morals. You, his wife and children, were his priority. On 14 November 1749, John Parke Custis drew up his last will and testament. Its purpose was served when he died on 22 November 1749. His will, witnessed by Thomas Dawson, George Gilmer, and John Blair, was proved 9 April 1750.[6]

1. For his faithful man servant Jack, also John Custis's illegitimate son, manumission (his freedom) a newly built home and a manifest of furnishings to be purchased from London, and two horses. He is to be under the supervision of Daniel Custis until he reaches the age of twenty and pro-

vided a handsomely maintained lifestyle. Please note, Jack has reached his legal age.

2. Anne Moody, twenty pounds annually.

3. Several other small allowances which have been allocated.

4. All other properties are the property of Daniel Custis.

It is my understanding there is a lawsuit brought about by Mr. Custis against Anne and Matthew Moody to regain the Custis family heirlooms John Custis gave to them. No resolution of that of which I am aware.[7] *If I can be of further help to you, please allow me to render my service,*

Your sincere servant,

Jonathan Milton

"Oh, how I detest that man! 'Your sincere servant'!" Martha cleared her throat, not realizing she was speaking in a rather loud voice. "He is only a sincere servant if it benefits himself. How dare he mention the illegitimacy of Jack! I'm surprised he didn't use the word "bastard." Thank heavens I haven't needed to confront him personally."

"Mis Custis, are you all right?" Dicey peeked around the door frame, her eyes squinting as she tried to determine if Martha was talking to someone else in the room or talking to herself. Martha waved her hand, motioning for her to come in.

"What is it, Dicey? Is there something I need to attend to?"

"There's someone here to see ya. He look like a sol'ier, Mis Custis."

"Goodness gracious, Dicey, show him in—quickly." Martha's heart began to race like the wind. "It is news about George, I'm sure."

A tall, thin, very young man entered the room, carrying his hat over his arm. The trousers of his uniform were shredded around his boots and his sleeves were tattered at the wrists. "I have a message for Mrs. Custis, Ma'am ."

"Yes, I am Mrs. Custis." Martha swallowed, but her throat was dry as she struggled to ask who the message was from. "Is it from Colonel Washington?"

"Yes, Ma'am, it is, Ma'am." He handed the ragged, soiled envelope to Martha.

She recognized his careful handwriting and blew the air from her lungs. "Thank you, young man. May I offer you food or drink before you return? Does the Colonel expect a reply?"

"No, Ma'am. My food and water supply are ample to see me back."

Martha's unsteady hands tore the envelope apart with trepidation. Without salutation, the brief note stated that the troops were marching west to Ohio and couriers were going to Williamsburg, and he would try to dispatch a few words when he could. He stated his thoughts were of her and the pledge they had made to one another. His prayers were that Providence would keep them both safe. He closed as her faithful and affectionate friend.[8]

"He is safe!" Martha clutched the letter to her breast and danced in a circle around the center of the room. "What am I doing? If anyone could see the Widow Custis now, they would think I'm acting like a lovesick ninny, and just after freakishly talking to Daniel all morning, longing for his comfort, I receive a weeks-old letter from a man I hardly know and have promised to marry, and my heart nearly leaps out of my bosom! Please, God, take away my madness and bring me back to the balance of rationality."

General Forbes and Colonel Washington pushed their men westward; their goal, to reach Fort Duquesne and face the French before winter. Road building, savage battles with Indians and French Canadians, miserable weather, and continual disagreements between Washington and Forbes left the morale and motivation of officers and enlisted men at an all-time low, along with the deprivation consisting of poor food, shelter, and poor leadership. One of the last battles was fought between a detachment of British soldiers and Virginia Militiamen fighting against each other. Mixed messages resulted in fourteen dead and twenty-six wounded before George, riding between the allies and swinging his sabre, shouted a cease-fire. Mid-November found the men closing ranks and ready to attack their destination, Fort Duquesne. Forbes, Washington (now a Brigadier General), and their staffs laboriously climbed the hill overlooking their prey. The view of the fort was obscured by low, sooty clouds. General Forbes, holding the spy glass steady, declared the clouds to be smoke. The two Generals, based on their observation, agreed the fort had been set on fire, then evacuated. Watching the billowing smoke, the men awaited word from the scouts sent ahead. The French had escaped capture by setting fire to the fort, climbing into canoes, and paddling up the Allegheny River to safety and surrender.

It was a hollow victory for the new General, lives saved after enormous losses. But in the end, no battle meant no honor gained.[9]

Five long years of military life had brought disappointment and disgust to George Washington. After the mop-up of the Fort Duquesne disaster, he mounted his horse and headed for Mount Vernon, suffering again from dysentery and pleurisy. Left with tenuous health, he felt the war had cost him much income because of his neglected farms. He rode home knowing he would resign from the military for good this time. His redemption would come as a successful husband, father, step-father and planter.[10]

Every day Martha, Jacky, and Patcy listened for sounds of horse hooves on the drive. Jacky, nearly four years old, stood guard on the porch as a lookout. Strange riders usually meant either a mail delivery or, hopefully, the colonel himself. Jacky's acute hearing could distinguish the sounds of each horse, and identify the rider if the person had visited the White House before.

The separation of George and Martha grew in time and distance. Six months had passed since his departure to the Ohio Valley, with infrequent correspondence. At first, his letters arrived on a weekly basis. As the situation darkened between the British Army and the French Canadians, the letter deliveries stretched over two weeks. As Christmas approached, nearly four weeks had passed with no word received from George. Martha felt bereft and fretful. She anxiously awaited the weekly Virginia Gazette to receive the war news, then after it arrived, she became reluctant to open it for fear the news was bad.

Frances Dandridge and the younger Dandridge children arrived at the White House two weeks before Christmas. The Custis White House brimmed with swags and della robia wreaths hung with fruits and nuts. Candles were in every window bidding welcome to all holiday visitors. The kitchen staff, busy baking breads, fruit cakes and tarts, kept a hot fire burning almost around the clock. Martha chose to busy herself supervising all the kitchen activity. Each morning after breakfast, she retired to the privacy of her room for her hour of reading Scriptures and saying prayers, mostly asking God to give her strength, calm, and reason while waiting to receive word either about George or from George. She knew her edginess transferred to her children. "Mother is such a comfort. Thank you for allowing me the privilege, dear God, of the companionship of her visit." Martha, on her knees in front of her Windsor chair, continued her morning prayer, reviewing her mother's words of solace the evening before in front of the warm fire.

"There can be no joy without sorrow, sunshine without clouds, spring without winter, my darling. There can be no daylight without darkness. Be patient."

Three days before Christmas, the Burwells, Bartholomew and his wife Mary, Frances and the two youngest Dandridge children, Martha, Jacky, and Patcy were gathered around the spinet singing, "Deck the Halls."

"Stop, everyone, stop!" shouted Jacky. "Listen, I hear horses!" He ran to look out the frosty window, cupping his hands around his eyes. "I can see a lantern. I am sure it is Colonel Washington, Mother."

Martha stopped playing the Christmas carol and ran to the window, wiping the condensation with her fist so she could see who was approaching in this darkest of winter nights.

Dashing through the unlighted passageway, Martha, with her mother close behind carrying a candle, hurriedly unlatched the door and ran onto the porch. Both Jacky and young Patcy joined her, straining to see the visitors. "I know it is Colonel Washington," Jacky told everyone as the family clustered around to determine the riders. "See! It is him, and Bishop is with him!"

The men slowed to a trot as they approached the house. George jumped from his mount and handed the reins to Bishop. "I did not expect such a homecoming. This is a most pleasurable surprise!" George removed his hat, caressed Martha's hand, picked up Patcy, and gripped Jacky's shoulder. "Patcy, I would never have supposed you would be speechless under any circumstances. No hello?"

"George, the words are locked inside my head. I don't seem able to express my surprise at your arrival, especially after dark." Martha endeavored to compose herself. "Your whereabouts has worried us all. The news has not been good."

"Didn't the courier deliver my last message?"

Jacky intervened. "No,Sir. My mother has been very worried about you. She has not smiled much for a very long time."

"Jacky, darling, thank you for the kind words of concern, but we must invite Colonel Washington inside where it is warm. You can help me serve a pot of hot tea."

All the Custis and Dandridge families finally retired, leaving George and Martha in front of the cozy fire to catch up and reacquaint themselves. "Patcy, I could not have chosen a better time for my return, your family here for Christmas, the White House looking so festive, and my homecoming . . . with your two children greeting me with such warm affection."

"George, my heart is overflowing. We have all been waiting word for some weeks. I did try to keep my concern from the children, but you now know I was unsuccessful at doing so. The children have given me such comfort during your absence." Patiently, Martha waited for him to speak about their future together. Her thoughts were tangled into a web of questions. *"Does he still wish for a marriage? When will he return to the war? Is his health still uncertain? How will he manage his election to the House of Burgesses? If we marry, where will we live?"*

"Patcy, dearest. The first thing we must settle tonight before retiring is planning our marriage. I have studied this question, and my choice, which I hope will be your choice, is to marry on Twelfth Night."

Astounded, and not sure which Twelfth Night he meant, Martha replied, "Which Twelfth Night . . . the one in two weeks, or wait for a year from now?"

"Definitely, in two weeks. Is that not a glorious day for a wedding?"

Struggling for words, Martha pushed her tongue to the roof of her mouth and swallowed hard. "Well, I suppose we can plan a wedding in two weeks—I mean . . . the invitations and all. Do you think we . . . or I mean . . . can I send messages to all the family and friends we want to join us?"

"Of course, and I will help with the festivities." Taking Martha's hand and pressing it to his lips, he held his eyes on hers and said, "Then it is settled. We will marry on January 6, 1759. [11]

Frances Dandridge sat sipping hot tea as she held her family Bible open to Psalms. The door opened and Martha entered, adjusting her mobcap. "Mother? I didn't expect to find you up so early."

"It was dark and dreary when I arose this morning. I could hardly sleep knowing the Colonel was here. I am so happy for you both."

"Mother, you will have to call him Brigadier Washington now that he has received a commission.[12] Isn't that splendid?" Martha reached for the teapot after she spread blackberry jam on a biscuit. "There is so much to tell you I hardly know where to begin. The most important news, however, I will discuss first. We have set our wedding date."

Frances reached for her daughter's hand, giving her a huge smile. "Oh, darling, I know how apprehensive you have been. When will it be?"

"In two weeks, Mother. On the sixth of January—Twelfth Night."

Frances sat up in her chair, trying desperately to hide her surprise. "Two weeks? That is hardly enough time to send invitations and prepare the food. Thank heavens, Mrs. Kidwell has completed your dress. Who will marry you? Reverend Mossum may be too busy on such short notice. Oh, how I wish your father was here. Who will escort you into the ceremony? It will have to be William. Yes, he will just have to come home and do that. Oh, my dear. Is this young man so crazed with you, he cannot wait for ample time to make proper arrangements? So many decisions."

"We will work through this frenzy together, Mother." Martha squeezed her hand, smiling. "There are many arrangements to be made and I have already planned to send invitations by messenger. George has been elected to the House of Burgesses, so he wants us to marry before he must be in attendance in Williamsburg. He has resigned from the military for good, Mother. He is not going back, ever! We will live in the House of Six Chimneys, and I have thought on how to make it ready for a bride and groom with a ready-made family of two children."

"I have so worried about where you would live if the two of you finally did marry. Thank heavens you are going to live in your home." Frances thoughtfully spread jam on a second biscuit and handed it to Martha.

"That will be the difficult part of our marriage, especially for my family. George is renovating his home on the Potomac. We will be moving to Mount Vernon when the Assembly ends, sometime in the spring. I will close the White House, Mother, but you must promise to visit us often."

To every thing there is a season,
and a time to every purpose under the heaven:
A time to be born, and a time to die;
A time to plant, and a time to pluck;
A time to kill, and a time to heal;
A time to break down and a time to build up;
A time to weep, and a time to laugh;
A time to mourn, and a time to dance;
A time to embrace, and a time to refrain from embracing;
A time to get, and a time to lose, a time to keep, and a time to cast away;
A time to be silent, and a time to speak;
A time to love and a time to hate;
A time for war and a time for peace.

A bookmark was placed in Martha's Bible as she finished reading from Ecclesiastes: "Yes, Lord, it is time for laughter, dancing, embracing, loving, and a time for peace. My head and heart anxiously look forward. But please allow time for me to look back. I will always need an opening to see Daniel and our two children peacefully with him. Amen."

She closed her Bible, rubbed her churning stomach and laid her head back on the pillows placed on her chaise, to review the day ahead. Tomorrow George would arrive for the wedding. "His brothers and sister will be with him, but not his mother. George must be very disappointed. The Fairfaxes declined the invitation also. I hope it is not because of me. I guess that is the reason my stomach is unsettled, all the misgivings about being the right choice for a man held in such high esteem, which seems to be building higher every day. I am thrilled the Governor of Virginia accepted the invitation. I must stop this nonsense. This day is so full of last minute preparations, I have no time for all this apprehension!"

5 January 1759 Tomorow George arrives for ar marrage the dae we become one. Mi hart an mi hed dont seem to be cooperating wit one another. The hart is talking an mi hed is not lisening . . . mi logic is being fooled by mi hart. George wil bee a good father to mi precious chilren an to ar future chilren together. He wil be a kindharted an well-intended husban. I wil promis to bee the same. but can we hav passion for one another? This, his first comitment to a woman? I no so litle of his early years an his of mine. I hav not met his mother or eny of his famly. Mother has askt so mane good questions about our short betrothment. Maebe in mi eagerness to find a father for Jacky and Patcy, I hav ben quik to answer afirmativly. Am I worthy of such a man? All Virginia seem to giv him such reverence since returning. He is a true hero now. and a new Burgess as well. What wil mi future be wit one so formidabl? Daniel wanted onle to devote himself to me and ar chilren. His home was where he wanted to be wit us. no outsid responsibiltys. Our marrage began wit establisht foundation. He new mi strenghs an accepted mi weakneses. We shared the same experiences. I hav agred to marry a man I hav onle seen four tims. What can he see in one to plump and roun, short of height and ordinary? Can it be caus the rumors of me being a rich woman? I no nothing of his early liaisons wit other women. Whi wud he chose me? Can mother and Nancy and Burwel be rite? Mi hart is working to convence me otherwis. I am puting mi hart an hed in yur hands LORD. Tomorow I wil be Martha Jones Dandridge Custis Washington "Come hell or high water," as papa uset to say. I giv thanks for all the ways you work an design the lif of each an evereone. I count mi blessings an put mi future in yur care an good wishes. I no yur decisions become my decisions. AMEN Patcy

Four AM The manel clock rang four bells an I hav yet to fall asleep. I wil tri to add to mi jornal som of the vagaries flying thru mi hed on this longest of nites. I think I was put on earth to wory. we had so litle time tagether. I strugle to remmeber his face. His mouth doesnt mov when he speeks. I always loved to watch Daniel talk wen his scar on his lip went up an down. George says he liks to danc but I cant think what well look lik tagather—him so tall an impresive in his blew an red uniform an me a moonish midge. Oh what nonsence this is. I do adore my dres. Mis Kedwil did a fin job wit the ecru brocade. Mi shoes match wit hi heels. I wil rap in mi hare the pearl necklas Daniel gave me when we marred. The chilren hav new cloths. Is he well? What if he is sick wit the disentary agin. I wil giv him nursing if so. Maebe he wont lik my wae wit cooking. I wil insist he drink red wine insted of milk for his flux. mi candl is berning down as mi eyes begin to drup. mi dere mother who alwaes has the words to comfort me an mi worys wud tell me that "worys alwaes go out the window and hapines ofen sneeks in thru an open door you didnt no you left open." Please GOD let her words bring me solace an SLEEP! Mi chilren wil be awake in 2 hours wit excitment wating for Gen. Washington.

The wedding celebration lasted three days. There was toasting, feasting, dancing, frolicking, and an explosion of laughing. George, loving the dance, showed his abilities with the minuet and the quadrille and danced with all the women, including the children. Martha was amazed at his resiliency and ability to continue the frenetic pace each day of the gala. All forty guests stayed throughout the three days, including the Royal Governor of Virginia.[13]

Martha was delighted with George's brothers, Sam, John, and Charles. His sister Betty's resemblance to George was undeniable. She walked and talked like him and had mannerisms just like his. The two women became close friends, and Martha learned that Mary Ball Washington was absent from the wedding because she felt abandoned by

George. His taking a wife, to her meant she had been replaced.

Martha watched her new husband, with his wit, charm, and grace, handle the guests, mostly members of her family, as old and dear friends. Jacky and Patcy ready were comfortable calling him Papa, with George responding enthusiastically. "This has washed the memories of the past six months away," George whispered into Martha's ear as he led her in the minuet. "Patcy, I feel exhilarated with my new beginnings—a lovely wife, the joy of parenthood, your brothers and sisters extending my family, meeting new friends and old acquaintances. My only regret would have been that your lovely wedding gown was not complemented by the suit of clothing I ordered from London before I left for the Ohio.[14] The delay of its arrival gave cause to wear my uniform, which is the only remnant in my life of the French and Indian conflict. I have removed it, Madame, if you haven't noticed, and plan never to wear another."

"I don't recall you mentioning the London order. Could it be possible it was on the manifest of a ship lost at sea?" Martha looked into the eyes of her new husband, feeling secure in knowing George had been sincere in requesting her hand before leaving for the front. "*Silly me,*" she thought, "*always the ninny, expecting the worst, causing my stomach to act like the rolling waves in a typhoon. I promise to be the best wife, sister-in-law, daughter-in-law, and mother to my children now and children yet to come*" she said to herself. They joined hands and raised their arms, meeting *almost* face to face as the dance ended, bringing closure to the wedding celebration.

One week later, Mr. and Mrs. George Washington packed their valises, dressed themselves and the children warmly, and made the day's journey into Williamsburg. Dicey and Oney rode in the coach with Martha, Jacky, and Patcy. George and Bishop rode their horses ahead of the Custis coach, setting the pace. It was a brilliantly sunny winter day, and with robes over the legs of the passengers, optimism reigned as a new adventure was unfolding for the Washingtons.

EPILOGUE

The story does not end there . . . Martha and George remained together until his death on December 12, 1799. Their forty years together brought fulfillment and disappointment, contentment and anxiety, courage and fear, accomplishment and failure, joy and sorrow.

The man labeled "First in war, first in peace, and first in the hearts of his countrymen," will live forever. His persona and position are engraved on the timeline of historic events. By circumstance he may be described as being a man born in the right time in the right place. His strength and patience originated in his youth as he learned to observe, listen and retain. As he matured, his immense size gave compelling presence, drawing attention to his every proclamation. "His mind was great and powerful," said Thomas Jefferson. "He was . . . a wise, a good and great man . . . On the whole, his character was, in its mass perfect . . . never did nature and fortune combine more perfectly to make a man great . . . "

Martha Custis Washington used her tiny feet to follow in his footprints as he walked into immortality. He was the leading man while she played the minor role: the dauntless soldier and the modest wife; George, the luminous dignitary, and Martha, loyal, but with an ill-defined position.

As the new country struggled to write the document that is our Constitution, George said "I walk on untrodden ground." The delegates to the Constitutional Convention wanted to call the new head of state "king." Unquestionably, this would have elevated Martha to "queen." George declined, saying, "One King George is enough." When the title of president was chosen, Martha was exiled into the shadowy darkness of unimportance. Women still had no place in a world dominated by men. However, she unknowingly became the trailblazer without a chart, the pathfinder without a compass.

During her lifetime, Martha would not realize where her own place in history would be. As one who began life in the hoi polloi of Virginian social strata, then rose to the height of wealth and prominence, she became one of the best-known American women of her time. She epitomized the role of wife, mother, grandmother, and hostess in Colonial times, with her cultivated manner and domesticity.

In most marriages in modern times, there are ups and downs. Two hundred and forty plus years ago things were no different. Martha's ability to fall back on her aristocratic training as Daniel Custis's wife held her in excellent stead when she married George. Her affable and gracious manner gave comfort to all their guests, whether at Mount Vernon, the General Headquarters of the Revolutionary War, or the new country's capital. Rarely did the Washingtons serve dinner without guests. Abigail Adams aptly described Martha as, "with modest and unassuming manner and great ease and politeness."

Surely, one of the great disappointments of Martha and George's life together was the failure to produce an heir. George was a devoted father to Patcy and Jacky, and like a father to Jacky's children. However, George did not ever have a child of his own. Martha outlived her two husbands as well as her two surviving children. Young Patcy died in her middle teens from epilepsy. Jacky married at age eighteen and fathered six children, two of whom died shortly after birth. He fought in the Revolutionary War as an aide to George, but died at age twenty-seven of camp fever shortly after the war ended. Two of Jacky's children lived with Martha and George until they reached adulthood.

During the Revolutionary War, Martha travelled to visit George wherever he was encamped in the wintertime. Fighting was curtailed during the harsh winters with snow-covered battlefields. After George became president, Martha moved to New York, the first capital city, then to Philadelphia where they resided until his presidency came to an end. Their remaining years were spent at their beloved Mount Vernon.

After George's death, Martha destroyed all their correspondence to one another except for several letters. Historians have debated her reasons for this destruction for nearly two centuries. It is a piece of their personal relationship that can never be known. There is renewed theorizing about George's feelings for Sally Fairfax, because some of his letters to her are in existence. One in particular, which was written shortly before his marriage to Martha, declares his feelings for her. It was not until 1958 that the letter was authenticated, says Willard Sterne Randall in his book, *George Washington, A Life.*

This void leaves many unanswered questions. Did Martha suspect George and Sally's attraction? Were his letters to Martha written in the idiom of friend to friend instead of husband to wife or lover to lover? Was Martha concerned about what future historians might write about her inability to use correct grammar and spelling in her letters to him? Did George express his concern about their letters in the hands of strangers? Or maybe the letters were so personal between the two she did not want to share them, knowing where George's place in history would be. Maybe that was one part of him she would never share with anyone but herself.

BIBLIOGRAPHY

Anthony, Carl Sferrazza. *First Ladies. The Saga of the President's Wives and Their Power.* New York: Quill, William Morrow. 1990.

Bennett, William J. *The Spirit of America.* New York: TOUCHSTONE. 1997.

Bergin, Mark; Humble, Richard. *A 16th Century Galleon.* New York: Peter Betruk Books. 1995.

Bradfield, Nancy. *Costume in Detail, 1730–1930.* Great Britain: Harrop Books Limited. 1968.

Brookhiser, Richard. *Founding Father.* New York: The Free Press, A Division of Simon and Schuster Inc. 1996.

Butterfield, Moira. *Look Inside, Cross-sections of Ships.* London, England: Dorling Kindersley Limited. 1994.

Carlson, Laurie. *Colonial Kids.* Chicago: Chicago Review Press. 1997. 2:6

________ *"Change from the Julian to Gregorian Calendar can Pose Problems."* The News Tribune. Sept. 12, 2001. P. 7, col. 1–6.

________ *"Decorations Evoke Feel of 18th Century Colonial Era."* The News Tribune. Dec. 17, 2000. P. 12, col. 5.

________ *"Descendants of Washington's Slaves Gather at Mount Vernon."* The News Tribune. Jan. 2, 2001. P. 4, col. 2–3.

Dunlop, Richard. *Wheels West 1590–1900.* New York: Rand McNally and Co. 1977.

Ellis, Joseph J. *Founding Brothers.* New York: Alfred A. Knopf. 2000.

Everett, Susanne. *History of Slavery.* Secaucus, New Jersey: Chartwell Books, Inc. 1991. 2:1, 5, 7

Fields, Joseph. *Worthy Partner, The Papers of Martha Washington.* Westport, Connecticut: Greenwood Press. 1994. 1:1, 3:5, 7, 9, 11, 12, 13, 20, 21, 3:36, 38, 5:8, 16, 17, 21-24, 44, 47, 6:1, 2, 3, 6, 7, 10

Flexner, James Thomas. *Washington, The Indispensable Man.* New York: Little Brown and Company. 1974.

Garraty, John A.; Carnes, Mark C. *American National Biography.*

New York and Oxford: Oxford University Press. 1999.

________Byrd, William. Vol. IV. Pp. 135–136. 1:6

________Parke, Daniel. Vol. XVII. Pp. 8–10. 3:16, 5:3/–5:4, 5,20

________Parke, George Washington. Vol.V. Pp. 928–929./

________ Spotswood, Alexander. Vol. XX. Pp. 494–496./1:12

________ Washington, Martha. Vol. XXII. Pp. 773–774./

Goor, Ron and Nancy. *Williamsburg, Cradle of the Revolution.* New York: MacMillan Publishing Company. 1994.1:7

Grass, Ruth Belov. *If You Grew Up With George Washington.* New York: Scholastic Inc. 1982.

Harwell, Richard. Abridged from Douglas Freeman. *Washington.* New York: Charles Scribners Sons. 1968.

Heyes, Eileen. *Tobacco USA.* Brookfield, Connecticut: Twenty-First Century Books, a Division of the Millbrook Press Inc. 1999.

Jernegan, Marcus Wilson.; Hart, Albert Bushnell, ed., Ph. D., LL.D, LITT.D. *Epochs of American History.* New York: Longmans, Green and Co. 1943. 1:11, 3:8, 28

Kalman, Nancy. *Historic Communities.* New York: Crabtree Publishing Co. 1992.

Kitman, Marvin. *The Making of the President.* New York: Harper and Row, Publishers. 1989.

Kolchin, Peter. *American Slavery 1619–1877.* Canada: Harper Collins Canada Ltd. 1994.

McPherson, Stephanie Sammartino. *Martha Washington, First Lady.* Springfield, New Jersey: Enslow Publishers, Inc. 1998. 1:2, 3, 3:35, 5:7

Meltzer, Milton. *Slavery, a World History.* New York: Da Capo Press, Inc. 1993.

Miller, John C. *This New Man, The American.* New York: McGraw-Hill Book Company. 1977. 1:10, 3:27

Porter, Roy, ed. *Medicine.* New York: Cambridge University Press. 1996. 3:2

Randall, Willard Sterne. *George Washington, A Life.* New York: Henry Holt and Company LLC. 1997. 1:14, 15, 3:4, 18, 23, 29, 3:31, 32, 4:2, 3, 5, 6, 7, 8, 10, 11-16, 18-20, 24-26, 5:13-15, 25, 26, 28-37, 5:40, 42,

43, 46, 6:4, 5, 8, 9, 12, 15

Rasmussen, William M.S.; Tilton, Robert S. *George Washington, The Man Behind the Myth.* Charlottesville: University Press of Virginia. 1999. *3:6, 17, 24, 25, 26, 30, 34, 4:2, 3, 5-8, 10-16, 18-20, 24-26, 5:6, 19, 36*

Sandoz, Mari. *The Beaver Men.* New York: Hastings House. 1964.

Smith, Carter, ed. *A Source Book on Colonial America.* Brookfield, Connecticut: Millbrook Press Inc. 1991.

________*Arts and Science. 2:4*

________*Daily Life. 2:3*

________*Governing and Teaching.*

Thane, Elswyth. *Washington's Lady.* New York: Dodd, Mead & Company. 1960. 5:39, 41, 45, 6:13

Truman, Margaret. *First Ladies.* New York: Random House. 1995.

Tunis, Edwin. *Wheels. A Pictorial.* Cleveland: World Publishing Co. 1955.

Wilson, Dorothy Clarke. *Lady Washington.* Garden City, New York, Doubleday 1984. 2:8

Wright, Louis B. *Everyday Life in Colonial America.* Toronto, Canada: Longsmans Canada Ltd. 1965.

________ *The Cultural Life of the American Colonies 1607–1763.* New York: Harper and Brothers. 1957. 1:7, 13, 16

FOOTNOTES

CHAPTER ONE

[1] Joseph Fields, *Worthy Partner* (Westport, Connecticut: Greenwood Press, 1994), p. 430. "Martha was born June 2, 1731, between 12 and 1 o'clock in a room at the east end of the house." She was born under the Julian calendar which was used until 1752 when the Gregorian calendar went into effect changing her birthdate to June 13, 1731.

[2] Stephanie Sammartino McPherson, *Martha Washington, First Lady (*Springfield New Jersey: Enslow Publishers, Inc, 1998), p. 18.

[3] Ibid., p. 18.

[4] Birthdate: Colonel William Dandridge, 1687, uncle of Martha.

[5] Birthdate: Nathaniel West Dandridge, 1728, first cousin, William's son.

[6] "William Byrd," *American National Biography,* 1999, IV, 135–136.

[7] Louis B. Wright, *The Cultural Life of the American Colonies, 1607–1763 (*New York: Harper and Brothers, 1957), p. 9.

[8] The new world colonists rushed to become owners of land surrounding the Cheaspeake Bay and its tributaries. Most plantations owners wanted available means to expedite the shipments of goods to England. Owning properties on the rivers meant building private docks so planters could transport their goods by the quickest means to reach the Cheaspeake and the English ships. The tidelands quickly became premium property with land prices spiraling.

[9] Ron and Nancy Goor, *Williamsburg Cradle of the Revolution,* (New York: MacMillan Publishing Company, 1994), p. 8.

[10] John C. Miller, *This New Man, The American* (New York: McGraw–Hill Book Company, 1977), p. 445.

[11] Marcus Wilson Jernegan, Ph.D. *Epochs of American History, The American Colonies 1492–1750* (New York: Longmans, Green and Co., 1943), pp. 407–412.

[12]"Alexander Spotswood," *American National Biography, 1999, XX, pp. 494–496.*

[13] Wright, p. 224.

[14] Randall Willard Sterne, *George Washington, a Life* (New York: Henry Holt and Company, 1997), pp. 68–71.

[15] Ibid., p. 35.

[16] Wright, pp. 5–6.

[17] Dorthea Spotswood and Nathaniel Dandridge were married June 18, 1747.

CHAPTER TWO

[1] Susanne Everett, History of Slavery (Secaucus, New Jersey: Chartwell Books, Inc., 1991), p. 67.

[2] "Tobacco," *World Book Encloypedia*, 1982, XIX, pp. 240–246.

[3] Carter Smith, Editor, *Daily Life, A Sourcebook on Colonial America* (Brookfield, Connecticut: Millbrook Press Inc., 1991), pp. 34–36.

[4] Carter Smith, Editor, *The Arts and Sciences, A SourceBook on Colonial America* (Brookfield, Connecticut: Millbrook Press Inc., 1991), p. 12.

[6] Laurie Carlson, *Colonial Kids* (Chicago: Chicago Review Press, 1997), p. 74.

[7] Everett, p. 70.

[8] Dorothy Clarke Wilson, *Lady Washington* (Garden City, New York: Doubleday, 1984), p. 3.

CHAPTER THREE

[1] "The John Custis Story," *Part I, The Web of Time*, 2002, IV, p. 1.

[2] Roy Porter, Editor, *Medicine* (New York: Cambridge University Press, 1996), p. 52.

[3] Joseph Fields, *Worthy Partner, The Papers of Martha Washington* (Westport, Connecticut: Greenwood Press, 1994), p. 430.

[4] Randall, p. 172.

[5] Fields, pp. 439–430.

[6] William Rasmussen and Robert Tilton, *George Washington, The Man Behind the Myth* (Charlottesville: University Press of Virginia, 1999), p. 81.

[7] Fields, pp. 426–427.

[8] Marcus Wilson Jernegan, *Epochs of American History* (Longmans, Green and Co. 1943), pp. 376–377.

[9] Fields, p. 426.

[10] There is little information available on the early life of Daniel Custis. The author's assumption is that there was enough money in the Custis estate to send him to England for higher education.

[11] Fields, p. 426.

[12] Ibid., p. 426.

[13] Ibid., p. 438.

[14] William Byrd had enormous propensity to admire women. His personal diary is filled with some of his conquests.

[15] Samuel Butler, 1612–1680. The date his poem was written is unknown.

[16] "Daniel Parke," *American National Biography,* 1999, XVII, pp. 8–10.

[17] Rasmussen and Tilton, p. 43.

[18] Randall, p. 72.

[19] Dennis Franklin, *The Virginia Colony* (Chicago: Children's Press, 1986), p. 26.

[20] Fields, pp. 422–426.

[21] Ibid., pp. 422–426.

[22] "The House That Byrd Built," *British Biographies: William Byrd,* 2002, p. 3.

[23] Randall, p. 68.

[24] Rasmussen and Tilton, p. 81.

[25] Ibid., p. 81.

[26] Rasmussen and Tilton, p. 46.

[27] John C. Miller, *This New Man, The American* (New York: McGraw–Hill Book Co, 1974), p. 323.

[28] Jernegan, pp. 328–329.

[29] Randall, p. 71.

[30] Rasmussen and Tilton, p. 46.

[31] Randall, pp. 68–73.

[32] Ibid., p. 72.

[33] Elizabeth Dandridge was born May 5, 1749.

[34] Rasmussen and Tilton, p. 81.

[35] McPherson, p. 23.

[36] Fields, p. 433.

[37] *Web of Time*, p. 5.

[38] Fields, p. 440.

CHAPTER FOUR

[1] Mary Ball and Augustine Washington were married March 5, 1731.

[2] Willard Sterne Randall, *George Washington A Life* (New York: Henry Holt and Company, 1997), p. 16.

[3] Ibid., p. 15.

[4] The Julian calendar was in effect when George was born setting the date of his birth as February 11, 1731. The Gregorian calendar went into effect in Great Britain and the American Colonies in 1752, changing his birthdate to February 22, 1732.

[5] Randall, p. 18.

[6] Ibid., p. 39.

[7] Ibid., p. 21.

[8] Ibid., pp. 22–23.

[9] Augustine Washington died on April 12, 1743.

[10] Randall, p. 25.

[11] Ibid., p. 35.

[12] Ibid., p. 19.

[13] Ibid., p. 37.

[14] Ibid., p. 35.

[15] Ibid., pp. 35–39.

[16] Ibid., p. 38.

[17] Douglas Southall Freeman, *Washington* (New York: Charles Scribner's Sons, 1968), pp. 9–19.

[18] Randall, p. 39.

[19] Ibid., p. 46.

[20] Ibid., p.45.

[21] Freeman, p. 18.

[22] Freeman, pp. 30–31.

[23] Ibid., pp. 62.

[24] Randall, p. 52.

[25] Ibid., p. 63–64.

[26] Ibid., p. 66.

CHAPTER FIVE

[1] "The John Custis Story," *Part I, The Web of Time,* 2002, IV, p. 2

[2] The John Custis will provided for Jack to receive a 500 pound bond and annual provisions.

[3] "Daniel Parke," *American National Biography, 1999, XVII, p. 9.*

[4] Ibid., p. 10.

[5] Ibid., p. 10.

[6] William Rasmussen and Robert Tilton, *George Washington, The Man Behind the Myth* (Charlottesville: University Press of Virginia, 1999), p. 43.

[7] Stephanie Sammartino McPherson, *Martha Washington, First Lady* (Springfield New Jersey: Enslow Publishers, Inc, 1998), p. 11.

[8] Joseph Fields, *Worthy Partner, The Papers of Martha Washington* (Westport, Connecticut: Greenwood Press, 1994), p. 436. Martha and Daniel's young son died on February 19, 1754.

[9] Douglas Southhall Freeman, *Washington* (New York: Charles Scribner's Sons, 1968), p. 36.

[10] 10. Ibid., p. 36.

[11] Ibid., p. 42.

[12] Ibid., p. 43. St. Pierre wanted George Washington to "continue north to Quebec and present to the Governor of Canada the communication from His Excellency of Virginia." George declined because his orders were to present the communique to the commander of the French camp.

[13] Willard Sterne Randall, *George Washington, A Life* (New York: Henry Holt and Company, 1997), p. 82.

[14] Ibid., p. 82. The actual number at that time was seven killed.

[15] Ibid., pp. 98–103.

[16] Fields, p. 436.

[17] Ibid., p. 436. August 31, 1754 was the actual date of John Dandridge's death, Martha's father.

[18] Frances Parke Custis, Martha's daughter, died in June 1755.

[19] Rasmussen and Tilton, p. 85.

[20] America Biography, XVII, p. 10.

[21] Fields, p. 437.

[22] Ibid., p.437.

[23] Ibid., p. 437.

[24] Ibid., p. 437. Daniel was buried at Queen's Creek Plantation, six miles north of Williamsburg. Young Daniel and Frances were also buried there. Years later the three were moved to the churchyard of Burton Parish Church in Williamsburg where they still remain.

[25] Randall, pp. 173–174.

[26] Ibid., p. 173.

[27] *The Web of Time*, p. 2.

[28] Randall, p. 167.

[29] Ibid., p. 167.

[30] Ibid., p. 167.

[31] Ibid., pp. 166–167.

[32] Ibid., p. 166.

[33] Ibid., p. 168.

[34] Ibid., p. 169.

[35] Ibid., p. 169.

[36] Ibid., p. 169.

[37] Ibid., p. 173.

[38] From: John Tayloe to William Byrd III., Williamsburg, 4/4/1758, in *The Correspondence of the Three William Byrds of Westover, Virginia, 1684–1776,* Volume II, edited by Marion Tinling (Charlottesville, Virginia: The University Press of Virginia, 1977), 646 & 646n.

[39] Elswyth Thane, *Washington's Lady* (New York: Dodd, Mead & Company, 1960), p. 3.

[40] Randall, p. 173. There is a lack of authentication of when and

where Martha and George actually met. Most historians cling to the Chamberlaynes as their meeting place. This "account was written seventy-five years later by her grandson, Daniel Parke Custis," says Randall.

[41] Thane, p. 6. Thomas Bishop was a man-servant to Major General Edward Braddock. When Braddock lay dying from his wounds, his legacy to George was Bishop and his saddle horse.

[42] Randall, pp. 173–174.

[43] Ibid., p. 177.

[44] Fields, p. 445.

[45] Thane, p. 22.

[46] Randall, p. 177.

[47] Fields, p. 448. George lost his first attempt to become a Burgess in 1755. When he made the decision to run again in 1758 he ran in absentia. George William Fairfax managed his campaign while the war continued in the Ohio Valley. George did win his seat. Records show his campaign cost him nearly forty pounds for sixty gallons of libation. Randall, p. 185. "To win, Washington laid out a considerable forty pounds to ply the voters with rum, beer, wine at what one observer called, "dull barbecue and yet duller dances."

[48] Fields, pp. 445–448. There is no definitive date when George actually proposed marriage. After their initial introduction, George visited the White House on March 25, 1758 and June 5, 1758.

CHAPTER SIX

[1] Joseph Fields, *Worthy Partner, The Papers of Martha Washington* (Westport Connecticut: Greenwood Press, 1994), p. 445. The time and place of the meeting and courtship of Martha and George is uncertain. There is little doubt that both knew of the other. George had a pervasive reputation as a Virginia war hero, Martha Custis, a very wealthy widow. The probability is that George would have heard about this young, attractive and *wealthy* woman on his visits to Williamsburg and in the ordinaries. The *Virginia Gazette* had numerous stories about the young Colonel Washington and his military exploits, as well. It is known they met in March 1758. George did visit the White House sev-

eral times. He ordered material that would be appropriate for a wedding suit in April 1758, so the assumption is he proposed sometime in March before returning to the war. Martha also ordered cloth for an elaborate gown.

[2] Fields, p.449.

[3] Ibid., p. xxxi.

[4] Willard Sterne Randall, *George Washington, A Life* (New York: Henry Holt and Company, 1997), pp. 178–179.

[5] Ibid., pp. 178–179.

[6] Fields, p. 433.

[7] Ibid., p. 433

[9] Randall, pp. 188–189.

[10] Fields, p. 451.

[11] George returned from the front early in December 1758. He made numerous stops before arriving in Williamsburg to settle his accounts before he resigned from the military. The stops included Belvoir, several ordinaries, probably Mount Vernon and perhaps to visit his mother. Historians assume he made a stop at the White House because the wedding was only two weeks away. He arrived in Williamsburg on either the 25th or 26th of December.

[12] Randall, p. 188.

[13] Thane, p. 15. There is no clear conformation that Martha and George married in her home, the White House. Because most marriages took place in the home of the bride, most historians assume that is where theirs took place.

[15] Randall, pp. 176–177.